The Health of the Nation – a policy assessed

Two reports commissioned for the Department of Health from the Universities of Leeds and Glamorgan and the London School of Hygiene and Tropical Medicine

London: The Stationery Office

ISBN 011 322256 4

CONTENTS

FOREWORD

It is a challenging task to evaluate a strategic policy initiative which was as wide-ranging as the Health of the Nation. The research teams whose reports are published together here, have demonstrated that systematic study can yield scientifically robust, and useful, insights into such major policy issues.

Information and views from a large number of people in sixteen local areas are reported here, and thanks are due to all those who helped with these studies. Their measured assessments have been captured in the reports to the benefit of all those working on this and successive strategies for health.

These studies were conducted at the same time as the Government initiated development work on a new health strategy for England, Our Healthier Nation. They will form an important strand in the thinking for that new strategy. The findings from this research are relevant not only to central government but to partnerships locally, on whose efforts the implementation of Our Healthier Nation will crucially depend.

Professor John Swales
Director of Research & Development
Department of Health

Universities of Leeds and Glamorgan

Investing in Health?

an Assessment of the impact of
the Health of the Nation

A report commissioned by the
Department of Health

Nuffield Institute
for Health,
University of Leeds.

Welsh Institute for
Health & Social Care,
University of Glamorgan.

AUTHORS

Professor David J Hunter*
Professor of Health Policy and Management

Professor Morton Warner+
Director and Professor of Health Strategy and Policy

Tony Beddow+
Senior Fellow

Professor David Cohen+
Professor of Health Economics

Dr Jim Connelly*
Senior Lecturer in Public Health

Brian Hardy*
Senior Research Fellow

Marcus Longley+
Associate Director and Senior Fellow

Dr Catherine Richards*
Visiting Lecturer in Public Health Medicine (on attachment)

Dr Mike Robinson*
Senior Lecturer in Public Health

Dr Wendy Sykes*
Visiting Senior Research Fellow

David Taylor+
Professor

Professor Rhys Williams*
Professor of Public Health and Epidemiology

Professor Gerald Wistow*
Director and Professor of Health and Social Care

* Nuffield Institute for Health, University of Leeds
+ Welsh Institute for Health and Social Care, University of Glamorgan

CONTENTS

APPENDICES

REFERENCES

ACKNOWLEDGEMENTS

This study would not have been possible without a large number of busy people giving freely of their valuable time in our field sites. We are indebted to them all and hope that what follows fairly and faithfully reflects their views. But they are in no way responsible for what follows.

We are also grateful to members of the Steering Group set up by the Department of Health to oversee the study. Their guidance and advice throughout have been helpful and have hopefully improved and strengthened the final report.

Nuffield Institute for Health,
University of Leeds.

Welsh Institute for Health & Social Care,
University of Glamorgan.

EXECUTIVE SUMMARY

1. Introduction

1.1   From 1992 to 1997 The Health of the Nation (HOTN) strategy was the central plank of health policy in England and formed the context for the planning of services provided by the NHS. Its importance lay in the fact that it represented the first explicit attempt by government to provide a strategic approach to improving the overall health of the population.

1.2   Under the Minister for Public Health, a new health strategy is being developed aimed at building on and extending The HOTN. The review of The HOTN commissioned by the Department of Health was designed to identify its achievements, failures, limitations and those elements that appeared to be working well and those where there was demonstrable room for improvement.

1.3   In carrying out the study, a multidisciplinary approach was adopted drawing on skills in policy analysis, public health and health economics. Fieldwork was conducted in eight health authorities and related agencies between September 1997 and March 1998. It involved extensive interviewing with key stakeholders and documentary analysis. Altogether, a total of 123 interviews were conducted.

1.4   Two specific aspects of the review of The HOTN centred on public health and health economics in order to demonstrate the impact of the strategy on health trends in the key target areas and on the extent to which health economics thinking and evidence impacted on local priority-setting and resource allocation decision-making. A third aspect of the review focused on policy analysis in order to describe and explain the influence of The HOTN on health authorities and other significant stakeholders at local level.

2. Principal Findings

2.1   The HOTN was widely welcomed - it was the first attempt to put in place a national health strategy based on WHO's Health for All. It had an important symbolic role.

2.2   The HOTN failed over its five year lifespan to realise its full potential and was handicapped from the outset by numerous flaws of both a conceptual and process-type nature. By 1997, its impact on local policy-making was negligible. It wasn't seen to count while other priorities, e.g. waiting lists, balancing the books, took precedence. The need for a fresh start was stressed.

2.3   The HOTN was regarded as a Department of Health initiative which lacked cross-departmental commitment and ownership. At local level, it was seen as principally a health service document and lacked local government ownership. Shared ownership at all levels both horizontally and vertically was stressed as essential for success.

2.4   The HOTN did not change significantly the perspective and behaviour of health authorities and did not fundamentally alter the context within which dialogue between health purchasers/providers and other partners took place.

2.5   The HOTN did not cause a major readjustment in investment priorities by health authorities. There was no relationship between resource use and outcomes and no evidence of a health economics perspective having been adopted.

2.6   The HOTN reinforced the changing role of health authorities, providing a framework within which the commissioning role was to be judged.

2.7   Some attempt was made to drive progress via the contracting process but it was minimal. The impact upon Trust and primary care teams' performance has been slight.

2.8   The HOTN did not seriously impact upon primary care practitioners either as commissioners or providers.

2.9   Community Trusts appear to have been most engaged via involvement in community development activities and health promotion programmes; acute Trusts have been largely untouched by the health strategy. The HOTN has been relevant only where it enabled pre-existing agendas to be furthered and/or as a source of new funds.

2.10   Local authorities in general perceived The HOTN to be dominated by 'medical conditions' and heavily 'medically led'. It was a cause for concern among those local authorities which believed that they contributed more to a health agenda in its broadest sense than health authorities.

2.11   Continual organisational turbulence frequently disrupted management teams and working alliances. It also contributed to lapses of corporate memory which hindered consistent data collection and recollection of events by interviewees.

2.12   The different agendas/drivers and cultures of health services and local government were complicating factors.

2.13   Pre-existing structures and challenges heavily influenced the starting point for joint working. For example, where local government had responded to WHO's Health for All initiative and had formed relationships with health authorities there was already joint machinery upon which to build. In these circumstances The HOTN had been possibly unhelpful. Where no such activity existed, The HOTN provided a suitable spur to joint action.

2.14   National targets were a useful 'rallying' point but local targets would have been welcomed within the national framework to reflect local needs.

2.15   Approaches to the translation of national targets to local level varied considerably. There was a general wish for greater freedom both to add target areas to the menu and to adjust targets in the light of local circumstances. There was criticism of the targets on technical grounds.

2.16   The performance management process was heavily geared to short-term outputs, largely driven by the Efficiency Index/Patient's Charter/financial management agendas and there was no extant performance management for strategic development and achievements for health as opposed to health services.

2.17   Lack of management guidance and incentives at local level were seen to be major failings of The HOTN. Local agencies did not have their roles, tasks and responsibilities clearly spelt out with a timetable to ensure that agreed targets or milestones were met.

2.18   Strengthening the capacity to deliver on the health strategy was seen to be a priority.

3.   Implications for Future Policy

3.1   There was a widespread desire for a fresh start and for new life to be breathed into the health strategy. The government's commitment to produce a new health strategy, which would both build on The HOTN's overall aims and objectives and extend and broaden these in an effort to tackle the poverty problem and the evidence of widening health inequalities, was welcomed.

3.2   There is a risk of 'initiative conflict' and overload as a consequence of the plethora of vehicles for collaboration which now exists. While offering rich opportunities to form and sustain partnerships, it is essential that the various initiatives are nested.

3.3   In particular, government needs to

♦   provide leadership by sending out clear, consistent 'corporate signals' and ensuring cross-departmental ownership

♦   establish shared ownership at all levels both horizontally and vertically and ensure that chief executives in health and local authorities are fully engaged and committed

♦   within a performance management framework, spell out as clearly as possible agency expectations, tasks and responsibilities

♦ consider carefully whether health authorities should have the lead role for delivering on the health strategy or whether this should not be a shared role between health and local authorities

♦ stress the importance of joint targets and joint monitoring with each stakeholder playing to its particular strengths

♦ ensure that primary care practitioners are on board with the strategy.

INTRODUCTION AND BACKGROUND

From 1992 to 1997 *The Health of the Nation* strategy, led and co-ordinated by the Department of Health, was the central plank of health policy in England and formed the context for the planning of services provided by the NHS. *The Health of the Nation* (HOTN) was important because it represented the first explicit attempt by government to provide a strategic approach to improving the overall health of the population in England.

Following the Minister for Public Health's announcement in July 1997, a new health strategy is being developed aimed at building on and extending The HOTN. A consultative document - *Our Healthier Nation* - was published in February 1998 to be followed by a white paper later in the year. While critical of The HOTN's limited vision for health and 'its reluctance to acknowledge the social, economic and environmental causes of ill-health' (Secretary of State for Health 1998, paragraph 4.12: 57), health ministers are committed to learning the lessons from the experience of implementing The HOTN. This will 'ensure a firmer evidence base for [their] policy' (paragraph 3.83: 53).

In presenting this assessment of The HOTN, we firmly believe that the insights derived from the experience of implementing the strategy at local level across the country contain important lessons from which the new health strategy can only benefit.

STUDY TERMS OF REFERENCE

The review of The HOTN commissioned by the Department of Health was designed to provide an assessment of the health strategy in order to identify its achievements, failures, limitations and those elements that appeared to be working well and those where there was demonstrable room for improvement.

Specifically, the study focused on structure (the resources employed to meet the The HOTN's objectives) and process (the interventions carried out in pursuit of the strategy) although, as we explain in sub-sections 3.11 and B.3.2 below, it has proved virtually impossible to make any robust causal connections between resource inputs and policy outputs or outcomes.

In addition to collecting information about the overall reception given The HOTN and its impact on a variety of local agencies, and key individuals within these agencies, the study considered the following issues to be of particular importance:

(a) how the health problems which constituted the key areas of The HOTN were conceptualised in terms of their incidence, prevalence, causation and consequences

(b) whether and how national targets were translated to local level

(c) whether The HOTN priorities replaced other topics which may have been of greater local importance as priorities

(d) how options for tackling The HOTN targets and objectives were generated, operationalised and selected

(e) how the chosen options were implemented and with what degree of success in process terms

(f) how effective and embedded local collaborative relationships have been in the pursuit of The HOTN targets and objectives.

In practice, it did not prove possible to address all these issues in equal measure. Part of the difficulty lay in getting access to reliable and consistent data in our chosen field sites. Consequently, the focus of the research has been on issues (b), (d), (e) and (f) above.

To implement the study terms of reference, a multidisciplinary approach was adopted drawing on the particular, and complementary, skills and expertise located within two academic centres: the Nuffield Institute for Health, University of Leeds, and the Welsh Institute for Health and Social Care, University of Glamorgan. The skills deployed comprised strengths in policy analysis, public health and health economics. A list of members of the two research teams is given in Appendix 1.

STUDY DESIGN AND METHODS

The study proceeded in two stages: a literature search of published material on The HOTN conducted for us by the Nuffield Institute's Information Resource Centre formed the background to our analysis of the data we have collected; and fieldwork in eight health authorities which involved extensive interviewing (one-to-one and group interviews) and documentary analysis. The fieldwork was conducted between September 1997 and February 1998. The results of the literature search are not presented here but an annotated bibliography, produced by the London School of Hygiene and Tropical Medicine in association with the Nuffield Institute for Health, is available upon request from Dr Naomi Fulop at the London School of Hygiene and tropical Medicine.

The eight health authorities were selected using a purposive sampling approach designed to ensure that a range of types of area were included in respect of:

♦ geographical location (one health authority from each of the eight health regions)

♦ population deprivation (four categories derived from the Jarman Deprivation Index)

♦ degree of established joint working (two categories based on 'soft' intelligence acquired through a previous research project carried out at the Nuffield Institute for Health).

The above strategy was based on the assumption that together these variables would deliver a mix of areas across which we would encounter all the main key issues associated with the implementation of The HOTN. This is reflected in our analysis which on the whole explores the aggregate picture presented by our sample areas rather than attempts to compare and contrast different health authorities.

Having selected our eight field sites, these were divided equally between the two research teams based in Leeds and Wales respectively. Interview guides (see Appendix 2) were prepared to promote consistency across the two research teams as well as coverage of agreed topics. Inevitably, differences did occur but the extent of divergence in the two teams' approach was minimised by frequent joint meetings. The interview guides covered the principal organisations we contacted: health authorities, NHS trusts, NHS Regional Offices, and local authorities. We also captured the views of GPs and other members of the primary health care team, adapting the health authority interview guide for this purpose. However, in the time available to us it was not possible to undertake in-depth coverage of primary care. We suggest that in the light of the 1997 NHS white paper and the future importance of primary care it be the subject of a separate research study. Interviews were also conducted with voluntary organisations where appropriate.

In each location semi-structured interviews were conducted with a range of key actors (a complete list

		Deprivation		
	High	**Medium**	**Less**	**Low**
Good Joint Working				
Poor Joint Working				

of roles interviewed across the eight locations is presented in Appendix 3). A total of 123 interviews and focus group meetings were carried out across the eight locations. Some of those interviewed, like health authority chief executives, directors of public health, and directors of health promotion, were obvious subjects. Other interviewees were chosen on the basis of their importance in a particular agency which became apparent on initial contact. In any case, apart from a few obvious roles there were no standard or consistent sets of roles when it came to The HOTN in any of our field sites.

The interviews combined one-to-one interviews and focus group meetings. A few interviews were conducted by telephone. Most of the interviews were tape recorded. Some of the tapes were transcribed and then analysed but in most cases detailed notes were made from the tapes organised according to a set of emergent critical themes which were refined and modified as the interviews proceeded. All fieldwork notes were exchanged among members of both research teams and formed the basis of the description of what happened (Part B) and policy action points (Part C).

Running concurrently with the literature review and field work was the acquisition and analysis of key documents requested from each health authority. These documents were chosen for analysis on the basis of likelihood of supplying information which could then be used to support or corroborate information on the key public health issues which informed the appropriate interview guide. As an illustration, we attempted to find documented evidence concerning the translation of national to local targets and target monitoring, the contribution of public health to local health needs assessments relevant to The HOTN, any focus on evidence-based practice in The HOTN areas, and the role of public health in bringing The HOTN within the commissioning process.

A checklist of essential documents sought was issued to each health authority in order to assist them in providing the research team with a complete set of documents (see Appendix 4). The researcher responsible for this part of the field work used a database of documents received to generate reminders for missing documents. Although none of our requests for key documents was denied, it was not always possible to locate or provide complete sets of documents (e.g. Directors of Public Health annual reports, strategy documents). This was sometimes because the archiving of material was weak, because key individuals had left the organisation and the corporate memory had disappeared with them, and/or because of organisational and boundary changes which had resulted in the loss of key documents. Whether such difficulties in obtaining key documents are in themselves significant and a possible indication of the low priority accorded The HOTN is impossible to say. More likely they reflect the considerable organisational turbulence to which the NHS has been subjected during the period of The HOTN. As far as possible, the documents were used to inform the topics covered in interviews.

The documents obtained also formed the basis of a quantitative analysis of secular trends for key target areas (data from the Public Health Common Data Set were used to supplement this for mortality from coronary heart disease, stroke and suicide and undetermined deaths) and an analysis of the extent to which, if any, there was evidence of the application of a health economics approach.

Two specific aspects of our review of The HOTN have centred on public health and health economics in order to demonstrate (if/where possible) the impact of The HOTN on health trends in the key target areas and on the extent to which health economics thinking and evidence impacted on local HOTN priority-setting and resource allocation decision-making. For reasons we report in Section B.3 below, neither of these quantitative approaches succeeded in revealing much about either the impact of The HOTN targets on health status or the expenditure flows which might have made it possible to determine whether health authorities were serious about implementing the strategy.

Public Health

Our primary focus has been to establish the extent to which national targets have been used to achieve measurable health gain at local level. This has been approached in four complementary ways (see also Box 1):

◆ an analysis of relevant documentation for each locality, including DPH annual reports and corporate contracts

◆ an assessment of the level of sophistication of translation of national to local targets, and of monitoring progress towards local targets

◆ a series of telephone interviews with past and present Directors of Public Health in each locality

◆ a checklist of key public health issues relevant to the above processes included in the interview guides composed for the site visits.

Our second focus has been to describe, using the sources of information described above, the way in which public health has contributed towards local health needs assessments relevant to The HOTN, and to what extent public health has contributed to the commissioning process in these areas.

The comprehensive time trend data, presented in Appendix 5, (Figures 1-5) for cardiovascular mortality, and for suicide and undetermined death mortality rates, have been assembled for the period 1986 to 1995 using the Public Health Common Data Set (Department of Health 1997). These key areas and targets were chosen to illustrate the importance of the number of expected events when specifying area targets. The findings are reported in subsection B.3.1 below.

Box 1 *Translating National Targets to Local Level*

Guidance was provided by the Department of Health for the translation of national HOTN targets to local level (NHSME 1993). This discussed 'top-down' and 'bottom-up' approaches as well as referring to, and making suggestions about, the problems of small numbers (using three year aggregations and rolling averages etc).

A number of approaches are theoretically possible. These span a wide range of sophistication:

◆ Ignore national targets and leave unspecified the reasons for doing so.

◆ Take no action in specifying local targets and state why this was not done. This was the practice in two of the localities studied. The reasons given were, in one locality, the realisation that, if the targets were met, this could not, with any confidence, be attributed to the activities of the health authority and, on the other hand, if they were not met, this could provoke unjustified criticism of the authority. In the other locality, setting local targets was considered to be a distraction from the local priority of tackling the 'broader determinants' (eg the influence of poverty on health).

◆ Simple transfer of national targets to local epidemiology using the percentage fall (in a mortality rate, for example) adopted nationally multiplied by the local base rate to calculate the local target. This was the most common approach.

◆ A variant of the above, making adjustments for local epidemiology. There is both an example of making a target more challenging by specifying a greater fall to be achieved locally (CHD in a district which knew it had a particular problem in that area) and an example of making a target less challenging by specifying a lesser fall to be achieved locally (cervical cancer in a district with a particularly high base rate). In these cases the local adjustment seems to have been arbitrary.

◆ Other techniques are the adoption of regionally determined targets in the place of national targets, concentration on the use of proxy indicators (prevalence of smoking, levels of physical activity, etc).

◆ Examples of all of the above, except the first, were encountered in our eight locations.

Health Economics

Health economics is about the relationship between resource inputs and health outputs. It normally adopts a society-wide perspective with a goal to maximising social welfare. Health is regarded as an output which can be produced using the resources of a wide variety of agencies in addition to formal health care interventions within the NHS. One measure of the success of The HOTN ought, therefore, to be in terms of the extent to which it has broadened the health agenda beyond the conventional focus that health is the responsibility of the NHS, to a point which ensures the most efficient production of health on a broader basis. The overall impression from this review of The HOTN is that it has achieved only limited success in this respect.

A full economic evaluation of The HOTN would assess the cost of the strategy (in terms of the resources used) against the health achieved. Such a task is not possible at this stage due *inter alia* to problems with data on both the input (cost) and output (health) sides, and to the large number of confounding factors.

An alternative to a full economic evaluation could be to identify expenditure changes which were due to The HOTN and relate these to proxy measures of achieved health gain. However, it became evident from a preliminary investigation of expenditure patterns that the data were revealing little of value and could potentially mislead regarding what effect The HOTN may, or may not, have had. This is explained more fully in sub section B.3.2, paragraph B.3.2.2 below.

This review of The HOTN aims to assess the extent to which the strategy has enabled central government to influence policy, especially at a sub-national level. An economic assessment of the influence of The HOTN ought, therefore, to be concerned with the extent to which local responses made use of (or at least were consistent with) economic thinking and principles.

From an economic perspective, The HOTN represented a major advance over previous strategic policy documents in its focus on health outcomes rather than processes and because of its explicit recognition that these outcomes are not produced solely by the NHS. The HOTN ought, therefore, to be conducive to the application of economic thinking which is based on the tenet that the resources to produce health outputs are finite and ought to be employed in a way which maximises the amount of health that can be achieved (see Box 2).

For the purposes of this review our principal interest has been in assessing the extent to which health economics *thinking* has been used, and the extent to which health economist *expertise* has been exploited in pursuit of The HOTN. We have approached this in two ways:

◆ 25 telephone interviews were conducted with staff working as commissioners or providers of The HOTN related services in the 8 locations to assess the nature and extent of formal links with health economists

◆ a series of checklist points were included in the interview guides to be discussed during all site visits in order to assess the extent to which health economics principles and thinking have been used.

Box 2   Contribution of Economic Analysis

♦   Economic analysis demands the assembly not only of comprehensive financial data sets relating to the provision of a service, but also of quantitative information relating to all other anticipated forms of cost and benefit. It also demands evidence of effectiveness - that is, that a given intervention results in an intended outcome or that a given policy has a desired political, financial or health impact. This opens the way to identifying areas of possible neglect or over-provision related to factors such as, say, provider-side rigidities or consumer-side information deficits.

♦   Economic analysis helps to show how behaviour relates to the incentives available to both individuals and groups within any given value framework. It can therefore help to inform management strategies and/or explain why policy may not in practice be implemented. It may also reveal policy distortions related to factors such as the electoral or other political incentives affecting decision-takers and service managers.

♦   Planning economic analyses should determine the types of data which will in future be needed to measure the costs and benefits of any given policy, as well as revealing the incentives people at all levels in a system may have for recording inaccurate or otherwise misleading information. Economists can define relevant data sets for use in future evaluations and help prevent the wasteful collection of meaningless and/or distorted figures.

♦   The process of health economic analysis can serve to bridge medical and social science. It could, therefore, help drive public health policy planning and implementation to becoming a more genuinely multi-disciplinary activity, operating across traditional academic and functional/financial interest boundaries in order to maximise opportunities for overall health improvement.

Policy Analysis

In assessing the implementation of The HOTN, we have adopted a policy analysis perspective which seeks to account for the inability of the orthodox 'top-down' view of policy formation and implementation to appreciate or comprehend the power of those on the periphery to shape policy and its implementation.   Such so-called 'street level bureaucrats' in practice exercise considerable discretion over both the implementation of policy and the substance of that policy (Lipsky 1980).   In studying implementation success and/or failure, it is important to be alert to the ability of those ostensibly charged with implementing policy to fail to do so for whatever reason. At the same time, 'bottom-up' approaches to implementation can represent a counsel of despair as they allow little scope for policy-makers with aspirations to effect substantive change being able to do so (Harrison 1998).

What is needed is a synthesis of the two perspectives - top-down and bottom-up - which allows insights derived from both to apply.   This might be termed the strategic approach (Harrison 1998). According to such an approach, implementation will shape policy but policy will also shape implementation and outcomes. While a top-down approach invariably fails to acknowledge how complex and messy the real world is, the bottom-up approach fails to appreciate how policy can set limits, and provide frameworks and resources within which implementation occurs. Gunn (1978) has identified 10 preconditions to achieve perfect implementation which are helpful in drawing attention to the variables to be addressed in explaining implementation failure (see Box 3).

Our findings on implementation of The HOTN at local level are presented in Section B.4 below.

Box 3   Preconditions to Achieve Perfect Implementation

♦   That circumstances external to the implementing agency do not impose crippling constraints.

♦   That adequate time and sufficient resources are made available to the programme.

♦   That not only are there no constraints in terms of overall resources but also that, at each stage in the implementation process, the required combination of resources is actually available.

♦   That the policy to be implemented is based upon a valid theory of cause and effect.

♦   That the relationship between cause and effect is direct and that there are few, if any, intervening links.

♦   That there is a single implementing agency which need not depend upon other agencies for success or, if other agencies must be involved, that the dependency relationships are minimal in number and importance.

♦   That there is complete understanding of, and agreement upon, the objectives to be achieved; and that these conditions persist throughout the implementation process.

♦   That in moving toward agreed objectives it is possible to specify, in complete detail and perfect sequence, the tasks to be performed by each participant.

♦   That there is perfect communication among, and co-ordination of, the various elements or agencies involved in the programme.

♦   That those in authority can demand and obtain perfect obedience.

Source: Gunn (1978)

Focus of Assessment of The HOTN

The remainder of this report is in three parts. Part A considers the purpose of The HOTN strategy, what it sought to achieve, and initial reactions to it upon its publication.   Part B reviews what happened in terms of the reception given The HOTN by local agencies, and the overall policy context in which the health strategy was launched. This was dominated by NHS structural and managerial reform as a consequence of the then government's introduction of the internal market. Finally, looking ahead,

Part C brings together and presents the key policy action points with the intention of promoting lesson learning and informing discussions underway on the forthcoming white paper, *Our Healthier Nation.*

PART A
WHAT WAS EXPECTED?

A.1   Origins and Synopsis of The Health of the Nation

A.1.1   The NHS reforms announced in the 1989 white paper, *Working for Patients*, were well advanced when the government decided to launch its health strategy.   It did so amidst criticism that the strategy should have preceded the organisational and managerial restructuring of the NHS and, in particular, the creation of a purchaser-provider separation in which the bulk of attention seemed to fall on the provider function.   The government's response to its critics was that the first two years of the reforms had been necessary to prepare the ground for the development of the purchasing function the centrepiece of which was the health strategy, *The Health of the Nation* (Mawhinney and Nichol 1993).   Health ministers at the time claimed that The HOTN was 'shifting the focus from NHS institutions and service inputs to people and health' (Mawhinney and Nichol 1993: 45).

A.1.2   The HOTN appeared as a white paper in 1992 following a green paper published in 1991 (Secretary of State for Health 1992). Drawing selectively on WHO's *Health for All* strategy, it was aimed at securing 'continuing improvement in the general health of the population by adding years to life and adding life to years'. The emphasis was on improving and maintaining health, not simply health care.   Five key areas of health were identified (see Box 4), chosen because

- ♦   they were major causes of premature death or avoidable ill-health

- ♦   they were ones where effective interventions should be possible offering significant scope for improvement in health

- ♦   it was possible to set objectives and targets in the areas and monitor progress towards them.

A.1.3   The key areas and associated objectives and national targets were tools for achieving the wider strategic aims of The HOTN which were to improve the nation's health in terms of life expectancy, reductions in premature death, and improvements in quality of life.   Settings such as schools, homes and workplaces were also identified where health promotion could show useful progress.

A.1.4   While the goals, objectives and targets in The HOTN were intended for the nation as a whole, the NHS had a central role to perform as the main provider of high quality health care.   It was therefore uniquely placed to promote health care. In order to assess and review progress, a monitoring framework was devised for the purpose. As part of the monitoring process, the Department of Health produced two progress reports in 1993 and 1995.   The HOTN has been a key strategic goal for the NHS since 1992 and has been included in successive NHS Priorities and Planning Guidance.

Box 4   Health of the Nation Key Areas and Main Objectives

A Coronary heart disease and stroke	*To reduce the level of ill-health and death caused by CHD and stroke and the risk factors associated with them.*
B Cancer	*To reduce death and ill-health from breast cancer, lung cancer, cervical cancer and skin cancer.*
C Mental illness	*To reduce ill health and death caused by mental illness.*
D HIV/AIDS and sexual health	*To reduce the incidence of HIV infection and sexually transmitted diseases; to provide effective diagnosis and treatment for HIV and STDs; to provide effective family planning services and to reduce the number of unwanted pregnancies.*
E Accidents	*To reduce ill-health, disability and death caused by accidents*

Source: National Audit Office (1996)

A.2 Reactions to The Health of the Nation

A.2.1 Reactions to the 1992 health strategy white paper were mixed, though by and large it was welcomed. The extremes have been summarised as follows

> *for some it was a bold initiative, setting out specific health targets for cutting mortality from the major causes of death and reducing risk factors across a range of illnesses and diseases. For others, [it] sidestepped issues such as the need to tackle poverty and deal effectively with equity.*
>
> (Appleby 1997: 24)

A.2.2 The HOTN received support from many quarters on the grounds that the emergence of an explicit national health strategy marked a significant turning point in shifting the emphasis in health policy from health care to health. But, while welcomed for its worthy aims and as a belated attempt to fill a serious strategic vacuum left by the organisational and managerial changes set in motion by the 1989 NHS white paper, The HOTN was criticised for its lack of innovation and narrow disease focus on individual lifestyles rather than on targets based on equity, community development, and environmental protection. Health inequalities and poverty were conspicuous by their absence. The focus of HOTN was on containing disease rather than on risk/behaviour modification (Holland and Stewart 1998). This was in contrast to the Faculty of Public Health Medicine's stance. The Faculty, report Holland and Stewart (1998: 154), wanted the targets and activities 'to focus on the factors that led to ill health - smoking, poverty, inadequate housing, for example, rather than on the disease and conditions that resulted'.

A2.3 When The HOTN appeared in 1992, it attracted considerable criticism from individual local authorities and their representative bodies. A survey of local authorities' views on The HOTN, conducted for the Health Education Authority and the Local Government Management Board, shows

that much of the criticism of the health strategy following its publication centred on four main issues (Moran 1996: 47):

- the health strategy was too narrowly focused on disease models and measurable disease-reduction targets, and failed to promote a positive view of health

- The HOTN neglected key socio-economic and environmental determinants of health

- because of its reductionist approach the health strategy failed to appreciate the potential local authority contribution to a national health strategy; local authorities had difficulty reconciling rhetoric about 'healthy alliances' with the allocation of lead responsibility to the Department of Health and the NHS

- no new resources were forthcoming to progress the health strategy.

Virtually all of these criticisms of The HOTN by local authorities have persisted over the years as our fieldwork, reported in Part B below, demonstrates.

A.2.4 The HOTN's preoccupation with the NHS and Department of Health were also viewed with concern by others since it seemed to confuse public health with the NHS. Moreover, there were reservations over the extent to which the NHS would in practice be capable of detaching itself from the pressures of providing health services in order to give priority to a notion of health which went far beyond its boundaries. Since the NHS has concentrated heavily on providing a treatment service and has, relatively, neglected the promotion and protection of the public's health few were convinced that it could or would make the necessary shift in thinking and resources. Regardless of whether or not it is right and proper for the NHS to operate in this way, it has had a disabling effect on health policy (Harrison and others 1991). The tendency to look upon the NHS as a catchall for all aspects of health - cure, care, prevention/promotion - may result in unreasonable, if not impossible, demands being placed upon it. This was certainly a frequently expressed view at the time of The HOTN's launch. Finally, while The HOTN made mention of a shared commitment and a concerted action approach, no attention was given to how collaboration might be achieved.

A.2.5   The targets themselves also came in for criticism on the grounds that they had been restricted by the limitations of routine statistics thereby excluding important areas about which there are no data.   Most of the available data measured the use of health services or mortality with very few measuring health or ill-health.   Nor could measuring outcomes, though regarded as desirable, be done because the data simply did not exist. The HOTN green paper asked what scope there would be for using indicators other than mortality for accidents such as measures of temporary or permanent injury, long absence from work or length of stay in hospital.

A.2.6   Our fieldwork interviews across virtually all stakeholder groups, including health authorities and providers, revealed strong support for The HOTN in terms of its principles and good intentions.   Its positive features were repeated frequently by interviewees and included its status as a national strategy for health, and its emphasis on prevention and promotion. The strategy was also seen to underwrite the role of the NHS as a health service and not simply an illness service. It focused attention on important health issues. One Director of Public Health's views were fairly typical

> as part of a continuum of developing
> any health approach to the
> management of health and health
> care, [The HOTN] has been a useful
> step....[A] step from no health policy
> toward a comprehensive health
> policy....[T]here had never been a
> national health policy before; this was
> their first shot. It had strengths and
> weaknesses, probably more
> weaknesses than strengths, and the
> charge on [the government] was to
> learn and review and re-establish and
> the new government is doing that.

A Head of Health Promotion's views were also fairly typical of the overall reception given The HOTN

> it was the first national strategy that
> was really about health, so I was
> completely delighted.... It was music
> to my ears just to have that
> recognition. For the first time it was
> recognised that the health service had
> more of a role than just managing
> health services. It looked at the
> health of the population.

A Chief Executive was less concerned with the choice of targets than with the fact that the strategy 'was focusing on areas that were recognised as important clinical and health issues'.

A.2.7   Within health authorities The HOTN was regarded by some of our interviewees as a powerful endorsement for raising the corporate profile of certain issues. A Director of Public Health suggested that

> it gave us something to fall back on in
> pushing areas that we had pushed for
> before but which perhaps we hadn't
> got very far with.

In general, those working in health promotion and public health were of the view that The HOTN, in the words of one Health Promotion Specialist, 'gave them a mandate to actually work and take things forward'. An area given a particular boost was the familiar one of joint working across agencies and sectors. A Head of Health Promotion saw the strategy as

> a tool to galvanise different
> organisations together, lever more
> money to ensure we all had a common
> language about how we were working
> together.

A Chair said that analysing local health status in terms of The HOTN targets provided a powerful focus for dialogue with the public at annual meetings.

when we got onto health and
differences between patches within the
area the audience came alive. They
were really interested in it, what they
could do and so on.

A.2.8   It was evident from our fieldwork interviews that The HOTN served an important symbolic role and was a catalyst to thinking at local level. It was possibly the best way to move things forward and, we were told, did influence the way people worked. But, at the same time, the strategy was seen as being 'about tomorrow' in a context where short-term pressures and demands were ever-present.

A.2.9   A performance framework for use by regional offices in reviewing health authorities was published by the NHS Executive in 1996. Clearly this was too late to influence the development of the implementation process. The value of such a framework in future is discussed in Part C.

A.3   Assessing Progress

A.3.1   An independent review of progress towards The HOTN targets was conducted by the National Audit Office (NAO) and published in 1996 (National Audit Office 1996). The NAO noted that the task of assessment was a complex one which 'should be approached cautiously. For some targets trends are not clear, or little historical data are available or the target date is further into the future, making assessment difficult' (NAO 1996, paragraph 8: 4). Appleby (1997: 26), in his review of The HOTN, comments that

although apparently successful in
terms of progress towards its targets,
attributing this purely - or even partly
- to the strategy itself is rather
difficult. The very fact - recognised
by [The HOTN] - that determinants of
health are multifactorial means that,
unless the environment is completely
controlled, it is very difficult to
ascertain which factors proved to be
the active ingredients.

On the strength of our experience in conducting this review of The HOTN, we would fully endorse both the NAO's caution and Appleby's reminder that any progress on the targets may have occurred irrespective of the strategy. Assessing progress in our eight locations has proved problematic for similar reasons (see further, Part B).

A.3.2   Key points from the NAO review were that many targets showed encouraging progress; progress towards some targets could not be monitored; the quantity and quality of data available were sometimes limited; the timescale for measurement was often long; some targets appeared to have been met already. In the last category, deaths from coronary heart disease in people under 65 merit a brief comment. Death rates have in fact been falling since 1979 and have continued to do so at about the same rate since The HOTN initiative commenced.

A.3.3   Areas where progress was limited were:

♦ obesity

♦ saturated fatty acids and total fat in the diet

♦ drinking more than the sensible level of alcohol

♦ smoking among children aged 11-15 years.

A.3.4   A similar picture is revealed in the Chief Medical Officer's Annual Report to the Secretary of State for Health, *On the State of the Public Health* (Calman 1997). While progress towards most of The HOTN targets has been made, with some having been met, adverse trends are evident in obesity, teenage cigarette smoking, and alcohol consumption among women.

A.3.5   Many observers have pointed to the absence of resources allocated to The HOTN which doubtless explains in part the disappointing progress made by the health strategy. However, Holland and Stewart (1998: 155) go further and allege that

*since the performance of health
authorities was judged on process
measures, such as waiting lists, or fiscal
measures such as savings made, there
was little incentive to develop new
programmes or change current ones
concerned with disease reduction and
health promotion. Public health effort
was also dissipated by the need to be
involved in contracting for services
rather than in promoting health.*

This leads Holland and Stewart to conclude that the specialty of public health medicine failed to grasp the opportunity presented by The HOTN, despite the importance of public health to the success of the strategy. Instead, public health physicians took on more and more tasks that could be defined as managerial.

PART B
WHAT HAPPENED?

B.1   Perceptions of Government Action

B.1.1 Although The HOTN, when it appeared in 1992, was presented as having the support of all central government departments this is not how it came across or how it was received at local level. Indeed, conflicts in policy across government departments ran counter to the spirit of The HOTN. By giving the Department of Health the lead nationally and the NHS (through health authorities) the lead locally, the clear message, whether intended or not, was that the health care system was firmly in the driving seat.   While others, notably local government, had an important contribution to make, it was perceived as being secondary to that accorded the NHS.   It was claimed that no serious attempt was made to secure shared ownership for the health strategy in a way which would give an unequivocal message to all those involved in promoting the nation's health that the government did not see either the Department of Health or the NHS as acting in isolation.

> *The HOTN became far too NHS focused when it should have been a whole society issue and a cross-departmental issue and a real inspiring challenge to everyone.   In the end it got dragged down into being just an NHS performance management target. Which is crazy given the multi-dimensional issues that needed to be tackled to really address the targets.*
> (Health Authority Chief Executive)

B.1.2   A Ministerial Cabinet Committee, representing 11 government departments, was established to oversee progress on The HOTN but it was not perceived by those in the field as having been very effective or even very visible. Knowledge of its existence was not widespread. Those of our respondents who had heard of it were somewhat dismissive: 'as far as I am concerned, it rarely if ever met and certainly never produced anything,

least of all leadership' (Director of Public Health). The notion of 'political leadership' was seen to be of crucial importance if The HOTN was ever to achieve its potential.   Without it, at local level

> *[we] just went through the motions doing what was simple, what came naturally but generally what wouldn't have much impact and didn't.*
> (Director of Public Health)

B.1.3   This point is echoed in the extreme sensitivity evident at local level in respect of the example set by central government whether it be on cigarette advertising, or environmental protection. In contrast, there is little corresponding awareness and understanding at the centre about the circumstances and mood of those 'at the coalface'.

B.1.4   With its emphasis on a disease model, and on targets which depended for their success on health service data, it appeared to many outside observers, and to those from other sectors and agencies, that for all its rhetoric The HOTN was less about health than about ill-health. One Health Authority Chief Executive went so far as to claim that a 'significant failure' of The HOTN was that local authorities did not receive the document with the result that from the outset there was 'no ownership' of it.

B.1.5   Our fieldwork suggests that given the way that The HOTN was presented and launched, an important opportunity was missed to build a broad coalition of support for the health strategy which was genuinely intersectoral. As one Community Trust manager put it

> *it would have been useful if [the health strategy] had been multi-agency. It could have been a joint health/local government strategy. There would have been more commitment from local agencies working together on targets....[Y]ou wouldn't have had to do so much work at grass roots level. It would have been more effective.... I would like to stress that we welcomed The HOTN approach but...everybody has got to be included in it - GPs, social services, education.*

A Director of Primary Care regretted the low profile The HOTN had among GPs in general and predicted much the same fate for its successor, *Our Healthier Nation*.

B.1.6   Nevertheless, as noted above, there was consistent evidence that the launch of The HOTN was greeted with considerable enthusiasm by directors of public health and members of district departments of public health and public health medicine.   This initial enthusiasm was usually sustained for a number of years in the face of several disruptive local reorganisations.

B.1.7   While a few of our local government respondents welcomed The HOTN for its value as a catalyst, the majority did not regard it as having had much, if any, influence on their health-related work. Typical comments from officers were: The HOTN was 'not a key driver'; it 'has been peripheral'; The HOTN is 'fairly invisible' and 'is never mentioned'; 'it's something "over there" in health'; it is very much a health authority-led initiative for which the health authority - not the local authority - is accountable; it is not particularly relevant or helpful; The HOTN 'was all about quite clinical targets' and focused too much on the performance of health services.

B.1.8   Not all the negative reactions were confined to local government.   Many of our health service interviewees harboured deep reservations about the thrust of The HOTN and the government's commitment to it reinforcing criticisms documented by, for example, Francome and Marks (1996).   In particular, the strategy was too focused on individual behaviour with little acknowledgement of the social factors that affect health.   Related to this concern was its disease focus.   One Head of Health Promotion saw the strategy 'as a rather conservative interpretation of health promotion' since it completely overlooked

> *treating people as whole people and looking at them within the context of their community and looking at community action, supporting the communities to change their own health.*

B.1.9   A view which came through our interviews quite strongly was that The HOTN was never the engine driving policy which some believed, or hoped, it would be.   This was in contrast to, for example, the government's approach to continuing care.   While a lot of things which went on could be seen to be related to The HOTN they were either already underway prior to the health strategy or had a life quite independent from it.   They were not being done 'under the banner' of The HOTN, as one respondent put it.   A respondent from a health promotion unit added

> *[The HOTN] hasn't any clout, it isn't consistently applied [by] all of the organisations you are working with....[I]t is so disease oriented and it is so detached from the work we are undertaking...with the homeless communities and the voluntary agencies that work with them...that it hasn't had any impact.*

B.1.10   Part of the problem also lay in the manner in which The HOTN was rolled out both initially and then over time.   A Director of Public Health made the point in the following terms

> *the trouble with The HOTN [was that] it produced a lot of words and the [NHS] Executive set up this...industry to produce guidance...which is lining the shelves.   Good work, big hand books, who...is going to read that?*

His views were echoed by other respondents.   A Director of Primary Care advised

> *don't just expect to produce a document and then just say 'get on with it', you've got to find the angle that switches them [i.e. GPs] on at a practical level.*

On the other hand, one Director of Public Health welcomed the supporting material produced at the time of the launch of The HOTN because it allowed her to 'give people an initial flavour of what was going on and the things they could be doing'.

B.1.11   The HOTN national targets received much critical comment from our respondents. We return to this issue in Part B, section 3 but a general criticism concerning the overall political perception of the strategy was that in the case of the targets for cancer, heart disease and stroke no additional action was required on the part of the NHS to achieve them.   Moreover, it seemed that the choice of targets was influenced more by ease of measurement than appropriateness.

> *We felt that some of the targets had been chosen simply because the information was there and it was easy, rather than looking at things that might have been a bit more difficult but perhaps would ultimately have given us something better to work for.*
>   (Health Promotion Specialist)

B.1.12   A particularly negative perception on the part of many of our respondents was that The HOTN, in the words of one,

> *has been an extant government policy, that is, it has never been replaced or withdrawn, but it has also never been assessed or monitored.*

B.1.13   Significantly, and although promised in The HOTN (in paragraph 3.7: 22), the guidance on 'policy appraisal and health' did not in fact appear until 1995 (Department of Health 1995). The guide, which appears not to be widely known, is concerned with appraising the health implications of policy. It is therefore central to the The HOTN's commitment to assess the health effects of policy making across government.

B.2   Sequencing of Policy Initiatives

B.2.1   The sequencing of policy initiatives at the time of the NHS reforms during the early 1990s proved significant in the signals sent out to the field, whether intended or not. First came the 1989 NHS white paper with its concentration on structural and managerial changes designed to introduce competitive principles into the NHS through an internal market system. The proposals were enshrined in the 1990 NHS and Community Care Act. Then, in 1992, after two years or so during which time the NHS was in the throes of considerable organisational and cultural upheaval The HOTN white paper appeared. For many health care practitioners, as well as those from other agencies, the health strategy came too late because by then the policy agenda had largely been determined by the changes in health care delivery arrangements (i.e. the policy means) rather than by health strategy developments (i.e. the policy ends).

B.2.2   Many of our respondents felt the timing of The HOTN was wrong because of the degree of turmoil within the NHS which was in the midst of major transformation. A Director of Public Health spoke for many when she said

> *The HOTN coincided with a period of great turbulence in terms of change of management, organisations and so on. These took their toll in terms of the work of the health authority and it is only in the last two years that things have begun to settle. Before we just seemed to be coping all the time with the effects of mergers, changes and whatever.*

There was also a view that initiatives from the centre were uncoordinated. In addition to The HOTN, there was the emphasis on clinical effectiveness and then clinical audit but none of these policy initiatives was linked to each other. Moreover, they may have contributed to the dissipation of public health effort noted by Holland and Stewart (1998).

B.3   Public Health and Health Economics Perspectives

B.3.1   *Public Health*

B.3.1.1   From an analysis of the time trend data (see Appendix 5), the numbers of expected deaths from coronary heart disease and stroke are much higher than those expected for suicide and undetermined causes.

B.3.1.2   Evidence from the case study material as a whole did not indicate that any significant impact on trends would be evident from reported activities. Furthermore, there was insufficient time since the strategy's launch to demonstrate a significant event, even if one might expect to observe it.   A number of *a priori* and *post hoc* reasons exist why it would be meaningless and misleading to undertake a detailed analysis of these trends for either assessing an individual district's performance or for comparing the districts under study.   Technical factors such as insufficient population sizes and low expected event rates constitute the principal *a priori* reasons.

B.3.1.3   The graphical data are nevertheless interesting for two reasons.   First, it can be seen that where the actual number of events is particularly small, such as deaths from suicide (Appendix 5, Figure 1), there are predictably large swings in observed numbers.   This problem might be approached through using three yearly averages but such a manoeuvre would make interpretation more, rather than less, difficult.   In addition, using actual figures, no significant time trends can be seen between health authorities for deaths from suicide and undetermined causes.   Second, some of the graphs (notably that representing death rates from stroke in people aged 65-74 (Appendix 5, Figure 2)) show an apparent tendency for variation in death rates between health authorities to reduce over time. This is due to regression to the mean and may be explained by our sampling procedure.

B.3.1.4   For deaths from asthma and tuberculosis (Appendix 5, Tables 1 and 2), numbers in all case study areas were very small, and again, there was little to be gained from analysing time trends. Rather, deaths from asthma and tuberculosis are better understood as avoidable deaths which require an individual analysis of the circumstances of that death.

B.3.1.5   The main interest within the public health component of this assessment of The HOTN is closely allied to the policy analysis task, in particular seeking to explicate the influence The HOTN policy had both within the public health function of health authorities and, as important, within the total organisation.

B.3.1.6   The documentary analysis did not reveal any independent, local assessment of the evidence as a basis for determining local strategies.   The intended forecasting exercise based on time series of national data was not undertaken because we were advised that the work was in hand within the Department of Health.

B.3.2   Health Economics

B.3.2.1   We felt it important to determine the extent to which Directors of Finance would agree or disagree with our contention that an examination of expenditure trends would reveal little, and may mislead in respect of any effect The HOTN may have had. Telephone interviews were therefore conducted with Directors (or Deputy Directors) of Finance from each of the eight locations.

B.3.2.2   Overall, there was strong agreement that an examination of expenditure trends would not be worthwhile. Reasons given by the interviewees to support this view can be summarised under four broad headings:

- ◆ **Attributing cause:** The HOTN was seen as having been a good framework for echoing/underscoring what health authorities were doing already, as well as acting as a catalyst to what they intended to do in future anyway. Labelling any resulting expenditure shift as being 'due to' or 'expenditure in support of' The HOTN could therefore mislead. For example, in one health authority a major investment in cardiology/cardiac surgery which had already been planned was re-labelled as expenditure in support of an HOTN target. Similarly, measures being taken within one trust to discourage smoking among its staff were re-badged as an HOTN expenditure.

- ◆ **Level of aggregation of expenditure data:** The level of aggregation of expenditure data means that changes in some narrowly specified expenditures might not be reflected in broader indicators. For example, one health authority had made a major investment in ambulance services in relation to the care of stroke patients specifically in pursuit of its HOTN target on strokes. The Director of Finance indicated that while evidence of this expenditure could be provided if specifically requested, it would not be revealed from any examination of general expenditure accounts.

◆ **Purchaser spending on contract versus provider spending on service:** There appeared to be a broad consensus that while health authorities might be certain of how much was spent on a contract, this was not matched by equal certainty regarding what happened on the ground. To quote one Director of Finance: 'I can tell you exactly how much we paid the Trust, but can't tell you exactly what they did with the money or even if they over or underspent.'

◆ **Changes in resource use:** Perhaps the most important reason why expenditure trend data might reveal little or even mislead regarding changes brought about by The HOTN is that changes in resource use often did not involve reallocations of money, i.e. the same people were now doing different things. For example, with respect to The HOTN target on accidents, a Director of Finance stated: 'I can guarantee that we are not spending any more money on accidents. However, we have set up an accident sub-committee specifically to address this target and have changed the activities of existing staff to support it.'

As an illustration of potentially misleading expenditure data, in one area family planning activities had traditionally been provided at both general practitioner surgeries and at GP 'outreach centres'. Expenditure on the outreach centres is recorded separately. Family planning activities undertaken at GP surgeries are recorded as General Medical Services (GMS) items of service.

In response to a HOTN target to reduce unwanted teenage pregnancies, a decision was taken to focus all family planning resources of the outreach centres onto young people, with adults being instructed to visit the surgery for family planning services.

This significant increase in resource use on teenage contraception at the outreach centres did not involve any change in expenditure on them. At the same time, the change in where adult contraceptive services were provided increased GMS item of service expenditure on family planning despite no change in the actual amount of this activity in the area.

B.3.2.3 One exception to the above was the use of growth monies. Several health authorities had used these specifically to support The HOTN initiatives, often calling for specific bids which, if funded, were subsequently evaluated and fed into contracts only if judged to be successful. Such activities were sometimes supported by a dedicated HOTN Project Officer. Growth monies, however, represent only something in the order of 1-2% of total expenditure, and several Directors of Finance pointed out that this was the only expenditure affected by The HOTN. A different set of pressures apply to the other 98-99% of expenditure

B.3.2.4 Formal links with health economists included direct employment of a health economist in-house (2 out of the 8 health authorities), use of at least one named external health economist adviser (in 7 health authorities) through formal links with university health economics units (in 4 health authorities).

B.3.2.5 The contribution of these health economists varied, but most interviewees were able to cite at least one example where health economic analysis had had a significant influence on local care commissioning policies. The authorities with formal links to academic health economists appeared to have a relatively mature approach to incorporating

Health Authority	Economist in-house	Named external economist adviser	Formal link with academic health economics unit
A	yes	no	no
B	no	yes	yes
C	no	yes	yes
D	no	yes	no
E	no	yes	yes
F	no	yes	no
G	no	yes	no
H	yes	yes	yes

health economist inputs into the overall activities of commissioners. They aimed at 'avoiding the tunnel vision of academics, but ensured that their insights were owned by all the team members'. Success in these collaborations was particularly felt where academic units had adopted pragmatic approaches to health economics, in essence providing it as a form of management consultancy.

B.3.2.6   The dominant view of interviewees, however, was that overall the role of health economists in the commissioning process had been only marginal. Commissioning was seen essentially as a political process within which established medical and other professional interests, information on the clinical (as opposed to cost) effectiveness of procedures, and the interventions of articulate local advocates of particular service developments have the greatest influence.

B.3.2.7   The overall contribution of health economics to The HOTN was perceived as being even less than that to health service commissioning generally. Reasons for this included both technical concerns (e.g. that The HOTN targets were based on 'guesstimates' of what might be achievable, rather than a rigorous analysis of marginal costs and benefits of alternative interventions) and practical concerns (e.g. the paucity of evidence on the effectiveness of health promotion, and concerns that a simplistic approach to evidence-based public health improvement will inappropriately alter the balance of activity away from community development and toward bio-medical interventions).

B.3.2.8   A minority of interviewees were opposed to the input of health economists, seeing health economics as an 'ivory tower' discipline with limited relevance to the day-to-day challenges facing bodies such as health authorities. There was outright hostility by some toward the use of certain health economics principles/techniques, for example Quality Adjusted Life Years (QALY) which was viewed by one interviewee as being unethical.

B.3.2.9   Apart from the use of health economist expertise discussed above, there was little evidence that health economic *thinking* had made any significant contribution to the way that The HOTN was perceived, priority areas were chosen, or targets were pursued.

B.3.2.10   Site visits were used to explore the extent to which three broad aspects of economics had influenced the way that The HOTN was tackled.

   ♦   *Were there any attempts to identify dis-investments or at least consider the opportunity costs of pursuing The HOTN targets?*

Achieving major changes in policy direction is difficult if new resources are not made available, and The HOTN was not accompanied by any major resource injections. This meant that strategy was supported either by growth monies alone (bearing in mind other pressures on these e.g. for waiting list initiatives) or through disinvestments to free resources to support investments in strategy.

Growth monies were, in fact, often earmarked for HOTN developments, usually under the control of dedicated HOTN officers. However, as these represented only small increases in total available expenditure the overall effect, even if all was used for HOTN initiatives, was likely to be small.

There were, however, a few notable examples of recognition that if The HOTN were to have any serious impact, then reliance on growth monies would not be sufficient and consideration would have to be given to disinvestments from some current activities which could then, in turn, be used to support investments to meet The HOTN priorities. One health authority, for example, set up a 'Priority Forum' that generated lists of low priority activities which had the potential to release significant resources but only for the resource-releasing specialty and not for more general use. Not untypically, however, the areas identified for dis-investment remained little more than guidance and it was left to medical staff seeking new developments to find the resources from within their existing practice. Despite the effort, the Deputy Director of Finance confirmed that there was little health authority push overall for a systematic approach to disinvestment. There was very strong agreement across all areas that The HOTN had not resulted in major disinvestments elsewhere.

♦ *Was the cost effectiveness of available interventions a factor in conceptualising problems and identifying priorities?*

Despite the fact that The HOTN did not contain any reference to cost effectiveness in its approach to the selection of target areas, it was possible that at local level consideration could have been given to cost effectiveness issues. If maximising health from limited resources was the aim, then prioritisation would be based on marginal benefit to marginal cost ratios of available interventions, rather than by the size of the problem or the measurability of effects. There was little evidence that this was the case and interviewees cited only a few examples where specific health economics studies had influenced the planning or executing of The HOTN related activities.

♦ *Was there an awareness of what was currently being spent in aggregate in any area (i.e. in hospital, community, primary care, local authorities, etc.)? Was any framework in place to consider shifts in the balance of expenditure between the different players?*

By focusing on health outputs rather than activities, The HOTN explicitly acknowledged that health gain in any strategic area was achieved through the efforts of many contributors. An awareness of who was currently doing what, and who was currently spending what in any area ought, therefore, to be a starting point for prioritising within the area. There was no evidence that such a 'programme' approach had been adopted in any of the districts examined.

B.3.2.11 Although a few attempts had been made to apply a 'marginal analysis' framework to consider potential shifts in the balance of expenditure, there were no examples of where this had been judged to have been effective. The overall impact of economic thinking and principles on The HOTN appears to have been limited

B.4 Implementation at Local Level

In assessing the implementation of The HOTN, none of Gunn's 10 preconditions for achieving perfect implementation (see Box 3, p22) were in practice met. Of course, Gunn's model is concerned with setting out the ideal conditions to be met if perfect implementation were to occur. In practice, such perfection is rarely, if ever, achieved. Moreover, as a top-down control model of implementation it only partially applies to The HOTN strategy which sought to combine a 'top-down' perspective with a 'bottom-up' one. This latter view holds that those implementing policy are often influential in shaping policy, and in determining its successful implementation. Insights from both perspectives are needed to illuminate what happened to The HOTN in practice, as the rest of this section seeks to demonstrate.

B.4.1   *Health Authorities in the Lead*

B.4.1.1   The HOTN strategy placed health authorities in the lead position as far as its implementation was concerned.   But this responsibility bestowed on health authorities has to be seen in the context of their overall remit which is substantial.   In total they have four major functions:

(i)   to provide a clear transparent link in the chain of public accountability from centre to periphery

(ii)   to discharge important statutory functions

(iii)   to undertake the role of the purchaser of health services

(iv)   to undertake the wider role of commissioning services and, working with other agencies, to impact upon the causes of ill health and promote health.

Our evidence showed that the last of these functions has regularly been subordinated to the third, and that these two functions are fundamentally different activities that may sit uneasily in the same organisation at a time when accountability demands are concentrated unevenly on functions (iii) and (iv).

B.4.1.2   In the light of this finding, a number of conclusions, many elaborated upon later in this section, can be drawn from the site visits made across the eight authorities and the documentary analyses conducted in each:

♦   The HOTN did not change significantly the perspective and behaviour of health authorities, and did not fundamentally alter the context within which dialogue between health purchasers/providers and other partners took place.

♦   The HOTN did not significantly cause any alteration to management structures within trusts or health authorities.

♦   The HOTN did not cause a major adjustment in investment priorities by the health authorities (see sub section B.3.2 above).

♦   The HOTN did, however, reinforce the changing role of health authorities, providing a framework within which the commissioning role was to be judged. Whilst of marginal benefit to some authorities, for others it prompted a more fundamental adjustment to their perspectives and *modus operandi*.

♦   A reasonable degree of analysis of The HOTN issues was carried out at health authority and regional office levels, and some accountability maintained whilst the RHA remained in operation. This later dissipated in some regions when RHAs were replaced by Regional Offices.   However, in at least one case greater importance seemed to be attached to the health strategy by the Regional Office than by its predecessor.

♦   Some attempt was made to drive progress via the contracting process but it was minimal. The impact upon Trust and primary care teams' performance has been slight.

♦   With few exceptions, The HOTN did not seriously impact upon primary care practitioners either as commissioners or providers.

♦   Community Trusts appear to have been most engaged, via involvement in community development activities and health promotion programmes; acute Trusts - especially the larger ones - have been largely untouched by the health strategy due to their preoccupation with waiting lists, the rising tide of emergency admissions, mergers, acute service reconfiguration, and repeated financial crises. The HOTN has been relevant only where it enabled pre-existing agendas to be furthered, and/or as a source of new funds.

B.4.1.3   Interviews with CHC representatives in the study districts tends to bear out these conclusions. Immediate crises (hospital closures etc) tend to 'soak up' the energies of the membership. They look for concrete issues:

> a *good example would be the whole thing around a primary care-led NHS.... People (in the CHC) can see it and understand it. They know what GPs are...... A much more realistic thing to take on...... HOTN is very much an NHS priority, but perhaps it wouldn't find its way onto our agenda.*

However, some CHCs attempted to 'follow progress on HOTN targets'; but most felt there was little awareness amongst the public - 'In the minds of the public it has probably faded altogether'.

B.4.1.4   In addition to the lead role status accorded health authorities, the study findings indicate three other important areas which have been problematic since the appearance of The HOTN in 1992. They are: the ownership of the health agenda by primary care; its ownership by local government; and the management of the health strategy both within and outside the NHS.   We consider each of these areas in turn.

B.4.2   *Ownership of the Health Agenda by Primary Care?*

B.4.2.1   The views of those involved in primary care, both at the delivery end and those at the authority level with responsibility for liaison/management, are especially important in the light of the 1997 NHS white paper's commitment to the introduction of primary care groups, and subsequently trusts, from April 1999. A key feature of the role of PCGs/Trusts will be to address the health needs of their populations. As our primary care interviewees revealed, overall The HOTN had minimal impact on GP practices.   One GP said that there was 'no connection (locally) between HOTN and primary care in any meaningful way'. Another commented that The HOTN 'did not obviously change GP behaviour'. These views were shared by interviewees in community trusts who claimed that 'preventive work is low on [GPs'] agendas'. A

Director of Primary Care suggested that primary care could be divided into three factions:

> Some *[GPs] saw The HOTN as a useful document that at least gave some coherence to national strategy. They might be cynical about the targets and argue that they do not pertain to where we are, but I would say that top group would probably say 'Yes...we have got heart disease, smoking and so on' but the vast majority of GPs probably just said 'Oh yeah, HOTN is out'. And then there is the cohort at the back who probably don't even know that it was around.*

B.4.2.2   One Chairman of the Local Medical Committee in one of our eight health authorities reported that active involvement by the LMC in The HOTN had ceased in 1995 when the director of public health had indicated that continuing involvement was no longer necessary.   The tangible benefits from an application of The HOTN had been few. One practice had acquired funds for extending counselling services as a result of linking this development to the mental health targets. Other changes in the organisation of mental health services, such as a psychogeriatrician visiting one general practice, had been easier to achieve as a result of The HOTN.   But no major changes could be detected in the key areas of accidents, coronary heart disease or cancer.

B.4.2.3   In another health authority, one GP reported that although The HOTN and what it was trying to achieve was seen as 'beyond our control', some targets were found to be useful and had a galvanising effect. The example given concerned stroke targets which had caused GPs to look at the quality of the stroke service locally and the role of community hospitals. Out of this exercise came a review of the overall approach to stroke management.

B.4.2.4.   Even in health authorities where GPs could appreciate the relevance of the key areas selected in The HOTN and the choice of targets difficulties remained in deciding, as a GP, how the particular targets could actually be delivered.   The

HOTN did not displace other priorities as it was difficult to translate its messages to small practice levels. Consequently, The HOTN ceased to be referred to on a regular basis by GPs although, as one put it, they would still regard a teenage pregnancy or a suicide in the practice as a 'failure' in The HOTN terms. On the positive side, it was suggested by several GPs that The HOTN strengthened what was already happening and allowed it to proceed.

B.4.2.5 Some of the targets, like accidents, posed particular difficulties for primary care because it was felt that on their own GPs could contribute little. Nevertheless, they stimulated awareness on the part of GPs.

B.4.2.6 The non-prescriptive nature of The HOTN was welcomed by some GPs in one health authority because this enabled the strategy to serve as a sort of umbrella under which practice plans could be shaped. In this same authority, the involvement of other primary care staff in The HOTN activity was variable. Some incentives existed which allowed health visitors to become involved in campaigns against exposure to the sun, smoking and accidents. Practice nurses were involved with seeking to influence diets.

B.4.2.7 One respondent summed up the views of all the primary care interviewees when he said that The HOTN's impact on primary care practices was minimal because

> primary care tends to be more reactive than proactive. At its launch [The HOTN] was not perceived to have a great deal of relevance to the average primary care professional.

B.4.2.8 The HOTN was seen by those in primary care as 'someone else's agenda' and as irrelevant because of its population focus, long time-scales and emphasis on non-medical interventions - all features which were opposite in character to the traditional GP practice. A Director of Primary Care said that GPs faced with patients coming through the door would 'concentrate on treating the sick rather than worrying about how to stop them getting sick'.

B.4.2.9 But those in community trusts felt that part of the problem of disengagement lay in strategy setting being seen as the prerogative of the health authority. The role and potential of community trusts and primary care had not been fully taken into account in determining strategy locally.

B.4.2.10 There was also a view that the targets themselves were deficient and not particularly relevant or achievable. They therefore did not engage effectively with GPs. For example, a GP was of the opinion that

> many of The HOTN targets were not thought through. There were grandiose ideas about reducing mental health burdens. But looking at something like suicide and The HOTN target, the average GP will see one potential suicide every 10 to 15 years. We have no evidence that any strategy we have makes any difference.

B.4.2.11 The consensus was that little would change in primary care unless the training of GPs actively encouraged a wider focus and strategic approach to public health. Training also needed to address the area of health promotion which was felt to be 'inadequate' and was given low priority at both undergraduate and post-experience levels. Lack of resources and failure of organisation of services were also seen as problems in engaging primary care. While practices lacked 'basic things' like 'premises, a nurse, computers' it was impossible to progress and do good preventive work. The feeling was that the government was only interested in pushing forward the leading edge of general practice/primary care while ignoring the basic issues which needed to be addressed.

B.4.2.12 Perhaps the most important issue to address in primary care came under the heading of 'culture'. As a Director of Primary Care explained

> you are talking about quite large cultural changes for part of the health service that didn't really consider itself as part of it until 1991 when FHSAs were created. That was the first time they [i.e. GPs] had management in

effect...There is some mentality about leave us alone and let us get on with our job. But I think that is less now. They understand they are fairly crucial to how we run the health service here and are taking ownership to a greater degree than they used to. But it is not easy for them to switch between looking after an individual to looking after public health in its wider sense.

A GP and part-time Medical Adviser claimed that GPs 'will always say they have no time for health promotion'. But the reasons for this need to be investigated. Time management and prioritisation may be the root of the problem. Also

what [GPs] may be saying is that they are so overloaded emotionally and physically in responding to the needs of what walks in through the door, and running a small organisation that they are responsible for that they don't have the inclination to take on this other bit of work. But I think that is a product of doctors' training in medical schools by tertiary specialists. And many people in general practice still see making the rare diagnosis as their raison d'etre. Whilst in fact what they should be doing is acting as public health catalysts for the population they serve. And that requires a huge culture shift. It's the wrong culture that gets you the responses that you are getting to the demands that are being made on them.

B.4.2.13 Our interviewees in primary care were critical of the dissemination of The HOTN which centred on the production of glossy support materials. They had no impact because support materials 'without some sort of focus and development and training behind it are useless' (GP and part time Medical Adviser). The root problem was one of lack of ownership of the health strategy:

You have got to involve people if you want them to take something on board. You have to involve them in developing it from the beginning, and involve them actively in its implementation.

B.4.2.14 A few of our respondents were primary care practitioners though not GPs. For them, too, The HOTN had not had a marked impact on their work. A partial exception was community-based nurses who had been influenced by the language of The HOTN and the initiatives it spawned. But elsewhere there was less enthusiasm. Among general dental practitioners, for example, in one health authority there was a feeling that The HOTN failed to appreciate the context in which they worked. The reality of general dental practice was one of restrictions, savings, capping and lack of resources. Working towards The HOTN targets in such an atmosphere was especially difficult and only made more so by the absence of oral health from the strategy. Among community pharmacists, the impact of The HOTN had been undermined as a result of there being no money or time to develop new services. Community pharmacists felt beleaguered and increasingly under pressure.

B.4.2.15 It was pointed out that the importance of The HOTN for GPs should not be looked at in isolation from the changes to the health promotion payments for GPs. Additional support was thought to be essential if GPs were to take The HOTN, or its successor, seriously. This need not take the form of additional funds but the availability of practical support for GPs.

B.4.2.16 Given the problem of engaging GPs and other primary care practitioners in The HOTN, the view was expressed that perhaps the primary care groups to be introduced in April 1999 offered more optimism about creating alliances across practices and primary care skills and contributing to the health plan, i.e. health improvement programme. However, as an extensive review of the state of primary care as it prepares for change shows, it would be misleading to understate the extent of the challenges, cultural, organisational and managerial, facing primary care, and those seeking to influence it, in the spheres of public health and strategy development (Marks and Hunter 1998).

B.4.3 **Ownership of the Health Agenda by Local Government?**

B.4.3.1 Local authorities across most of the study sites perceived The HOTN to be dominated by 'medical conditions' and heavily 'medically led'. This was a cause for concern, especially among those authorities which believed that they contributed more to a health agenda in its broadest sense than health authorities and gave tangible evidence of actions in the field of health. Many, indeed, identified the WHO *Health For All* ethos and principles as closer to their conception of a health strategy.

B.4.3.2   A general view expressed by local authorities was that 'health' needs to be much more broadly conceived than hitherto, with health promotion being seen as an issue of general community well-being - an area of significant local government concern. The point is nicely captured in a 1993 environment sub-committee report entitled 'The Health of the Nation - One Year On'. It states that

> *although the Government is taking the lead in implementation and the NHS has an important part in this, local authorities have a vital contribution to make in improving the nation's health, building on traditional essential services such as environmental health, planning, housing, education, social services, youth services, emergency services, accident prevention, transport, waste management, trading standardsand leisure and recreation facilities.*

B.4.3.3 The view of one current local authority leader - echoed by many other interviewees, officers and members - was that 'we see it as a town-wide corporate responsibility to be involved in health'. In his view The HOTN targets showed 'that health is not the prerogative of just the NHS'.

B.4.3.4   A perceived leadership role for local government finds expression in a number of forms. Although none of the local authorities in our sample had a corporate health strategy as such - i.e. an extant poling document - most had one of two things which comprise a corporate health approach:

♦   other corporate strategies which singly or collectively address health issues, *inter alia*, Anti-Poverty Strategies, Economic Regeneration Strategies, Agenda 21 Strategies

♦   'Quality of Life' mission statements or guiding principles.

The second of these is the overarching framework which embraces The HOTN and other health related issues within local authorities. Responsibility is most often spread across Chief Officers and, therefore, departmental budgets which provides for a degree of corporateness.

B.4.3.5   The hope was expressed that local government would explicitly have increased responsibility - joint not sole - for public health in its broadest sense, i.e. dealing with the determinants, the root causes of ill-health, not the effects.

B.4.4   *Ownership by Opportunism*

B.4.4.1   The HOTN was no exception amongst government initiatives in being perceived by many groups from the standpoint of their own vested interests.   Hence interpretations as to its operationalisation varied. A comment from one respondent was replicated at many sites

> *one of the errors that some made in interpreting The HOTN was to see it as a health promotion strategy ....*
> *Others saw it as a medical strategy where doctors decided how to do things differently. Neither of those approaches was going to make a difference.*

B.4.4.2   General practitioners, in particular, still discontent from the imposition of a new contract, were prepared to expand health promotion activities as a means of hiring new staff, particularly practice nurses, and expanding their businesses.

B.4.4.3   But it was Departments of Public Health (or Public Health Medicine), following the Abrams Report, that were given the lead position within health authorities for taking The HOTN forward, and for working collaboratively across agency boundaries (Department of Health 1993).   They often became, or were seen to become, the natural protagonists for the new health movement.   So began the development of linkages between public health directors and consultants in public health medicine on the one hand and departmental directors within local authorities on the other; and between health promoters, located in a variety of health service or university settings, and community developers in local government, where their perspectives were aligned in favour of a non-biomedical model oriented towards self-empowerment.

B.4.4.4   For Health Promotion Departments or sections, in particular, The HOTN appeared as a policy blessing to often deeply-held beliefs. As one Head of Health Promotion put it, echoing the voices of many '(I saw it) as an opportunity for funding health promotion, for publicity and for promoting health promotion. It has been a vehicle for this. It has enabled debate and raised awareness'.

B.4.4.5   For many respondents, with the power of hindsight, herein lay the crux of problems that were to follow: fragmentation of ownership, and a failure of corporate alignment between health authorities and local authorities. One response again summarises many:

> *if this was a serious policy at the top of*
> *the government's agenda, then it is the*
> *top of the organisations that need to*
> *deliver the alliances.*

B.4.4.6   Part of the problem in securing 'top of the office' leadership and support in respect of The HOTN lay in the tendency for the strategy to be 'ghettoised' by health authorities, that is, maintained as part of the portfolio of responsibility but effectively sidelined from the real business.   This was underlined by assigning responsibility for The HOTN to parts of the health authority, notably public health and health promotion, which often lacked any real power in organisational terms.

B.4.4.7   Our findings on ownership can be summarised as follows:

♦   Although the reasons for the relatively small number of target areas in The HOTN were understood, there was a

view that health and local government could have tolerated a wider menu that allowed all players to find a role in The HOTN.

♦   Many respondents, from both the health service and local government, felt that some targets should have been clearly allocated to local government, e.g. accidents. Additional targets were also proposed, including: pollution/air quality (being cited by respondents from all disciplines as key health areas); and the quality of life of the 'added years' that would derive from a concentration upon caring for elderly people.

♦   The attitude of elected local authority councillors, only partly determined by party   affiliation, was a critical element in the pace, timing and nature of local partnership. Some local authorities maintained an active involvement in health matters because they sought to influence health in order to improve local health status. Others, for a variety of reasons, were reluctant to engage in meaningful action on The HOTN.

♦   Local politicians were motivated much more by local health issues affecting their area and responded to these rather than national targets. Local ownership of local challenges proved, on the whole, a much more potent force than national exhortation to achieve national targets.

♦   Specific arrangements for health promotion partnerships and alliances between health authorities, trusts, local authorities, primary care and the voluntary sector were unclear.

B.4.4.8   Key findings on the health authority/local authority interface can be summarised as follows:

♦   Continual organisational turbulence frequently disrupted management teams and working alliances, and long term planning had been virtually abandoned in many areas in the face of continual upheaval and instability.

♦ The different agendas/drivers and cultures of health services (centralised and professionally centred) and local government (community based, party political) were complicating factors. Many respondents stressed that, unless local authorities were given a statutory duty to perform, members would most often give low priority to non statutory functions.

♦ Pre-existing structures and challenges heavily influenced the starting point for joint working. Where local government had responded to WHO's *Health for All* and had formed relationships with health authorities there was already joint machinery upon which to build; and in these circumstances The HOTN had been possibly unhelpful. Where such activity and alliances were absent, The HOTN provided a suitable spur to joint action.

♦ Voluntary organisations had been involved in different ways; some had been involved in key areas and had been supported with long term finance. Others were given short term assistance but were 'wheeled in on days like today [i.e. the evaluation interview] to show what the authority has done'.

B.4.5 *Management Issues Within and Outside the NHS*

Handling the Agendas - the Need for a Policy Synthesis

B.4.5.1   Throughout the late 1980s and 1990s, public sector reform has been high on the government's agenda. The NHS, in particular, has been subjected to almost continuous organisational and managerial change. The crowded management agenda for both the NHS and local government, accompanied by high levels of organisational turbulence and personnel disruption, led to a

concentration upon the immediate and operational rather than the strategic and developmental.

B.4.5.2   One Social Services Director summed up the feelings of many respondents across all the sites visited. Whilst on one hand praising the thrust of much of The HOTN, he felt there was an initiative overload, and a need to 'nest' the various ideas in circulation. He explained his concern in these terms

> *how many initiatives can any area*
> *sustain at any one time? We almost*
> *seem to be into initiative conflict,*
> *whereby the health authority call a*
> *meeting under 'HOTN' and talk about*
> *XYZ, and then the Borough call a*
> *meeting under 'Agenda 21' and talk*
> *about YXZ, and then I call a meeting*
> *under 'Community Care Planning' and*
> *talk about ZXY, and then Community*
> *Safety comes along... and we're all*
> *talking about the same things, with slight*
> *peripheral variation, with the same*
> *people, under different title... At some*
> *point, somebody has to ... start to decide*
> *on some kind of hierarchy or nesting of*
> *initiatives.*

Few interviewees claimed to have a clear idea of what each of the initiatives comprised, let alone how each related to the others.   Indeed, there was an expressed wish for some clarity on this issue from the government.   But it would require a corporate approach at the centre which has hitherto been woefully lacking.

B.4.5.3   But this still leaves open the issue of leadership of the multi-agency agenda required by the targets in The HOTN. Many respondents from local government, but also significant numbers from within the NHS, concluded that the health service has rarely shown a capability or capacity for leading consistent interagency strategic change designed to improve the public's health. It has always been diverted or thrown off course by the pressing demands of the sick. They have dominated the policy agenda both nationally and locally.

B.4.5.4.   Successful interagency working has to overcome problems of compartmentalised thinking, concerns about ownership and responsibility for costs. As one quite representative health authority Chair put it,

> *there is an overall problem in the way in which local services are delivered. We tend to think in compartments. Even though health and social services work more closely now. There is constant concern about cost-shifting. Who is really responsible? Where the bottom line is for paying for it. And therefore there is a sensitivity all the time.*

B.4.5.5   Weaknesses in partnerships working were reported particularly to affect key areas such as accident prevention that depend on interagency collaboration:

> *it has been all right with heart disease, strokes, sexual health and so on. People have recognised them as areas where we have problems that we need to address. But I can't say the same thing for accidents. That is the one I feel needs real commitment to push forward because it is much more nebulous, and because our part in it isn't quite so clear cut and involves much more partnership working. And to be honest I don't really feel we have followed through with a lot of that. We are not much further forward with partnerships than we were when HOTN came out.*

B.4.5.6   A shared strategic approach and vision are important to effective joint working and they proved difficult to implement. One Director of Public Health summarised the typical problem common to many situations:

> *although we have some very good working relationships and have lots of meetings, especially with social services, they are very operationally based groups. So we tend to talk about - for example - care in the community schemes, or charging policies, those kinds of things. But I don't think we have really developed a clear strategic*

> *approach with our partner agencies. We work well on the ground, but we haven't got a shared vision.*

B.4.5.7   Human resources issues were a source of difficulty - especially for small health authorities - in establishing partnerships and alliances, particularly where the onus was put on public health directorates. The following illustrates the problem:

> *perhaps we haven't led as much as we should and perhaps we haven't inspired that strategic approach, but it really has been quite hard on the ground with really only two or three of us in the public health department to make that input.... There are not a lot of us to go out and do all this persuading and influencing.*

B.4.5.8   A considerable load has been placed on health authorities in terms of showing other agencies the relevance of The HOTN to their work and in encouraging ownership. A common theme was health authorities having to 'sell' The HOTN. In the words of one Head of Health Promotion:

> *I worked hard (with local authorities) to say 'look we are delivering HOTN, but it is completely underpinned with Health for All principles'. And I worked to gel those two agendas together - to help the local authorities feel they owned it and to run with it.*

Targets and Target Setting

B.4.5.9   The HOTN targets were viewed as the centrepiece of the strategy. With this visibility and the associated publicity came mixed reviews. Whilst generally it was felt The HOTN 'had grand aims [but] very little in terms of actual mechanisms to make it happen', according to one Social Services Director, and they [the targets] were 'something for us to aim at', in the words of a Director of Public Health, both echoing common sentiments, there were a number of more detailed items which the government will need to consider as it prepares for the forthcoming white paper.

B.4.5.10   Views were mixed on the subject of the value of targeting and the targets themselves (see Box 1, p9) echoing other reviews of central guidance on targets (e.g. Barnes and Rathwell 1993, Harvey and Fralick 1997). A summary of one perspective from local government suggests

a strength of HOTN was its broad programme areas, with clear targets, around which organisations and people could coalesce. But the establishment of some more specific mechanisms would have helped - i.e. corporate and joint structures and budgets for grasping what can be done and then planning action, with linkages between activity and outcomes.

B.4.5.11   But another respondent, in contrast, asks why there should have been an interest in The HOTN targets. The response of one Director of Social Services represents a position taken by many across local government and those within public health departments:

everybody wants there to be less cancer and less heart disease...[but] the truth of the matter is that just by setting those targets doesn't actually mean that you tackle the things that would really make a different to those things at all..... what we know is that if you really wanted to make an impact on people's health you would first and foremost fix their housing; secondly, you would create jobs and put people into employment so they could get themselves out of poverty; thirdly, you would provide education, not just about health but about a range of other things; and fourthly, and last, you provide better access to primary health care - but you do the other three first, and then you'd have a healthier nation.

What it was felt was needed was 'a nested strategy where the more specific clinical issues are clearly located within the rather vaguer, longer-term, preventive rather than curative, activities'.

B.4.5.12   If there was some strength seen in having national targets as a vehicle to encourage organisational coalescence, there was a general criticism at the failure to encourage local target setting. Chief Executives from both health authorities and local authorities are represented by one of them who said

you do need a national overlay. If there are some national targets that's helpful; but that's a blunt instrument unless you have something at local level which faces up to the individual characteristics of the local area... There needs to be enough room for manoeuvre locally to interpret national pressures, national targets, standards, policies... to fit local need.

This was a message echoed repeatedly by members and officers alike from all the case study areas.   It was also confirmed by an earlier study commissioned by the NHS Executive on effective healthy alliances for The HOTN (Nuffield Institute for Health 1997). This report noted that The HOTN 'became crucial and important when it was a locally owned agenda for health improvement, reflecting local priorities and supported by key local people and organisations'.

B.4.5.13   The greatest number of observations and criticisms came in terms of the technical and scientific rationality of the actual targets, and over the choice of the inclusion of one target in particular, namely, for suicide reduction. These matters have been considered above in Section 3 on study design and methods.   Suffice it to say here that, as one Director of Public Health put it, summarising the position of many respondents:

......it is fair enough to have population based targets for health improvement, but if they don't require the health service to respond in a different way then they are not challenging enough and it is a reasonable criticism of Health of the Nation. It didn't provide sufficient requirement to change, to seriously affect the mainstream work of health authorities. For cancer, heart

disease and stroke no additional action was required because the targets were simply an extrapolation of the line.

B.4.5.14 Finally, there were difficulties in forming alliances with two tier local authorities. As a Director of Public Health explained,

two tier local government is a complete shambles in terms of determining who is in charge and it has got to be changed. We have tried to get ownership at County level and although the chief exec utive is willing, his members are not interested - they don't get votes for it. Why should they be interested - it is not one of their responsibilities. So we have tried also to get the (numerous) district councils interested and have succeeded in one or two. But most of them are simply housing bodies and once they have sold their houses they are just planning bodies. They don't run services and they don't make decisions that affect people in their everyday lives. Why should we build alliances with them? I fear the present government only sees unitary local government in London and the metropolitan cities. They don't seem to understand this is a big problem they have inherited.

B.4.5.15 However, this is perhaps a rather narrow view, and one limited to the potential impact of NHS interventions alone. There were some fine examples of joint agency health strategies for coronary heart disease and stroke which could be attributed to the healthy alliances arrangements in place, and these might well be expected to impact locally, both in a quantitative reduction of morbidity, and in improvements in quality of life for sufferers and their carers.

B.4.5.16 With a single exception, we could find no support for the inclusion of the suicide reduction target. It was held to be 'a bad indication of anything'. Suicide was not seen as the problem but rather 'the normal functioning of normal people who are under stress.' Mental illness and its consequences, it was felt by many of our

respondents, must be separated from the more frequent problems associated with emotional health and relationship difficulties, and targets should have been set with these areas in mind. The challenge, however, is to avoid stigmatising those with a mental illness by creating a division between them and those with emotional problems. Both varieties of mental illness require to be coped with through a multi-sectoral approach.

B.4.5.17 The sole exception to the lack of support for the suicide reduction target welcomed a focus on serious mental illness (as opposed to the 'worried well') and felt that the suicide target was an appropriate one highlighting the distress of people with severe mental illness and the failure of society to deal with it.

B.4.5.18 Our findings on targets can be summarised as follows:

♦ Approaches to the translation of national targets to local level varied considerably.

♦ Those sites which devoted considerable effort to local targets at first were diverted from this by other priorities as time went on.

♦ There was a general wish for greater freedom both to add target areas to the menu and to adjust targets in the light of local circumstances. 'Well performing' areas already exceeding national targets would have selected higher local targets, perhaps based upon a percentage increase in performance from a historic baseline. Similarly, 'poor' performers would have been more comfortable setting achievable local targets that might be below the national figure. Indeed, this had been locally negotiated in some areas, although there seemed to be an extreme reluctance in all sites to move away from the nationally devised targets, particularly where (though unusually) performance management was highly monitored by regional health authorities/regional offices.

♦   Numerical targets encouraging a change in outcome indicators ought to have been complemented by service targets in relation to particular programmes or activities, and local partners encouraged to set targets.

♦   Many respondents were critical of the targets on technical grounds, for example the suicide target mentioned above. Other targets, again as mentioned earlier, were clearly derived from existing trend lines which, whilst politically comfortable, raised cynicism among professional staff.   Also, because they remain 'rare' events at a local level changes due to 'chance' are difficult to unscramble from 'real' change.

B.4.6   *Performance Management, Continuity and Sustainability*

B.4.6.1   As described earlier, the management agenda in both the NHS and local government was exceedingly busy and turbulent in the early 1990s. But every new initiative brought its own excitement and particular demands.   The HOTN strategy proved to be no exception.

B.4.6.2   Two quotations serve to define the time boundaries of that excitement and describe well the situation found at most sites.   In the words of a respondent working in a joint finance post, it involved

> *not just taking the targets as given, but making very careful analysis of those targets. Looking at the data that we had about how those problems were manifested in our area, and also looking at the other dimension in terms of the particular communities that were experiencing those problems and thinking about how to develop programmes that were going to address those targets. By looking very locally at the way that we responded.*

B.4.6.3   But another individual, taking on a public health role towards the latter part of 1995, reported

> *by the time I took it over it was old hat and there was no excitement left around the implementation. What I have done principally is to monitor progress against national targets ... it has been a monitoring exercise largely as far as I have been concerned.*

B.4.6.4   In our study of the management effort that went into implementing The HOTN between 1992 and 1997, we focused on three elements:

♦   the evidence base and intelligence functions of commissioners

♦   NHS commissioning and contracting, as a means of meeting policy objectives

♦   monitoring the performance of commissioners, providers and local authorities.

We consider each of these in turn.

B.4.6.5   The use of evidence for implementation lay mainly in Departments of Public Health and was variously provided to health authorities and local authorities.   However, the findings suggest:

♦   that these functions have not, in practice, been sufficiently available to local authority and other partners, and that a different organisational model would be required if public health is to provide a commonly-owned intelligence function responsive to locality-based issues and with an agenda rooted in responding to local health challenges

♦   that attempts to use an evidence-based approach to investments was limited in terms of formal arrangements with health economics (academic support) to help evaluate investments. However, even now, it must be noted that techniques that clearly link choices of investment options, service outputs and outcomes are still relatively undeveloped as the following comment demonstrates *without...evidence it is harder to put strong strategies and initiatives together. We need more research and better communication about what works and doesn't work.*

(Head of Health Promotion)

♦   it was unclear to what extent these academic resources had been influential, or even whether all authorities with access to such support had found them useful

♦   many investments were still made as a response to other pressures (e.g. emergency admissions, waiting lists, new therapies) with The HOTN often being deployed to lend credence to a desired expenditure that already had strong support - often among key stakeholders in provider trusts

♦   although authorities had tried to link investments to actions and service output which in turn affected outcomes, it was clear that all faced challenges in how certain they could be about the strength of the linkages.

B.4.6.6   Commissioning and contracting were perhaps the most underdeveloped items of all of the features of the 1990 reforms, and the link between the two was ill-formed in many parts of the country, including the study sites. The corporate contract between RHAs and, from 1996, Regional Offices and health authorities was the principal vehicle for including The HOTN and keeping track of progress towards meeting the targets.   However, the strategy was not high in the contract.   In informal dialogues between the Regional Office (RO) in one region and health authorities The HOTN was almost an afterthought from 1996 onwards.   Other work took priority, e.g. the mental health strategy.   With very few exceptions, at a regional level a service-driven agenda has predominated.   To some extent, the ROs took their cue from the NHS Executive where issues concerning The HOTN were handled at a more junior level.   Interest in progress with The HOTN at the 'top of the office' was minimal.   There has therefore been little official monitoring of RO

performance in regard to The HOTN by the NHS Executive.

B.4.6.7   Other key findings were:

♦   the performance management process was heavily geared to short-term outputs, largely driven by the performance index/Patient's Charter/financial management agendas, and there was no extant performance management for strategic development and achievements for health, as opposed to health services

♦   repeatedly, respondents referred to the formal performance management processes in disparaging terms. 'We feed the beast. I give them the information they seem to want.' 'We've written it in the contract but it doesn't mean anything.' 'We have made efforts to introduce The HOTN through the contracting process but who reads the contracts?'

♦   there was some evidence in the written material of a 'hoped for' world, whilst other systems continued to chart the 'real' activities - the commissioning and contracting processes functioned in a way almost divorced from The HOTN

♦   in primary care, GPs were reported as becoming more aware of population issues, but performance management of independent contractors remained problematic - '(even obvious) items such as asthma weren't on the agenda, and where targets were set they were perceived by GPs to be outside their remit', said one Medical Adviser

♦   for large acute trusts there was little or no reforming or realignment of activity, and in community trusts pre-existing activity was given the convenience label of The HOTN. 'HOTN was not a clarion call for the trust, but a source of money', said one acute trust respondent; 'it does not feature in the trust's Mission Statement'

♦   joint working with local authorities, where it occurred, was most often a community trust/local authority initiative - rarely were acute trusts involved.

B.4.6.8   Monitoring can take on a number of guises: of people meeting their work objectives, of whether or not organisations - local authorities and NHS agencies - meet theirs. In general monitoring progress in respect of The HOTN targets and objectives was regarded as an exceedingly difficult and diffuse process for reasons already stated earlier. This then made it easier to get diverted into responding to local crises and issues identified by, for example, the health authority as requiring attention. In some health authorities, The HOTN as a corporate concern simply got swamped by so many other intervening developments, often of a more tangible nature that, in the words of one Chief Executive, 'Directors can get their hands on'. In such an environment, 'agendas are crowded out'.

> *Every month there is a cry of what can we cut off our agenda. We can't have 20 items. Sometimes the things you really ought to have on the agenda get left off because they don't absolutely have to be dealt with.*

B.4.6.9   Concern was expressed over the monitoring of contracts generally, including the health promotion part of them. A Head of Health Promotion said, when commenting on their contracts with trusts which included health promotion, the problem was in part a capacity one but also one of priorities.

> *We have a large number of trusts and only a small department - how do you monitor what is going on in the trusts? Our chief executives and their chief executives, at the end of the day, are answerable for waiting times and bed-days rather than 'have you got a smoking policy implemented throughout your hospital, or have you done that work on diet?' There just isn't that same level of urgency and accountability.... You can go on banging away at a contract but if they feel it is something*

> *they do not particularly want to do or is not today's priority then they are not going to get it done - or they might get it done but they won't sustain it.*

B.4.6.10   For Directors of Public Health and Health Promotion it was reported that The HOTN was firmly planted in their objectives from the outset and still is, although 'we've stopped talking about it in these terms' said one fairly representative chief executive. For most directors, including Chief Executives, it has tended to fade away as an item for active discussion. One Regional Director explained that while attention paid to The HOTN was quite high in the early years towards the end of the last government it dropped off considerably and fell out of the Director's priorities by 1996. It did, however, continue to be maintained in the induction arrangements for non executive directors.

B.4.6.11   For local authority departments, The HOTN either did not feature at all or a *Health for All* approach took precedence, or, more usually, it was incorporated into other health strategies where they existed.

B.4.6.12   For health authorities, one public health director summed up the impact of performance management discontinuity on The HOTN as follows:

> *when the regions were merged in 1994, as far I am aware everything stopped on the regional overview of Health of the Nation, and the co-ordinating role and monitoring was all but abandoned as almost everyone at the RHA left.*

B.4.6.13   Our findings point to many important lessons to be learned from the way The HOTN was implemented locally from 1992 onwards. These can inform future policy. Suggested lessons for policy are explored in the next and final Part.

PART C.
IMPLICATIONS FOR
FUTURE POLICY

C.1   Why a Checklist?

C.1.1   The principal purpose of this review of The HOTN has been to learn lessons from the experience of implementing the health strategy at a local level with a view to influencing future policy, in particular the forthcoming white paper, *Our Healthier Nation*. From our analysis of the material collected from our eight field sites, and presented in Part B above, we have derived a checklist of policy action points which we consider to be of critical significance in respect of both The HOTN's successes and its failures.   They offer important lessons for future policy.   Most of these have already been mentioned or alluded to in Part B but we have grouped them together in this final part to highlight them and for ease of access.

C.1.   As we have reported in Part A above, there is much to welcome and applaud in The HOTN and it should not be forgotten that, as most of our interviewees were quick to point out, it marked the first attempt by any government to put in place a health strategy which derived its inspiration, at least in part, from WHO's *Health for All* initiative.   But as our findings unequivocally show, The HOTN failed over its five year lifespan to realise its full potential and was handicapped from the outset by numerous flaws of both a conceptual and process-type nature.   Indeed, by 1997 The HOTN appeared virtually moribund in the eyes of many of our respondents, its impact on local policy-making negligible.   Many of those interviewed stressed the need for a fresh start and desperately wanted new life breathed into the health strategy.   They therefore welcomed the government's commitment to produce a new health strategy which would both build on The HOTN's overall aims and objectives, and extend and broaden these in an effort to tackle the poverty problem and the stark evidence of widening health inequalities.

C.1.3   For lesson learning to be effective it is necessary to identify and confront problems and failures, to admit to their existence, and to acknowledge that their resolution lies in being open and honest about what past experience has to offer in guiding future policy.

C.1.4   During the final stages of our field work, the green paper, *Our Healthier Nation*, appeared. Inevitably there were comments on it and comparisons made with its predecessor, The HOTN. Just as the sequencing of events had been unfortunate at the time of The HOTN's appearance (see Part B, section B.2 above), many comments centred on a widespread perception that history was repeating itself.   The view expressed by a Director of Public Health was fairly typical:

> *I suppose the weaknesses of the chronology in the early 1990s have just been repeated and are very regrettable. A logical approach to setting health and health care policy is to set up health policy first, then R&D, then [the] structure [of] the NHS. In 1989 to 1992 it was exactly the other way round and I am afraid they have got it wrong this time, too.*

Like many others, this respondent welcomed the green paper and generally supported its overall thrust and approach. His concern was over the sequencing of policy statements, with the NHS white paper and circular on Health Action Zones having regrettably preceded the green paper, despite ministers' initial intentions. This had left many in the field wondering where the green paper actually fitted in. Predictably, this sequence of events was already resulting in a situation where 'structure is dominating' and proving to be 'a massive distraction to health policy'. The concern expressed was that 'health policy takes second place again' in a context where 'the big picture' is one of 'developing the NHS'. A Director of Public Health put the dilemma unequivocally as follows:

> *we need this initiative [i.e. the green paper] now like a hole in the head. It should have come last year, we were poised for it then, we were ready, we were waiting, we would have done it well.*

C.1.6   A Director of Primary Care confirmed the fear that NHS structural reconfiguration would dominate the agenda. He was firmly of the opinion that the development of primary care groups, as set out in the NHS white paper, should proceed in the context of the green paper but noted that GPs' perception of the green paper was to believe that

> *it is somebody else's agenda - it's big, it is not [about the] individual doctor/patient relationship...They can't see how it relates to their day-to-day business...and this is something we didn't learn from the first time around.*

While the development of PCGs might encourage a population focus within primary care and a weakening of the focus on individuals, the counter-argument was the concern among many GPs about their diminishing advocacy role in respect of individual patients compared to the greater good of the population. For the new health strategy to succeed in a primary care context, it is a matter of continuously 'drip feeding' it.

C.1.7   Some disappointment was expressed in the targets, for example in the absence of a more imaginative approach in the area of disability. The focus of the targets is on reducing mortality.

C.1.8   The need for central government to give a lead was emphasised by many respondents but mixed with cynicism that it would succeed. The view was expressed that a performance management structure for central government was needed 'to underline their commitment to the policy'. A Head of Health Promotion wanted national policy to reflect what was being asked of local agencies and individuals themselves.

> *The general public and the professionals working on health promotion just see total hypocrisy, and you have to have faith in the people who are setting these strategies that they are putting their money where their mouth is. If the... government do that then they should have an inter-departmental group that looks at all their policies...so that at that level you are putting in place things that ultimately would benefit the health of the population.*

C.1.9   For some, the green paper was 'still The HOTN minus one or two things'. The real test of the government's resolve would come over 'how it is going to address inequalities' and how it is 'going to work to make sure that the right policies and structures are in place to ensure that'. (Head of Health Promotion).

C.1.10   As we reported in subsection B.3.2 above, a widely expressed view among senior finance staff was that the limited use of health economics thinking (see Box 2, p21) in implementing The HOTN was due at least in part to the absence of mechanisms which would allow expenditure data to be related to outputs rather than to activities. Several health authorities had in fact made attempts to establish such 'programme budgeting' mechanisms but with little success due mainly to difficulties encountered and the need to respond to other pressures.

C.1.11   There was broad agreement among Directors and Deputy Directors of Finance that a programme budgeting approach would have been helpful in their pursuit of The HOTN, particularly if the programmes had included expenditure by non-NHS agencies. There was similar agreement that allocating expenditure to health gain related programmes now will assist any future evaluation of *Our Healthier Nation*. Several examples were cited to support this contention. One Director of Finance explained that an anticipated large increase in expenditure on statins would clearly have to be accompanied by disinvestments elsewhere in the cardiovascular disease area, but without a programme budget it was difficult to identify where these disinvestments might take place. In terms of the example given in paragraph B.3.2.2, p 22 above, the Deputy Director of Finance pointed out that a programme budgeting system would have allowed the expenditure on outreach centre staff to be shifted from the adult to the teenage contraception sub-programmes. This would have captured the change in resource use and would have facilitated consideration of further marginal shifts between these programmes.

C.1.12   The importance of such a programme-oriented approach becomes all the greater for a future evaluation of *Our Healthier Nation* with its shift away from a medical orientation to health and towards a greater emphasis on the economic, social and environmental causes of ill-health.

C.1.13   Further key lessons for future policy are presented in a checklist format in the next section.

C.2   The Checklist

C.2.1   *Central leadership, ownership and lead role locally*

There is a risk of 'initiative conflict' and overload or the occurrence of a policy mess as a consequence of the plethora of vehicles for collaboration which now exists, e.g. HAZs, HIPs, HLCs, SRB, Agenda 21 and so on.   This range of policy instruments presents rich opportunities to form and sustain partnerships, and to experiment with different models.   But it is essential that the various initiatives are nested and that clear lines of accountability both upwards to central government and downwards to local communities are in place.

Government therefore needs

(a)   to send out clear, consistent 'corporate' signals and ensure cross-departmental ownership (e.g. whereas the Scottish green paper *Working Together for a Healthier Scotland,* is signed by all members of the Scottish Office Ministerial team, the English green paper is signed by two Health Ministers; even the English white paper has a foreword by the Prime Minister) - the importance of such signals, though largely symbolic, cannot be overestimated

(b)   to establish shared ownership at all levels both horizontally and vertically and ensure that chief executives in health and local authorities are engaged and held accountable; as the Scottish green paper states: 'a strategy

for all must be a strategy by all' (The Scottish Office Department of Health 1998, paragraph 5)

(c)   to spell out as clearly as possible agency expectations, tasks and responsibilities; there should be a statement of specific roles and a timetable designed to articulate the achievement of the targets set out in the white paper

(d)   to give careful consideration to whether health authorities should in fact have the lead role for delivering on the health strategy, or whether this should not be a shared role between health and local authorities; the CMO's project to strengthen the public health function in England mentions the possibility of joint appointments between the NHS and local authorities (DoH 1998) while the Scottish green paper suggests other mechanisms to strengthen cross-agency links in public health

(e)   to address the ownership of the health agenda by local government; local authorities are not seeking an exclusive responsibility for health but a joint responsibility; the stress should be on joint targets, joint monitoring, a wider responsibility for health, and statutory responsibility for partnership.

C.2.2   *Interfaces, partnerships, alliances*

Building and sustaining partnerships and alliances is critical to the success of a health strategy since it is by definition multifaceted.   What is needed is a development strategy in order to equip managers and practitioners with the requisite skills and competencies.

There is therefore a need

(a)   to acknowledge, and be sensitive to, the different cultures in health and local authorities respectively

(b)   for policy-makers and managers to act on the evidence where it already exists, as in the case of successful alliances where an evidence base demonstrating the success criteria is available

(c)   to draw on work on effective healthy alliances for The HOTN like that produced by the Nuffield Institute for Health's Community Care Division for the NHS Executive; alliances are likely to succeed where the following nine elements are in place (Nuffield Institute for Health 1997):

-   clear and agreed goals and focused activity
-   clear link to The HOTN agenda
-   senior management commitment and appropriate involvement
-   partnership working and ownership amongst relevant agencies
-   a project management approach and a project manager
-   agreed intermediate outcomes with timescales
-   good and timely communication
-   learning from performance
-   allowing sufficient time.

C.2.3   *Information, intelligence, R&D, use of evidence, gaps in evidence, targets*

There is a need to consider the following points:

(a)   nationally determined targets were acknowledged to be useful in some circumstances as a 'rallying point' or on which to hang existing or developing programmes of work

(b)   national targets are important but local targets should be encouraged within the national framework in recognition of local needs

(c)   the narrowness of The HOTN's focus and targets and whether those set were sufficiently challenging (e.g. the CHD target clearly was not which rather weakened support for, and confidence in, the strategy)

(d)   whether the inclusion of suicide as a target is appropriate: if its removal is not an option then other targets stressing measures of well-being should be included

(e)   individual lifestyle and community development approaches: consider whether these should be combined rather than remain polarised which is unhelpful and wasteful of scarce resources - they should be viewed as complementary; there is no need, nor does it make sense to polarise the medical and social models of health - it is not a case of either or but of ensuring that both are recognised for what they each contribute to improved health

(f)   making the lead role likely to be assigned to public health within health authorities a responsibility that should be shared across health and local authorities

(g)   strengthening the public health function so that it can engage the whole board of directors of health authorities in relating to local authorities

(h)   setting up new data capture mechanisms if the new health strategy is to be evaluated at some point in the future; a data system (e.g. a programme budget approach to recording expenditure as suggested above) which relates resource use to outcomes is a helpful prerequisite.

C.2.4 *Performance management, continuity and sustainability*

Lack of management guidance and incentives at local level were arguably the major failing of The HOTN.

There is therefore a need

(a)   to require that local strategies and targets be set to which both health and local authorities, as well as the voluntary sector, would define their contribution - they would each be responsible to their own organisations, as well as to the joint working group, for performance accountability, and this would also overcome the negative criticism, levelled by many, of green paper targets which might be seen as representing a biomedical model

(b)   to make the delivery of the health strategy matter by establishing clear milestones but at the same time ensure that these are sufficiently flexible to allow for micro-level activities, involving, for example, neighbourhoods, which do not lend themselves to an orthodox performance management framework based on easily measurable and standardised factors

(c)   to resist allowing other agendas or the urgent (e.g. waiting lists, mergers acute sector reconfiguration, establishing PCGs, clinical governance) forever to drive out the important. This fatally weakened The HOTN because it clearly didn't count at the end of the day, especially to chief executives

(d)   to acknowledge The HOTN's important symbolic role: it legitimised activity and put health on the national

and local policy agendas for the first time - its weakness was that it was not regarded as core business and ceased to be taken seriously

(e)   to consider instituting a regular and independent policy audit of the new strategy if it is to be taken seriously locally and if commitment to it is to be sustained

(f)   to consider how a health economics approach may be helpful in the event of introducing an audit

(g)   to acknowledge that stability is an important aspect of ensuring continuity; the high turnover of key staff was a contributor to corporate amnesia

(h)   to avoid over-reliance on 'product champions' or social entrepreneurs since it induces a false sense of permanence; invariably when such charismatic individuals depart, the project collapses - embedding the health strategy principles in the culture of the organisation and its management is vital

(i)   to give early attention to strengthening the capacity to deliver on the strategy: unless policy intentions and resource flows are aligned then the prospect of the strategy being taken seriously must be remote; the CMO's project to strengthen the public health function is a recognition of this reality but it is only a start

(j)   to strengthen the ability of the public health function so that multi-disciplinary work can be carried out, taking full advantage of local expertise available

k)   to consider the role and value of the HEA, which is not mentioned in the green paper, *Our Healthier Nation*, in any assessment of past HOTN achievements and possible future developments; it could contribute to the strengthening of infrastructure where weaknesses (many of them noted above) are to be found.

C.3   *Looking to the Future*

C.3.1   The emerging agenda for encouraging partnerships and alliances across both central government departments and local agencies (horizontal integration), and between national and local levels (vertical integration), provides for many exciting opportunities.   No previous government has succeeded in achieving partnership working on a sustained basis despite occasional attempts to do so but then none has embarked on such an ambitious reform strategy.

C.3.2   Reflecting on the future, and on possible developments arising from the green paper as it progresses through to white paper status, we think it wise that attention be given to evaluation of the new programme and actions now under consideration. As we have noted, our assessment of The HOTN has been hindered by a lack of appropriate data. It would be helpful, therefore, to consider what types of data are required, whether there is a need for routine or special collection approaches, and the time frame that is of interest. Some information might be required quickly by both the government and managers whilst other information can be provided in the medium term for planners and policy-makers. Epidemiologists and economists often need to have a longer term perspective if their respective contributions are to be useful and trends are to be discovered.

C.3.3   We believe that if an evaluation culture is built into the new health strategy then there is every prospect of real and sustained improvements in the health of the population occurring. The health policy agenda is an exciting one. No other government has succeeded in securing change in the health status of its population on such a scale. All the more reason, then, for ensuring that the lessons from implementing the HOTN are learned, and any corrective action taken, as the strategy is implemented in the years to come.

APPENDIX 1

Members of the Research Teams

Nuffield Institute for Health, University of Leeds

Professor David J Hunter (Principal Investigator)
Professor of Health Policy and Management

Dr Jim Connelly
Senior Lecturer in Public Health

Brian Hardy
Senior Research Fellow

Dr Catherine Richards
Visiting Lecturer in Public Health Medicine (on attachment)

Dr Mike Robinson
Senior Lecturer in Public Health

Dr Wendy Sykes
Visiting Senior Research Fellow

Professor Rhys Williams
Professor of Public Health and Epidemiology

Professor Gerald Wistow
Director and Professor of Health and Social Care

Welsh Institute for Health and Social Care, University of Glamorgan

Professor Morton Warner (Co-Principal Investigator)
Director and Professor of Health Strategy and Policy

Tony Beddow
Senior Fellow

Professor David Cohen
Professor of Health Economics

Marcus Longley
Associate Director

David Taylor
Professor

APPENDIX 2

Interview Guides

Health Authorities

How significant a problem is each of the health issues seen to be locally? Evaluated in what terms?

What analysis of the key areas (targets) did the authority do?

Was the health authority's 'mission statement' revisited in the light of HOTN?

Was the 'mission statement' of, and/or corporate contract with, the Regional Health Authority (Regional Office from April 1996) revisited as a result of HOTN?

Were there any identifiable incentives that influenced the way HOTN was put on the agenda and subsequently handled?

In pursuing local policies have specific local objectives/targets been set? Or has the framework been set by national targets?

To what extent have decisions about local objectives in respect of the key issues been a joint endeavour between local agencies?

Did you conduct (ask for) any programme (service) reviews? Did you think any were necessary? Why did you (didn't you) ask for (conduct) a programme (service) review?

Have you any idea what is currently being spent in any key area (target) - in hospital, community, primary care for treatment; primary, secondary and tertiary prevention, palliative care and so on? If so, have you any idea of the relative size of the expenditure as compared with other key (or non-key) areas (targets)?

To what extent have locally important health issues been 'displaced' by HOTN priorities?

To what extent have HOTN key issues been 'overshadowed' by health matters considered locally to be of greater importance?

More generally, to what extent has the pursuit of HOTN priorities been at the expense of other important agency (HA, LA) activities? Or is it HOTN priorities that have suffered through such activities?

How far has HOTN been a focus for initiatives relating to 'healthy schools' and 'healthy workplaces'?

Does the authority have an explicit policy for promoting the health of its own employees?

Were HOTN targets built into provider contracts? If so, how were they expressed?

How much heed was paid to HOTN in formal dialogues between the RHA/RO and health authority?

How often did HOTN key areas (targets), and assessments of progress towards meeting them, appear on the authority's agenda?

How many investment decisions were explicitly made with HOTN key areas (targets) in mind? Have investment patterns changed? If so, can you provide evidence?

Did the DPH's annual report change to deal with progress in responding to HOTN key areas (targets)?

Did the annual report of the health authority address HOTN topics?

How, if at all, have any local initiatives been evaluated? With what result?

What has been the impact on local initiatives of alliances between agencies?

To what extent have gains resulting from local initiatives been set against the costs of attaining them? How do they compare?

Can you identify any expenditure which was specifically undertaken in the pursuit of a HOTN target? If yes, please give examples.

Can you identify any expenditure reduction (or proposed increase that didn't go ahead), ie disinvestment, specifically as a result of a HOTN target being pursued?

Is it possible to identify with examples any expenditure shifts or co-funding between health and social services - or any other agencies - in pursuit of an HOTN target?

Are you aware of any changes made within the DoH/NHS Executive to track or monitor the impact of HOTN on management priorities and action?

What changes were made to information systems in order to monitor progress with HOTN targets?

What demands were made by and upon the RHA/RO in respect of HOTN reports?

How did the RHA/RO approach the implementation of HOTN?

Were HOTN milestones established and if so by whom?

Was the health promotion function modified to respond to HOTN targets? If so, how?

Were HOTN targets reflected in the guidance given to GP fundholders?

Were HOTN targets related to the required performance of GPs?

Have data been gathered locally that allow interventions to be evaluated in terms of health outcomes - final [most unlikely], intermediate or proxy? With what result?

Concluding Questions

What problems has HOTN created for your organisation?

What positive aspects and opportunities has HOTN created for your organisation?

Local Authorities

Is there a corporate health strategy? Is it part of a broader strategy such as anti-poverty work, Agenda 21, economic regeneration, the authority's mission statement or business plan? Or is it a separate strategy focused on health issues?

If a health strategy exists, which is the lead department for it? Which is the lead committee for health work?

Is health promotion work recognised as a specific area of activity in the local authority? If so, what are the main areas of health promotion work?

Which departments are most involved in health promotion work?

Is there a centrally held corporate budget specifically for health promotion? If so, what is its source?

What mechanisms, if any, do you use for working with the health authority on health promotion strategies and action?

Can you give any examples of areas where you have successfully influenced health authority priorities and plans for health promotion?

What impact has HOTN had on the authority's health promotion activity? For instance, has it made you more or less likely to undertake health promotion work? Has it increased the amount of inter-agency or health alliance working?

How far has HOTN been a focus for initiatives relating to 'healthy schools' and 'healthy workplaces'?

Does the authority have an explicit policy for promoting the health of its own employees?

Have any other health initiatives or strategies either nationally or internationally (eg WHO's Health For All) had an impact on your work?

NHS Trusts

What changes in practice were made in the Trust in response to HOTN key areas (targets)?

How significant is HOTN seen to be for the Trust? Does it feature in its 'mission statement' or business plan?

Has HOTN influenced the priorities of the Trust?

How many investment decisions were explicitly made with HOTN key areas (targets) in mind? Have investment patterns changed? Can you provide evidence?

How far has HOTN been a focus for initiatives relating to 'healthy schools' and 'healthy workplaces'?

Does the trust have an explicit policy for promoting the health of its own employees?

Do HOTN priorities get reflected in contracts with the health authority(ies)? If so, how?

Is the Trust able to show how interventions associated with HOTN have impacted on outcomes?

Concluding Questions

What problems has HOTN created for your organisation?

What positive aspects and opportunities has HOTN created for your organisation?

NHS Regional Offices

How were key areas (targets) for achievement set within the Region

Did the RO (and the RHA before it) revisit the corporate contract with health authorities as a result of HOTN?

Has the RO's approach to HOTN been substantively different from that adopted by the RHA?

How much attention is/was paid to HOTN in formal dialogues between the RO/RHA and health authorities?

Has the RO/RHA initiated any regional level structure to engage partners outwith the NHS?

How is the impact of HOTN on management priorities and action tracked and monitored?

What demands have been by and upon the RO/RHA in respect of HOTN reports?

How has the RO/RHA approached the implementation of HOTN?

APPENDIX 3

List of Roles Interviewed

TYPE OF INTERVIEWEE	A	B	C	D	E	F	G	H
Chairman, Health Authority			G	I	I	I	I	
Chairman, Trust		2 x I					I	
Chief Executive, Health Authority	G, I	G	G	G, I	G	G	G	G
Chief Executive, Trust			2 x I		2 x I		G	
Consultant/Director of Public Health	G	G	2 x I	G, I	G	G, I	G	G, I
Director of Finance, Health Authority		G	I		G		G	
Other Health Authority Director		2 x G			I, 3 x G	I	2 x G	I
Other Trust Director	2 x I	4 x G	I	6 x I	I, 3 x G	4 x I	7 x G	2 x G, I
Chief Executive, County Council			I					I
Chief Executive, Metropolitan Borough Council			I			I	G	
Chief Executive, Other Local Authority	I							
Local Authority Member						2 x I		I
Director of Education			I				G	
Director of Social Services	2 x I		I		G	3 x I	I	I
Director/Assistant Environmental Health	I		2 x I		G	I	I, 2 x G	
Other Local Authority Senior Officers		5 x G		3 x I	3 x G		3 x G	3 x I

TYPE OF INTERVIEWEE	A	B	C	D	E	F	G	H
Medical Trust Officers			I		G			
GP	I	7 x G	I	I	2 x G			
Voluntary Sector	I	10 x G	I	2 x I		I	2 x G	I
Health Promotion	G, I	I	I	I	I	I	I, G	I
HOTN Co-ordinator			I				4 x G	
Local Medical Council Representative			I		G		I	
CHC Member	I							
CHC Chief Officer				2 x I		2 x I		
Other Primary Care Practitioner		2 x G			3 x G			I

Key: I = Seen individually
G = Seen in a group of 2 or more people

APPENDIX 4

Health of the Nation (HOTN) - Essential Document Checklist

Name of Health Authority ....

1. Health Authority map showing local authority boundaries
    (with names/details of re-organisations)

2. HOTN-relevant reports to the
    Health Authority
    (title and dates)

3. DPH Annual Reports
    1991   _____
    1992   _____
    1993   _____
    1994   _____
    1995   _____
    1996   _____

4. Health Authority Purchasing Intentions
    1990   _____
    1991   _____
    1992   _____
    1993   _____
    1994   _____
    1995   _____
    1996   _____
    1997   _____   (Strategic Framework)

5. Health Status Information documents
    (titles and dates)

6. Corporate Contracts
    1990/91   _____
    1991/92   _____
    1992/93   _____
    1993/94   _____
    1994/9   _____
    1995/96   _____
    1996/97   _____
    1997/98   _____

7. Specific Contract documents
    (titles and dates)

8. Reports on alliances/joint
    developments in HOTN areas
    (titles and dates)

APPENDIX 5

Comprehensive Time Trend Data Tables for Stroke, CHD, Suicide, Asthma, Tuberculosis.

<u>Note</u>: *The 8 health authorities in our sample have been coded A, B, C, D, E, F, G, H.*

Figure 1

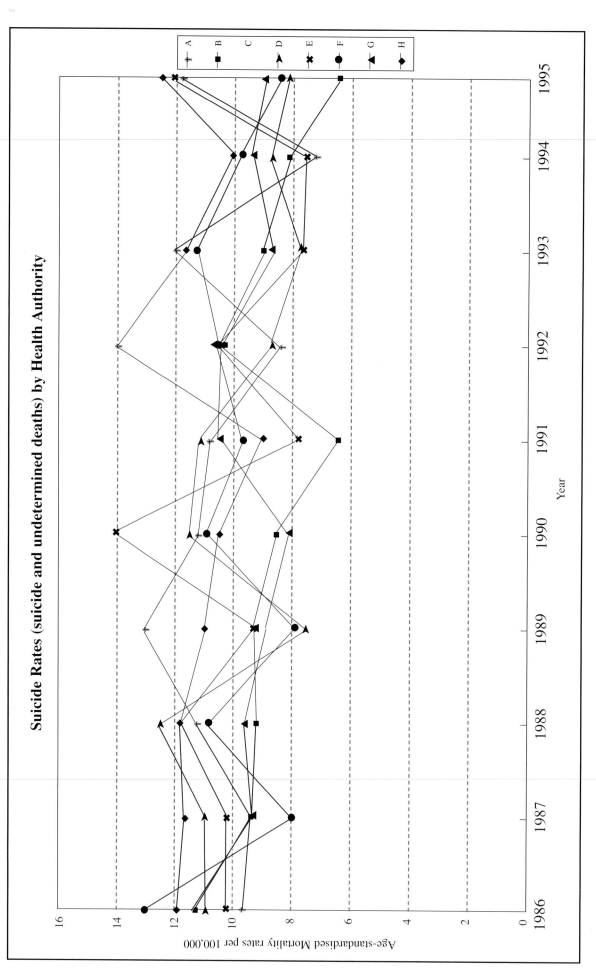

Suicide Rates (suicide and undetermined deaths) by Health Authority

Figure 2

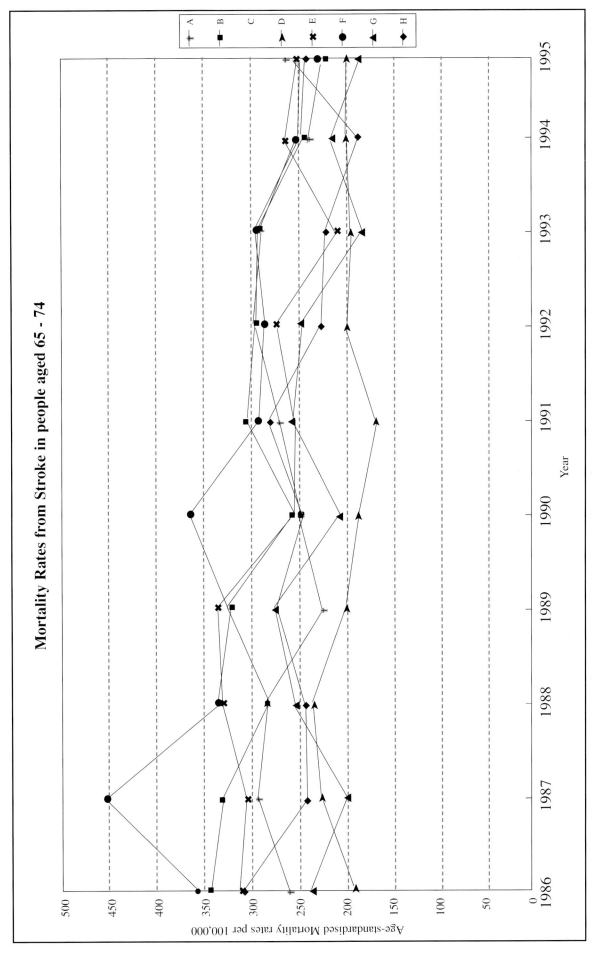

Mortality Rates from Stroke in people aged 65 - 74

Figure 3

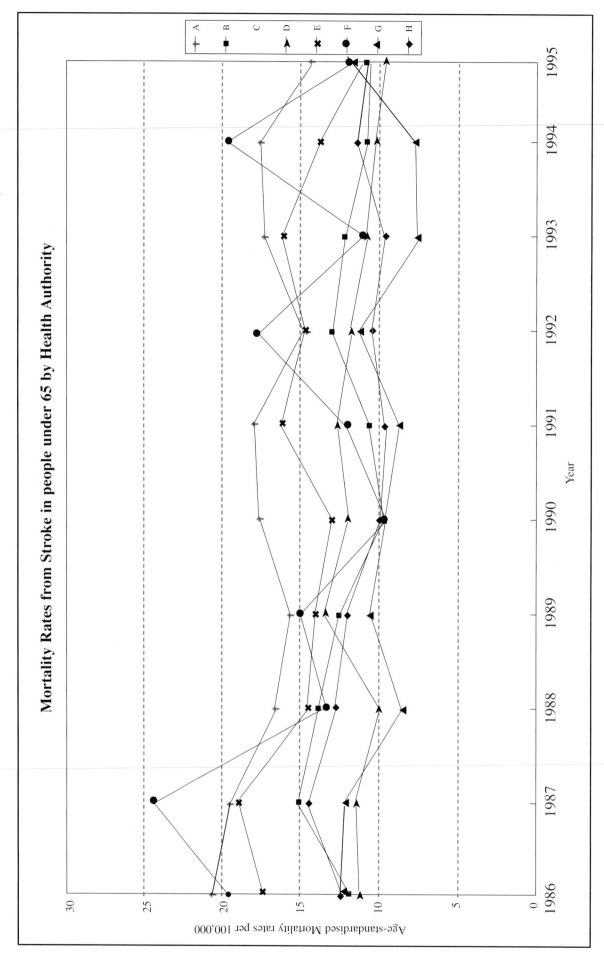

Figure 4

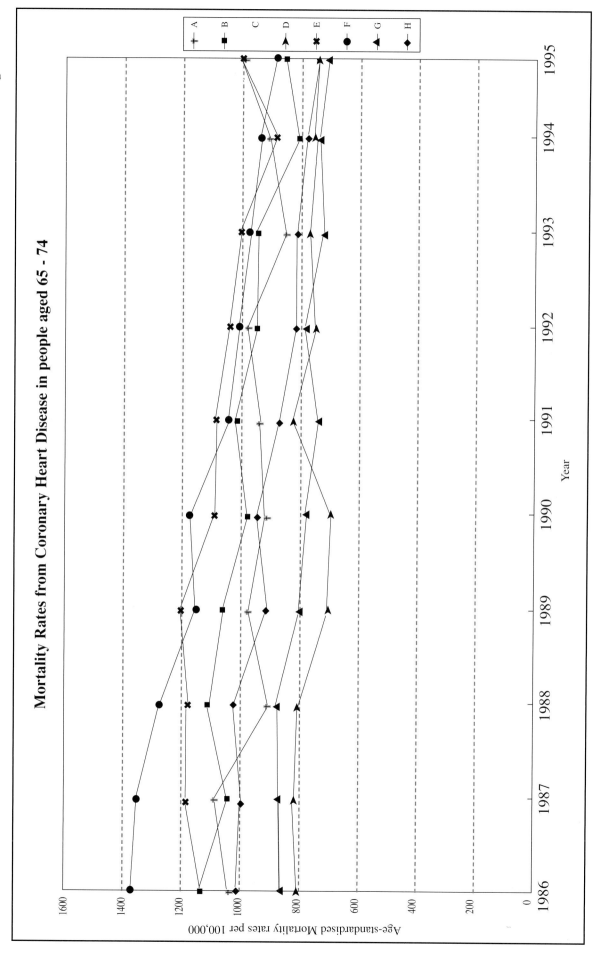

Mortality Rates from Coronary Heart Disease in people aged 65 - 74

Figure 5

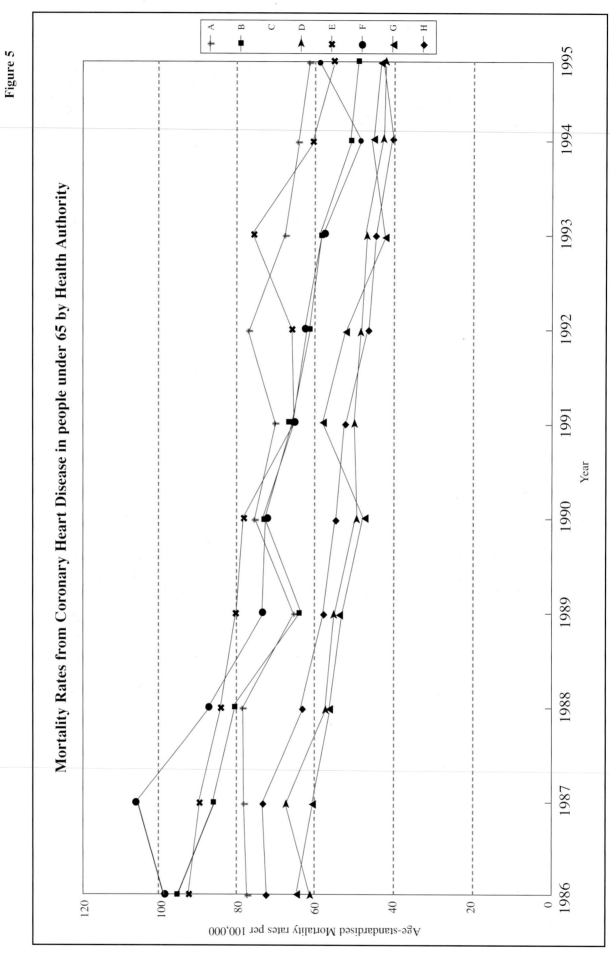

Mortality Rates from Coronary Heart Disease in people under 65 by Health Authority

Table 1   ASTHMA persons 5 - 64 (1993 - 1995)

Health Authorities	(observed)	Standardised Mortality Rates	95% (confidence units)	
			Lower Limit	*Upper Limit*
A	(15)	245	137	404
B	(03)	101	20	294
C	(05)	100	32	233
D	(06)	93	34	202
E	(03)	69	14	201
F	(03)	52	10	151
G	(03)	48	10	139
H	(01)	20	0	112

Table 2   TUBERCULOSIS persons 5 - 64 (1993 - 1995)

Health Authorities	(observed)	Standardised Mortality Rates	95% (confidence units)	
			Lower Limit	*Upper Limit*
A	(15)	425	238	702
B	(09)	229	105	435
C	(03)	97	31	227
D	(02)	77	15	224
E	(02)	61	7	220
F	(01)	48	1	265
G	(01)	29	0	158
H	(00)	0	0	101

REFERENCES

Appleby, J (1997) 'Feelgood Factors' *Health Service Journal*, 107: 24-27

Barnes, R and Rathwell, T (1993) *Study to Assess Progress in the Adoption and Implementation of Health Goals and Targets at the Regional and Local Levels.* Leeds: Department of Health and Nuffield Institute for Health

Calman, Sir K (1997) 'On the State of the Public Health', *Health Trends*, 29 (3): 67-79

Department of Health (1993) *Public Health: Responsibilities of the NHS and the Roles of Others.* Advice of the Committee set up to undertake a review of HC(88)64 (The Abrams Committee report)

Department of Health (1995) *Policy Appraisal and Health.* A Guide from the Department of Health. London: Department of Health

Department of Health (1997) *Public Health Common Data Set 1996: England, Volume II.* Produced by the National Institute of Epidemiology, University of Surrey

Department of Health (1998) *The Chief Medical Officer's Public Health Function Review in England.* London: Department of Health

Francome, C and Marks, D (1996) *Improving the Health of the Nation.* London: Middlesex University Press

Gunn, LA (1978) 'Why is Implementation so Difficult?' *Management Services in Government*, 33: 167-76

Harrison, S (1998) 'Implementing the Results of Research and development in Clinical and Managerial Practice'. In: Baker, M and Kirk, S (eds.) *Research and Development for the NHS: Evidence, Evaluation and Effectiveness.* Second edition. Oxford: Radcliffe Medical Press

Harrison, S Hunter, DJ Johnston, IH Nicholson, N Thunhurst, C and Wistow, G (1991) *Health Before Health Care.* Social Policy Paper No. 4. London: Institute for Public Policy Research

Harvey, J and Fralick, E (1997) 'Targeting Neglect' *Health Service Journal*, 107: 26-27

Holland, WW and Stewart, S (1998) *Public Health: The Vision and the Challenge.* The Rock Carling Fellowship 1997. London: The Nuffield Trust

Lipsky, M (1980) *Street Level Bureaucracy.* New York: Sage Foundation

Marks, L and Hunter, DJ (1998) *The Development of Primary Care Groups: Policy into Practice.* Birmingham: NHS Confederation

Mawhinney, B and Nichol, D (1993) *Purchasing for Health: A Framework for Action.* Leeds: NHS Management Executive

Moran, G (1996) *Promoting Health and Local Government.* A report prepared for the Health Education Authority and the Local Government Management Board. London: Health Education Authority

National Audit Office (1996) *Health of the Nation: A Progress Report.* HC 656 Session 1995-96. London: HMSO

Nuffield Institute for Health (1997) *Effective Healthy Alliances for the Health of the Nation.* A Performance Management and Self Audit Workbook for Commissioners of Healthy Alliances. A Report for the NHS Executive. Leeds: Nuffield Institute for Health

Secretary of State for Health (1992) *The Health of the Nation. A Strategy for Health in England.* Cm 1986. London: HMSO

Secretary of State for Health (1998) *Our Healthier Nation: A Contract for Health.* A Consultation Paper. Cm 3852. London: The Stationery Office

Secretary of State for Scotland (1998) *Working Together for a Healthier Scotland.* A Consultation Document. Cm 3854. Edinburgh: The Stationery Office

London School of Hygiene and Tropical Medicine

Evaluation of the Implementation of *the Health of the Nation*

A report commissioned by the Department of Health

AUTHORS

Dr. Naomi Fulop (Principal Researcher)[1]
Senior Lecturer.

Julian Elston[1]
Research Fellow.

Martin Hensher[2]
Health Economist.

Professor Martin McKee[1]
Professor of European Public Health.

Rhiannon Walters[2]
Consultant/Researcher.

[1] Department of Public Health and Policy.
[2] London Health Economics Consortium.

CONTENTS

LIST OF FIGURES

ACKNOWLEDGEMENTS

The project team would like to thank all the people in the case study districts who gave up their time to be interviewed, and others who spent time collecting documents and financial data. We would also especially like to thank the following individuals for the considerable help they gave with aspects of the expenditure analysis:

Nick Adkin Immunisation and Communicable Disease Branch
Department of Health, Wellington House

Dr John Ferguson   Medical Director
Prescription Pricing Authority

Sammy Foster Breast Screening Programme Team
Department of Health, Skipton House

Paul Gilbert
Sean Gregory Financial Returns, SPB ATA
Department of Health, Quarry House

Linda Johnson-Laird Department of Health, Wellington House

David Lambert Population Estimates Unit
Office for National Statistics

Damon Palmer

Karl Payne   FPA PES 3
Department of Health, Quarry House

LIST OF ABBREVIATIONS

AIDS/HIV - Acquired Immune Deficiency Syndrome/Human Immunodeficiency Virus

APHR - Annual Public Health Report

CCP - Community Care Plan

CHC - Community Health Council

CHD - Coronary Heart Disease

CMO - Chief Medical Officer

DAT - Drug Action Team

DfEE - Department for Education and Employment

DoE - Department of Environment

DoH - Department of Health

DPH - Director of Public Health

EHO - Environmental Health Officer

FHSA - Family Health Service Authority

GDP -Gross Domestic Product

GMS - General Medical Services

GPs - General Practitioners

HA - Health authority

HAZ - Health Action Zones

HCHS - Hospital and Community Health Services

HFA - Health For All by 2000

HIP - Health Improvement Programme

HLC - Healthy Living Centre

HOTN - Health of the Nation

HP - Health promotion

IHD - Ischaemic heart disease

KAB - Knowledge, Attitude and Behaviour

LA - Local authority

NHS - National Health Service

OHN - Our Healthier Nation

OPCS - Office of Population Censuses and Surveys

PBMA - Programme Budgeting and Marginal Analysis

PH - Public health

PHC - Primary Health Care

R&D - Research and Development

SMR - Standardised Mortality Ratio

SRB - Single Regeneration Budget

TEC - Training and Enterprise Council

UK - United Kingdom

UPA - Under-Privileged Area score

US - United States of America

VSC - Voluntary Sector Council

WHO - World Health Organization

EXECUTIVE SUMMARY

Background

The Health of the Nation (HOTN) strategy for England was launched in 1992. It focused on five key areas, setting out overall objectives for each, with 27 individual targets monitored by the Department of Health's Central Health Monitoring Unit. Although there is information on progress towards meeting these targets, the HOTN strategy has not been evaluated as a method by which central government influences national and local policy.

This study aims to provide a review of the HOTN strategy which will complement current monitoring of progress. It aims to provide an analysis of the mechanisms by which the strategy has been implemented at the local level.

Locations

The study was undertaken in eight districts, with one selected at random from each NHS region. The districts selected have a fairly even distribution of structural and demographic characteristics including the OPCS Area Classification, Jarman scores and standardised mortality ratios (SMRs). All except one experienced a real budgetary increase, averaging 9.7% over the study period (1991-97).

Methods

133 semi-structured interviews were conducted in the eight districts covering all sectors. 189 documents were collected. A comprehensive dataset from health authority, former FHSA and trust accounts, AIDS Control Act Reports and resident population estimates were obtained for each district. Local expenditure data were obtained to varying degrees of completeness in all health authorities.

How the policy was perceived

Those interviewed were clearly committed to intersectoral work for health improvement and interviews supported a view that positive experience of partnership for other purposes such as drugs action or economic regeneration were beneficial to partnership for health improvement. There was some support for the proposal that directors of public health be appointed jointly by local authorities and health authorities, as an enabling structure for *Our Healthier Nation* (OHN). Communication of HOTN by the Department of Health to most potential partners for health improvement was poor. Information about the health strategy should be more relevant and accessible, particularly to key players outside the health service

The present targets had little credibility, and most of the sample would like to see the indicators changed. Introduction of performance management of OHN in the health service and other sectors would be seen as demonstrating top-level commitment, provided it is introduced with a sophisticated understanding of agencies' ability to achieve performance management objectives

Interviewees would like central government to take a stronger role in improving health, at every level, and to avoid conflicts between policies of different government departments.

The sample supported more resourcing for a national strategy for health, but nearly half qualified their replies to specify prescribed and purposeful spending to support structured action for health improvement at the local level.

A strategy structured by a matrix approach (see Figure 8.1) which combines diseases, settings and population groups at its highest level could be flexible and successful in winning the support of a wider range of partners.

Impact of HOTN

HOTN was perceived as increasing prevention activity overall, particularly in relation to the key areas and alliance work. In particular, HOTN was perceived as enabling health promotion efforts to be prioritised and to improve co-ordination. There is some evidence for ownership of HOTN outside HA departments of public health, particularly through purchasing plans and contracts with providers but there are also areas where ownership appears weaker, such as a lack of reference to HOTN in corporate contracts and general practice reports. The impact of HOTN on key policy documents did, however, increase over the study period, peaking in 1993 but then falling off slightly.

Per capita expenditure and health promotion expenditure as a proportion of total NHS for both 'narrow' and 'broad' measures of health promotion show a slight increase over the study period to a peak in 1994/5 with a gradual tailing off, so there is little evidence to suggest that HOTN had anything more than a limited influence on patterns of resource allocation at local level. Analysis of individual health authorities' patterns of expenditure suggests that population-based health promotion may be a 'soft target' and may be reduced to achieve savings. Expenditure on HIV/AIDS prevention activities increased its share of total population-based health promotion funding suggesting that some HAs are using this ring-fenced budget to cross-subsidise other health promotion activities. This raises the issue of the importance of ring-fenced resources in the implementation of a national health strategy

Mechanisms for implementation developed at local level

The different extent to which HOTN was used to focus activities for health improvement and intersectoral health strategies was reflected in varying management structures for HOTN. Health strategies and alliances developed by the health authorities can be categorised as: i) taking place under a heading other than HOTN; ii) under the specific heading of HOTN or; iii) HOTN 'plus', where local key areas were added to the original five. The use of contracts to involve NHS Trusts in the implementation of HOTN varied greatly - but there is support for integrating OHN explicitly into new commissioning arrangements. General practitioners tend to focus on the health promotion tasks under their contracts, and did not give strong priority to strategic action for health outside this framework.

HOTN appears to have stimulated and focused intersectoral health strategies in some districts, while others have been able to progress strategies without this stimulus. Health authorities have not found it easy to involve the police and private sector in health partnership. Police forces and some businesses are willing to engage in partnership, but prefer working on specific measures to less well-defined 'strategic' partnerships. Six out of eight HAs had explicitly earmarked funds for alliances; amounts ranged from £2,000 to £200,000, suggesting that they were used in very different ways. Over a third of interviewees (38%) mentioned the need for a statutory framework to allow key local participants, particularly local government, to work intersectorally for health with the support of their formal system.

Only one HA operated a designated HOTN budget covering all HOTN development activities. Five other HAs had allocated partial (non-staff) budgets for development in certain key areas. Current budgeting and financial reporting mechanisms need considerable improvement if they are to be effective in supporting decision-making across multiple settings and agencies. The absence of any requirement to monitor spending on HOTN development ensured that it is impossible to identify or compare the resources invested in the implementation of the strategy. If current financial monitoring and budgeting systems do not change, the same fate will inevitably befall OHN implementation.

Factors influencing implementation of HOTN

The following key factors emerged as influencing the implementation of HOTN: lack of resources; support from central government; organisational structures within or between organisations; the quality of partnerships; commitment of organisations and individuals; demographic characteristics of the local district, and LA cultural and political factors.

Resources - lack of resources were cited by one-third of interviewees as a barrier to implementation. This was supported by the expenditure analysis which indicated first that population based health promotion may be a 'soft target' and may be reduced to achieve savings, and secondly that HIV/AIDS prevention funds were being used to cross-subsidise other health promotion activities.

Organisational structures - at the interface between organisations, coterminosity in general was perceived as facilitating implementation of HOTN. However, at an individual district level, unitary districts were not any less likely to perceive structural factors as barriers to HOTN implementation. Within HAs, organisational restructuring and staff turnover were perceived as negatively affecting implementation. Within LAs where directorates worked independently of each other without a strong corporate approach, HAs found it difficult to develop relations across these LAs.

Quality of partnership - perceived as important for implementation of a health strategy. Partnerships need to be reinforced by a supportive culture and incentives for partnership (such as those provided in SRB).

Commitment - data indicated a range of perceived commitment to HOTN with health promotion departments perceived as having the strongest commitment followed by public health departments and HAs overall. Commitment by senior staff and key individuals was perceived as an important facilitating factor for HOTN.

Demographic characteristics - divisions between affluent and deprived areas in their districts were identified as influencing implementation of HOTN. Deprivation can be seen as a factor which can mobilise intersectoral action on health.

Local authority cultural and political features - the political complexion of LAs may affect implementation of HOTN, although this was a stronger factor in some districts than in others. LAs which had a tradition of commitment to health promotion had better relations with their health authorities.

Impact on non-HOTN areas

Compared to the level and type of activity in the HOTN key areas, strategic activity and activity involving alliances and targets, or based in innovative settings is low in the non-key areas (childhood immunisation, asthma, diabetes). There may have been a slight increase in 'HOTN-type'

activity where these areas are designated as local key areas. Work on the non-key areas is based largely on well established mechanisms in primary health care. These mechanisms need strategic management that is probably best ensured at the national level. The inherent characteristics of these three areas probably led to the development of a different pattern of activity

Lessons learned for implementation of a national health strategy

There are ten key lessons for the new health strategy.

(i) A range of models of implementation of OHN should be supported to allow for variation in local circumstances and previous developments in health strategy.

(ii) OHN should address the underlying determinants of health and inequalities. A matrix model has many advantages, enabling explicit consideration of both disease and population-based models of health.

(iii) There is an unresolved issue about where responsibility for the strategy should rest and the placement of the public health function should be kept under review in the light of changes in the NHS.

(iv) Regardless of the detailed arrangements within the NHS, communication needs to be improved to widen ownership of OHN outside the NHS

(v) If the momentum of the strategy is to be sustained, it needs to be firmly embedded in a performance management framework. This should include monitoring the process of implementation as well as the outcome, and should enable resources connected with the strategy to be identified, isolated and monitored.

(vi)   Targets are a necessary tool for prioritisation, but must be credible and local development of local targets should be encouraged.

(vii)   There is a need for a statutory framework to encourage key local agencies, particularly local government, to work in partnerships for health. Other incentives for partnerships should also be considered to support the commitment of individuals and organisations necessary for implementation.

(viii)   Central government has a key role to play but it is essential that there is a consistent message across government that is in support of OHN. Central government should also foster the development and dissemination of an evidence base.

(ix)   It will be important to increase the role of key stakeholders, in particular the public, the private sector and those working in primary care.

(x)   Consideration should be given to ring-fenced funding for the implementation of OHN in order to give priority to this activity.

1. BACKGROUND AND METHODS

1.1 Background

The Health of the Nation[1] (HOTN) strategy for England, launched in 1992, built on the World Health Organisation's 'Health for All Strategy'[2] and similar developments in the US[3]. It focused on five key areas, setting out overall objectives for each, with 27 individual targets monitored by the Department of Health's Central Health Monitoring Unit. While data are available to monitor targets and describe activities[4,5,6,7,8] the HOTN strategy has not been evaluated as a method by which central government influences national and local policy.

The HOTN strategy sought to widen the responsibility for health, and this emphasis was reflected in the Ministerial Committee which was intended to oversee the development, implementation and monitoring of HOTN. This was supported by three Working Groups which focused on the public health dimensions of HOTN; the monitoring and review of progress towards the achievement of targets; and the contribution of the NHS to the implementation of HOTN. At a local level health authorities were given the responsibility for co-ordinating implementation of HOTN through alliances with other organisations such as local authorities, voluntary organisations, and the private sector.

Following the election of a Labour Government in May 1997 and the appointment of the first ever Minister for Public Health, the Government announced its intention to launch a new health strategy *Our Healthier Nation*[9]. The strategy will address important underlying causes of mortality and morbidity. A Green Paper[10] was published in February 1998 as part of a major consultation process. Following this, the White Paper launching the new strategy is due to be published in September 1998. Other important policy developments which intersect with the public health strategy are the proposals set out in *The new NHS White Paper*[11]; the consultation paper on assessing performance in the NHS[12]; the emerging findings

from the Chief Medical Officer's report on the public health function[13]; and the Acheson inquiry on health inequalities.

This report presents the results of an evaluation of the HOTN strategy, commissioned by the Department of Health. The evaluation has assessed how the strategy has worked at local level and draws lessons for the development of the new strategy. An annotated bibliography of the research papers, studies and documents quoted in this report is available from Naomi Fulop at the Department of Public Health and Policy, London School of Hygiene and Tropical Medicine.

Previous research on the implementation of HOTN

Much research and comment on HOTN has centred on its contents and, in particular, on the key areas and targets. The manner of its implementation, especially at national level, has received little attention[14]. A review of the research literature was undertaken in order to identify the available evidence on the degree of implementation of HOTN, factors affecting the implementation process and on the economics of HOTN. A search of *Medline, HealthStar* and *Health Management* databases (1986-1997) was undertaken using the following search terms:

- Health of the Nation
- Implementation
- Alliances
- Partnerships
- Health strategies
- Evaluation
- Intersectoral
- Healthy Cities
- Public Health
- Health Promotion
- Health Expenditures
- Data Collection [economics, methods]
- Economics
- Economic Evaluation
- Programme Budgeting
- Program Budgeting

A number of studies indicate the degree to which HOTN has been implemented locally in the UK. A study in North Thames which used in-depth qualitative methods across a broad range of organisations found that there was widespread commitment to HOTN and local health strategies both within and outside the NHS, and a great deal of activity within the five key areas, but concluded that HOTN had presented an enormous challenge to the NHS to integrate health promotion into its activities as it is dominated by a culture of treatment[15]. This finding was supported by an NHS review, commissioned in 1994, for which Chief Executives and Directors of Public Health from 15 health districts were interviewed. They broadly welcomed the policy and supported the choice of the five key areas[16]. Examples of changes achieved within the HOTN framework were cited. However these were usually marginal. Participation and commitment from local partners was also patchy. The review also noted that there was much less support for local targets due to their inherent variability when applying them to small populations. This view is supported by a recent survey of health authorities in England and Wales which found that only 28% had adapted HOTN targets to take account of local circumstances, although 40% had adopted the national targets[17]. Reasons given included lack of baseline data and difficulties in measuring progress. The generalisability of this survey was, however, undermined by the poor response rate (38%).

Facilitators and barriers to intersectoral work

While the studies outlined above attempted to gauge the degree of implementation, only the North Thames study and the NHS review evaluated the process of implementation and the factors which have helped or hindered it.

In the North Thames study, the authors identified a number of tensions affecting implementation including those between different organisational cultures and agendas; those between different approaches to health and illness; and those between competing public health and financial priorities. They identified three key factors for successful implementation: senior managers committed to the strategy; integration of the health strategy into the work of the whole organisation (through job descriptions or departmental priorities); and

development of good working relationships between organisations around shared agendas (working 'bottom up' as well as 'top down'). Barriers to successful implementation included differing political orientation of health and local authorities; the pace of organisational change, which hampered the development of stable relationships; and lack of funding.

The NHS review found lack of direction from central government limiting local authority involvement. Additional barriers to implementation included insufficient investment in achieving population behavioural change; lack of wide ownership of HOTN polices; and turbulence in the NHS managerial environment.

An important feature of the HOTN strategy was the emphasis on Healthy Alliances - bringing together individuals and organisation to tackle health problems[18]. This was seen as the means by which the HOTN goals were to be met[1]. A number of studies have evaluated inter-agency working[19], although most focused on the intersectoral collaboration encouraged by WHO's Health For All (HFA) and Healthy Cities initiatives. They have generally focused on the factors which impact on successful collaboration itself, rather than the outcomes of that collaboration. Several of these studies were initiated prior to the publication of the HOTN Green and White Papers or shortly afterwards but their findings are still relevant. Despite this, their findings are remarkably similar and support the growing consensus around conditions for improved collaboration[20]. It is important to recognise, however, that these emerging key issues do not stand alone but are inter-connected[20] and relate to either partner organisations or the individuals within them. These issues are summarised below[15,16,19, 20, 21, 22, 23, 24, 25].

- ◆ **goals;** acknowledgement and acceptance by alliance partners of differing organisational goals[15, 20, 23, 24,] recognising that all parties have something to gain and contribute from partnership[24]. Lack of mutual recognition or competing goals, even within organisations, may hamper collaboration[20].

- ◆ **values and vision;** commitment of organisations and individuals, especially senior staff is thought essential[15, 19, 20, 24.] Different approaches to health and illness and differing organisational cultures and political orientation can also hinder collaborative work[15].

♦ **relationships;** tolerance of other participants is essential. Good working partnerships are fostered by openness, trust and regard for others. Previous history of intersectoral work is thought to be important in preparing the ground for collaboration[20]. The purchaser-provider split can militate against joint work[24].

♦ **skills;** communication, political and strategic planning skills as well as the ability of individuals to 'network' is thought crucial to alliances[20, 23, 25]. These skills make for effective personal and professional relationships between individuals and organisations[23] and can be learnt[20].

♦ **approaches;** agreeing the terms of reference for collaboration is considered crucial e.g. 'top-down' versus 'bottom up' approaches[15, 20]. Joint decision making and shared agenda setting, whether for establishing strategies or implementing projects, help create equal partnerships and facilitate alliances[5, 20, 24.] Commitment of resources can act as an incentive for partnership[24.]

♦ **structure;** group or project structure are highly significant[20]. Different levels of collaboration have different implications for planning and action. Although the literature does not prescribe any one structure for alliance working, a 'task focus' and a degree of formalisation is an essential attribute[20]. Integration of the strategy into whole organisation is also helpful[15].

♦ **wider context;** central government direction and wider ownership of policies directed at intersectoral working are important[16]. Government committed resources/funds provide a powerful incentive to joint work[16, 24] but are not essential[20]. Competing public and financial priorities or pressures can obstruct alliances[15, 24,] while organisational change can hamper the building of stable relationships required for partnership[15, 16].

Evaluating outcomes, or effectiveness, of alliances is problematic[19.] The success of intersectoral work has largely been based on an act of faith. Systematic and rigorous evaluation of alliances is needed before it is possible to judge if the outcome of joint efforts is worthwhile[24]. However, monitoring and evaluating healthy alliance work presents a major challenge, requiring the development of novel instruments and indicators[26]. Work in this area has been beset by disagreement over which indicators and criteria to use in order to measure the effects of alliances in a meaningful way[27]. Funnell *et al*'s work on evaluating healthy alliances in terms of their outputs (policy change, service /environment change, skills development, publicity, contact and knowledge, attitude and behaviour change) and process (commitment, community participation, communication, joint working and accountability) is a positive step in this direction[28].

Economic evaluation

No studies with a primary objective of addressing the impact of HOTN on expenditure, resource use or investment could be identified. The Department of Health made an estimate of the costs of health promotion in HOTN key areas in a progress report to the Public Accounts Committee[29]. This estimate attempted to identify programme expenditures by the local NHS for 1996/97 on 'identifiable health promotion expenditures' in each key area (e.g. anti-hypertensive drugs for CHD, the cancer screening programmes, family planning services for HIV and sexual health etc.), as well as centrally funded health promotion initiatives. By far the largest single component of this estimate was the cost of anti-hypertensive pharmaceuticals, at £350 million - all other components in the estimate summed to a total spend of £384 million on HOTN related 'health promotion' activities.

A study by three NHS Executive Regional Offices[30] analysed management expenditure on different functions by health purchasers (in a sample of 11 health authorities and 9 GP purchasers); their analysis included an estimate of the management resources devoted to developing and implementing HOTN activities. On average, the HAs in this study spent £9.93 *per capita* on overall management functions; of this, £0.17 *per capita* (or 2% of management expenditure) was devoted to HOTN, in the form of achieving targets, health promotion commissioning and inter-agency working, and contribution to HOTN from other HA functions (e.g. needs assessment, mental health etc.). In addition to this HA expenditure, GP purchasers spent £0.12 *per capita* on HOTN, or 3% of their total purchasing management costs of £5.41 *per capita*. Clearly, these estimates reflect only the management costs of strategy development and implementation at local level.

Finally, the study in North Thames region[15] attempted to assess the relationship between HOTN and resource allocation decisions. The key findings of this study were that shifts in resources had tended to manifest themselves in terms of staff time and priorities, not direct cash expenditures; that disinvestment or reinvestment of budgets was rare; that most shifts in resources had been marginal and 'not substantial'; that HOTN had preserved budgets which were at risk; and that it had proved very difficult to shift finance from health services into health improvement measures.

All of these studies dealt only with expenditures made by or within the National Health Service. No studies from the UK were identified which examined expenditures on health promotion or public health functions *across* agencies. There are, however, models from elsewhere that demonstrate the strengths and weaknesses of the methods that could be used. One US study reported the results of a pilot project in eight states which sought to estimate the resources expended on ten core public health functions[31]. A parallel study describes the considerable difficulties in 'measuring' public health activities in the US[32]. The functions covered by the expenditure survey included a wide range of services delivered by state, county and city agencies, which in the UK would have been

delivered by both the NHS and local authorities. There are no British studies to compare with these US results but it is interesting to note that their estimated expenditure of $44 *per capita* on these core public health functions represented only 1.25% of estimated total US health expenditure of $3500 *per capita*.

Given the absence of expenditure studies on HOTN *per se*, the wider literature on programme budgeting and marginal analysis (PBMA) was investigated. Donaldson[33] describes PBMA as 'the economics approach to priority setting'; it allows a picture to be drawn of where resources are being expended, while illustrating the choices which are open through changes to the allocation of resources. PBMA is often approached in terms of constructing a matrix of 'programmes' defined with reference to diseases (or disease groups), client groups or age groups (e.g. Madden *et al*[34], Miller *et al*[35]). Indeed, PBMA can be used across agency boundaries to indicate overall resource use. For example, Jones and Wright[36] present an approach to combining data from health and local authorities for expenditure on services for people with learning disabilities. However, only one of the studies identified[37] mentioned the Health of the Nation explicitly, and then only tangentially. This study described how a PBMA exercise conducted in East Sussex Health Authority indicated that only 0.15% of HA spending was on health promotion, prompting the HA to redirect one third of its growth funds to health promotion the following year 'under the Health of the Nation banner.'

Overall, whilst it is clear that some form of PBMA approach is required to identify resource use and impacts related to HOTN, few if any such exercises have been conducted. The direct implication of this result was that a novel approach to data collection would be necessary to conduct the expenditure analysis proposed by the current review.

1.2 Aim of the present study

This study aims to provide an analysis of the mechanisms by which the HOTN strategy has been implemented at local level, which will complement current monitoring of progress.

While there are data on the progress that has been made towards achieving the targets set out in the strategy, there has been little evaluation of its organisational elements. Using a variety of methods, including in-depth interviewing, documentary analysis, and analyses of expenditures, this study provides lessons for the implementation of the new strategy *Our Healthier Nation*. While the study is concerned with the implementation of the HOTN strategy at the local level, it has also, inevitably, raised issues concerning implementation at national level.

Research Questions

(i)   What has been the impact of the HOTN strategy at the local level in terms of changes to policies, services, behaviours/ideas, changes in organisation and shifts in resources, both within and outside the NHS?

(ii)   What mechanisms have been developed at local level to produce this impact and are they sustainable?

(iii)   How useful are the key components of HOTN at the local level? What are the views of key actors locally concerning the limited range of key areas; target setting, healthy alliances? How might these be improved?

(iv)   Which factors within the strategy have facilitated change and what have been the barriers to change? Which factors external to HOTN have facilitated or provided barriers to change? What can be learned from the best practice within the key areas?

(v)   How does HOTN relate to other structures for health promotion such as the GP contract? What impact has HOTN had on areas outside the five key areas such as asthma, childhood infectious diseases and diabetes?

(vi)   What information do we need in the future to be able to evaluate the new strategy?

1.3   Methods

Theoretical Approach

Given the problems of evaluating such a strategy in terms of the many confounding factors and the difficulty of ascribing causality, the theoretical approach of the study is 'contextualism', which is defined as the analysis of organisational change in terms of the context and process, as well as its content. The aim of data collection is to allow analysis which will identify patterns in the process of change and the 'how' and 'why' as well as the 'what' of policy changes[38] - an approach which has been applied to the study of health care organisations[39]. The focus of the study will be on the *perceptions* of key actors at the local level on the impact of the HOTN and *documentary evidence* of such impacts, including evidence of policies and activities and, where possible, data on expenditure.

Within the given time constraints, the research questions have been addressed in the following ways:

Case studies in eight health authorities

The objective of this part of the study is to provide an in-depth analysis of how HOTN has been implemented at a local level. It seeks to identify best practice and mechanisms to overcome barriers to change. This has been achieved through an overview of how HOTN has been implemented within each district, and specifically an analysis of how each district has implemented the strategy in relation to the five key areas and three areas outside HOTN: asthma, childhood infectious diseases and diabetes.

Selection of case studies

The eight districts were selected at random, stratified by region (giving one health authority for each region). By selecting at random, we expected to obtain a mix of urban and rural authorities, and to reflect the range of different organisational relationships between health and local authorities (unitary, two-tier etc.). This has been achieved (see Chapter 2).

Data collection

Data have been collected in three ways:

i) semi-structured interviews with the key actors in health authorities, local authorities, provider trusts, GPs, relevant voluntary organisations, police and the private sector.

ii) analysis of documents.

iii) expenditure analysis.

Interviews

The aim was to conduct 15-20 interviews in each district with key actors from the following organisations: health authorities, local authorities, provider trusts, GPs, CHCs, relevant voluntary organisations, police and the private sector. The organisations and key actors included are listed in Appendix A. Semi-structured interview schedules were developed for each type of organisation - these included a set of core questions which were addressed to all respondents. The interview schedule used for the Directors of Public Health is shown at Appendix B. Other schedules were adapted from this.

Interviewees were identified through 'snowball sampling'[40] i.e. the initial respondents were asked to identify key informants within the health authority and in other organisations. However, attempts were made to conduct interviews with each of the organisations/groups listed above whether or not they had been involved in HOTN, in order to avoid selection bias in which those with greater involvement with or knowledge of HOTN were preferentially included. Therefore, where contacts were not identified by initial interviewees, contacts within these organisations were identified by other means.

Analysis of documents

A list of documents as requested from the eight health authorities which included purchasing plans, annual public health reports, corporate contracts, and community care plans for the years 1992/3 to 1996/7. The full list of documents appears at Appendix C. Three types of documents were

requested across the full five year period: purchasing plans, annual public health reports (APHRs) and corporate contracts. For other types of documents, such as contracts and general practice reports, examples only were requested.

Expenditure analysis

A pilot financial data collection exercise was conducted in one of the study districts during late 1997, in order to identify available sources of information on health promotion and HOTN activities, and to define a feasible approach to data collection and analysis. This pilot exercise highlighted the very patchy availability of data at local level and the extreme difficulty of obtaining local historical data for periods longer than two or three years.

As a direct result of this pilot phase, it was decided to use centrally held data from authority and trust annual accounts to develop a common dataset relating to NHS funded health promotion and preventive activities in the eight study sites. Data were extracted from the archived health authority, FHSA and trust annual accounts held by the Department of Health's Authority and Trust Accounts (SPB ATA) team at Quarry House. A detailed list of the data extracted is presented at Appendix D. These data were extracted for each year from 1991/92 to 1996/97 for each study HA, FHSA and local NHS trust. This dataset was then supplemented where possible with more detailed local data. A detailed list of the local data required was developed and revised (both lists are presented at Appendix E). Health authority finance departments co-ordinated the collection of these supplementary data in all of the sites. Not all elements of the local dataset could be provided in each district. Where local data was missing or inadequate, national estimates were used in their place.

Population data for each district were obtained from published sources[41] for the years 1991 to 1994, and directly from the Office for National Statistics Population and Vital Statistics Division for 1995 and 1996. Gross Domestic Product (GDP) Deflator and Hospital and Community Health Services Pay and Prices Index series were provided by the NHS Executive Headquarters.

Data analysis

Data from semi-structured interviews and documentary evidence have been analysed using both quantitative and qualitative methods. Closed items have been analysed quantitatively using EPI-INFO. Open items have been analysed using qualitative methods based on concepts of 'grounded theory'[42] which enable the common themes to be drawn out. Two members of the research team developed the analytic categories, according to an agreed framework and with subsequent review by other members of the team. The use of different sources of data and methods ('triangulation'[43]) has assisted in the validation of results.

For financial data, aggregates were constructed using the dataset described above for expenditure on:

♦ Total local NHS services - Hospital and Community Health Services (HCHS) and Family Health Services (FHS).

♦ Population-based health promotion activities (i.e. designated health promotion work by HA and trust health promotion units).

♦ General Practitioner health promotion activities.

♦ Primary prevention services used by individuals, i.e. family planning (trust and GP), cervical cytology and breast screening programmes.

♦ The childhood immunisation programme.

These aggregates were converted into constant 1991/92 prices using the Hospital and Community Health Services Pay and Prices index. Simple time-series analysis of these aggregates was then undertaken to explore trends in expenditure *per capita*, and the share of health promotion and preventive activities within total NHS expenditure.

Where local data supported such an analysis, resources explicitly earmarked for HOTN purposes were identified, and related to the main expenditure aggregates.

2. DESCRIPTION OF THE CASE STUDY DISTRICTS AND DATA COLLECTED

Key points

District characteristics

◆ districts selected have a fairly even distribution of structural and demographic characteristics including the OPCS Area Classification, Jarman scores and standardised mortality ratios (SMRs). They are slightly biased towards those with higher Jarman scores and higher SMRs.

◆ all HAs experienced a real increase in *per capita* spend.

◆ on average, real *per capita* spending rose by 9.7% over the study period.

Data collected

◆ 133 semi-structured interviews were conducted in the eight districts covering all sectors.

◆ 189 documents were collected.

◆ a comprehensive dataset from health authority, FHSA and trust accounts, AIDS Control Act Reports and resident population estimates were available for each of the eight districts.

◆ local expenditure data were obtained to varying degrees of completeness in each of the eight health authorities.

2.1 Introduction

This chapter contains a description of the case study districts in terms of their socio-demographic characteristics and their NHS expenditure. Finally in this chapter, the three types of data collected (interviews, documents, expenditure) are described in terms of their range and completeness.

2.2 District characteristics

Socio-demographic characteristics of the case study districts

The local authority structure, economic classification and demographic composition of the case study Districts A to H are shown in Table 2.1. The random selection of the eight health authority areas has resulted in a fairly even distribution of structural and demographic characteristics. Two of the six broad categories of OPCS Area Classification are not represented (Mining and Industrial and Inner London). The Under-Privileged Area (UPA) decile scores show that higher scores - indicating higher GP workload - are over represented by the health authorities districts A to H. Similarly, the distribution of SMRs (all cause, all ages) is also skewed to the higher end (SMR greater than 100).

Total NHS expenditure by health authority

Estimates of total expenditure *per capita* by the NHS locally were created by combining HA expenditure with FHSA expenditure for each year until 1995/96; this created a direct equivalent for global HA expenditure in 1996/97. In the case of one HA where complex boundary changes had taken place, expenditure and populations were disaggregated to provide a direct equivalent in earlier years of the 1996/97 composition of the district.

Table 2.2 shows cash expenditure *per capita* in 1991/92 and 1996/97. During the study period, the NHS weighted capitation formula for HCHS allocations was in force, with its explicit aim of achieving long-term shifts in funding towards areas of higher need. Spending in Authority A stands out as having increased by a very much smaller rate in cash terms than in the other seven HAs. Interestingly, however, the change in relative positions vis-à-vis *per capita* expenditure affected mainly the four HAs in the middle of the range - the two top spenders and the two bottom spenders have not changed.

Table 2.1 The demographic characteristics of health authority districts A to H

District	Local Government	OPCS Area Classification	Population (1000s)	UPA Score (Decile)	SMRs (Quintile)
A	Unitary	Most prosperous	250-300	1	1
B	Unitary	Services & Education	450-500	9	2
C	Unitary	Mixed economies	700-750	8	3
D	Two-tier	Resort & Retirement	550-600	6	2
E	Two-tier	Mixed Urban & Rural	550-600	5	3
F	Two-tier	Mixed Urban & Rural	650-700	5	1
G	Unitary	Manufacturing	250-300	6	5
H	Unitary	Resort & Retirement	300-350	7	4

All data taken from the Public Health Common Data Set Indicators (1996), Department of Health

SMRs - All causes, all ages

Key: UPA Scores: Under-privileged area (Jarman) score

  SMR: Standardised Mortality Ratio

Table 2.2 Nominal NHS expenditure *per capita*

Health Authority	1991/92	1996/97	% Change	Change in Rank
A	489.38	596.21	21.8	3 ➡ 6
B	511.01	685.09	34.1	1 ➡ 1
C	503.41	675.81	34.2	2 ➡ 2
D	466.25	633.93	36.0	4 ➡ 3
E	430.58	580.08	34.7	8 ➡ 7
F	434.54	569.14	31.0	7 ➡ 8
G	456.38	607.64	33.1	5 ➡ 5
H	453.34	628.93	38.7	6 ➡ 4

When nominal *per capita* spending is converted to real spending at constant 1991/92 prices, it can be seen that, over the study period, all HAs experienced a real increase in *per capita* spend. On average, real *per capita* spending rose by 9.7% over the study period, equivalent to a real spending increase of 1.94% per year. Clearly, the effective freeze on any growth in Authority A is evidence that the allocation formula has achieved some 'bite' over this period.

2.3 Data collected

Interviews with key informants

A total of 133 interviews were conducted in eight different sectors within and outside the health service between September 1997 and January 1998. Of these, 121 were face-to-face, nine by telephone and three used both methods. Within the health service, the key informants in health authorities,

Table 2.3 Real *per capita* spending (1991/92 prices)

Health Authority	1991/92	1996/97 α	% Change
A	489.38	491.92	0.5
B	511.01	565.26	10.6
C	503.41	557.60	10.8
D	466.25	523.04	12.2
E	430.58	478.62	11.2
F	434.54	469.59	8.1
G	456.38	501.35	9.9
H	453.34	518.92	14.5

α constant 1991/92 prices, deflated by HCHS Pay & Prices Index trusts (acute, mental and community), general practitioners and Community Health Council (CHC) officers and members were interviewed. In total, this amounted to 76 interviews. There was one refusal, by the CHC in Authority A. Outside the health service the majority of interviewees were from local authorities (unitary, county and district) comprising 37 interviews, while key informants in voluntary organisations, the police and the private sector made up the remaining 20 interviews. Table 2.4 shows the number of interviews conducted in each of these sectors. A more detailed breakdown is

NHS White Paper was published and it was discussed by interviewees in subsequent interviews.

Documents

Health authorities were asked to provide a set of documents as described in Chapter 1. Table 2.5 shows the types and numbers of documents provided by health authority. The numbers of missing documents are shown for the three types of documents which were requested across the full five year period (91/2, 92/3, 93/4, 94/5, 95/6) i.e.

Table 2.4 Number of interviewees within each sector and their distribution by district.

District	HA	Trusts	GPs	CHC	LA	Vol. Orgs	Private Sector	Police	Total
A	5	3	1	0	5	1	1	1	17
B	5	4	1	1	3	3	0	0	17
C	6	1	2	1	4	0	1	0	15
D	5	2	1	1	3	1	1	1	15
E	5	3	2	1	6	1	0	0	18
F	4	2	1	1	5	1	1	1	16
G	4	2	1	1	7	1	1	1	18
H	6	1	1	2	4	1	1	1	17
Total	**40**	**18**	**10**	**8**	**37**	**9**	**6**	**5**	**133**

Key:
HA - Health Authority
Trusts - Acute, Community and Mental
GP - General Practitioners

CHC - Community Health Council
LA - Local Authorities; Unitary, County, District
Vol. Orgs - Voluntary Organisations (including umbrella organisations)

given in Table 9.1 at Appendix A. Information has also been obtained on approximately 97 different projects which are related either to HOTN work or alliances.

It is important to note that interviews took place prior to publication of the Green Paper, *Our Healthier Nation*, so reference could not be made to it. During the interview period, however, *The new*

purchasing plans, annual public health reports (APHRs) and corporate contracts. As the table indicates, some health authorities could more easily provide this documentation than others. Organisational changes and changes in physical location were the most common reasons for missing documents. Corporate contracts were more likely to be missing than purchasing plans and APHRs.

Table 2.5 Health authority district A to H. Number of documents provided.

Health	A	B	C	D	E	F	G	H	Total
Purchasing plan (missing)	3 (2)	5 (0)	3 (2)	3 (2)	1 (4)	5(0)	4 (1)	1 (4)	**25 (15)**
APHR (missing)	3(2)	5 (0)	4(1)	4 (1)	5 (0)	3 (2)	3 (2)	3 (2)	**30 (10)**
Corporate contract (missing)	1 (4)	4(1)	3(2)	4(1)	2 (3)	4 (1)	4 (1)	2 (3)	**24 (16)**
Five year strategy	1	0	0	1	1	1	0	1	**5**
Community care plan	1	6	5	3	1	4	3	1	**24**
Other HOTN documents	1	13	6	9	3	1	14	1	**48**
Provider Contract	0	2	0	1	5	1	2	1	**12**
FHSA annual plan	0	0	1	2	0	0	0	0	**3**
GP practice report	3	5	0	0	0	3	4	3	**18**
Total (missing)	**13**	**40**	**22**	**28**	**18**	**22**	**33**	**13**	**189 (41)**

Expenditure data

Local expenditure data were obtained to varying
degrees of completeness in each of the eight health
authorities. A comprehensive dataset from health
authority, FHSA and trust accounts, AIDS Control
Act Reports and resident population estimates were
available for each of the eight districts. Table 2.6
summarises the key categories of local data obtained
to date for each of the study districts (above and
beyond the common study datasets):

Table 2.6 Availability of local expenditure data

Health Authority	Target Populations	Health Promotion α	Contraceptive Prescribing by GPs	School Health Services
A	Complete	Complete	Partial	Nil
B	Complete	Complete	Partial	Nil
C	Complete	Complete	Partial	Nil
D	Partial	Complete	Partial	Nil
E	Partial	Complete	Partial	Partial
F	Complete	Complete	Partial	Partial
G	Partial	Complete	Partial	Nil
H	Complete	Complete	Partial	Nil

α Health authority health promotion

Data on contraceptive prescribing expenditure for
each district for 1996/97 were provided by the
Prescriptions Pricing Authority, along with national
data from 1992/93 onwards. The Department of
Health provided data on total costs of vaccine supply
and coverage by the childhood immunisation
programme.

3. HOW THE POLICY WAS PERCEIVED

Key points

♦ The study found little support for a strategy based solely on a disease -based model. A strategy structured by a matrix approach which combines diseases, settings and population groups could be successful in winning the support of a wider range of partners.

♦ HOTN targets had little credibility, and the majority of the sample would like to see the indicators changed.

♦ Introduction of performance management of OHN in the health service and other sectors would be seen as demonstrating top-level commitment provided it is introduced with a sophisticated understanding of agencies' ability to achieve performance management objectives.

♦ Interviewees were committed to alliance work for health improvement and interviews supported a view that positive experience of partnership for other purposes such as drugs action and economic regeneration was beneficial to partnership for health improvement.

♦ There was strong support for a statutory framework to allow key local participants, particularly local government, to work in partnership for health.

♦ There was some support for the proposal that directors of public health be appointed jointly by local authorities and health authorities, as an enabling structure for OHN.

♦ Communication of HOTN to most potential partners for health improvement was poor. Information about the health strategy should be more relevant and accessible, particularly to key players outside the health service.

♦ Interviewees would like government to take a stronger role in improving health, at every level, and to avoid conflicts between policies of different government departments which obstructed their work.

♦ The majority of the sample supported more resourcing for a national strategy for health, but nearly half qualified their replies to specify prescribed and purposeful spending to support structured action for health improvement at the local level.

♦ Interviewees stressed that a new health strategy should be evolutionary rather than revolutionary, allowing review of current practice in order to build on successful activities as well as flexibility to identify local priorities.

3.1 Introduction

All interviewees were asked two sets of questions which sought their opinions on health strategies. The first asked for their views of HOTN, drawing on their experience in their present post and any previous one. The second asked what interviewees would like to see in OHN. Both asked about the same features of a health strategy - key areas, settings, targets, encouragement to form alliances and partnerships, and communications about the strategy such as roadshows and documents. Interviewees were also asked some more general questions which allowed them to give views on the strategy as a whole.

3.2 Key areas

Respondents overwhelmingly thought the HOTN key areas identified important problems - 119 of the 126 respondents who answered this question agreed with this (Table 3.1).

These responses are typical in showing that many positive views are qualified:

Certainly, CHD is important for [District C], cancer as well, within an inner city area and within ethnic minorities. And the ways services need to be

Table 3.1 Do the key areas identify important problems?

	Number	Percent
Yes	119	90
No	4	3
Don't know	3	2
Missing	7	5
Total	133	100

(All interviews)

Table 3.2 Could the key areas have been based around population groups, or something else, rather than around diseases?

	All		Public Health Health Promotion		Local authority/ Voluntary Sector	
	Number	Percent	Number	Percent	Number	Percent
Yes, population groups	34	26	5	23	14	30
Yes, something else	13	10	3	14	6	13
Arguments on both sides/can't decide	20	15	5	23	8	17
Matrix/Must use many approaches	9	7	2	9	2	4
Doesn't matter where you start	9	7	3	14	0	0
Yes possibly	5	4	0	0	3	7
No, disease-based areas are right	31	23	3	14	10	22
Don't know	4	3	0	0	1	2
Missing	8	6	1	5	2	4
Total	133	100	22	100	46	100

(All interviews)

sensitive to individual populations and ethnic minorities. (Chief Officer of a CHC)

Yes - but there are more issues which cause more problems - they are the prevailing problems - wide issues - poverty, unemployment, social exclusion. (Assistant director, council for voluntary services).

A quarter of interviewees (34/133) thought the key areas in HOTN should have been focused on population groups rather than diseases, and another 10% would want them to cover some other dimension, including 'issues' such as poverty and housing, which are mentioned in the Commission for the Environment report *Agendas for Change*[44]. Contrasting views are illustrated in the following quotations:

It should be based around people and geographic areas. In health authority B you have two towns. If you look at the east to west side, there's a divide. The abortion rate in under 16s has increased, there's been a rise in teenage pregnancies in the past ten years. For stroke and CVD, all the rates in the east come out higher. This is where our poverty,

unemployment are very high. Unemployment is 27-30% in parts of [the east of the borough]. (Head of health and safety, borough council)

Yes- it should have addressed social ills - housing (my priority), unemployment. HOTN was very convenient for measurement taken but didn't address the input things (Local government officer)

A Director of Public Health made a distinction between a medical perspective and a broader one:

Do the key areas identify important problems? *From a medical viewpoint yes. Mental health consumes resources, and cancer and CHD are two most important causes of mortality and morbidity.* Could the key areas have been based around population groups, or something else, rather than around diseases? *The determinants of health were not given much attention, the Black report and Margaret Whitehead's work for David Player [The Health Divide] were ignored - an excuse for those who saw it as a Tory document to ignore it.*

Table 3.3 Should the government keep all existing key areas?

	Number	Percent
Yes	63	47
No	47	35
Don't know	11	8
Missing	12	9
Total	133	100

(All interviews)

Table 3.4 Should there be new key areas?

	Number	Percent
Yes	97	73
No	13	10
Don't know	10	8
Missing	13	10
Total	133	100

(All interviews)

Table 3.5 Is the encouragement to work in 'settings' helpful in delivering the strategy?

	All		Public Health Health Promotion		Local authority/ Voluntary Sector	
	Number	Percent	Number	Percent	Number	Percent
Yes	71	53	12	55	24	52
No	39	29	9	41	13	28
Don't know	8	6	0	0	1	2
N/A	15	11	0	0	0	0
Missing	0	0	1	5	8	17
Total	133	100	22	100	46	100

(Selected groups)

A quarter of interviewees thought the present disease-based approach was right, with intermediate positions including ambivalence ('*there are arguments on both sides*'), indifference ('*it doesn't matter where you start as long as you take action*') and a belief in a matrix or combined approach (Table 3.2). Proportions supporting disease-based areas were similar among interviewees based in health promotion and public health on the one hand, and respondents based in local government and the voluntary sector on the other.

This issue is closely connected to the question of who takes the lead on a health strategy - one with disease-based key areas fits within a health authority agenda better than a local authority one.

Just under half of the respondents would keep all the existing key areas in the new strategy (63/133) (Table 3.3).

Asked about whether they would favour new key areas, three quarters (97/133) said they would - suggestions included environment, inequalities/poverty, respiratory diseases and the elderly (Table 3.4).

Those who were against the introduction of new key areas mentioned continuity and maintenance of a manageable number of priorities among their reasons. In connection with both this question and the question about maintaining existing key areas, some, particularly those outside the health sector, said they needed to trust the opinions of experts.

3.3 Settings

Matrix approaches to health promotion, including for example the European Commission's health promotion programme[45], and many local approaches, often include settings as a dimension along with diseases or health problems and population groups. Over half of

Table 3.6 Should the strategy include work through settings?
If so, should the settings be added to or strengthened

	Should be included		Should be added to		Should be strengtherned	
	Number	Percent	Number	Percent	Number	Percent
Yes	91	68	40	30	27	20
No	9	7	9	7	9	7
Don't know	8	6	2	2	2	2
Missing	25	19	82	62	95	71
Total	133	100	133	100	133	100

(All inerviews)

Table 3.7 Are the targets credible?

	Number	Percent
Yes, all	15	11
Yes, most/some	37	28
No	48	36
No, but they are important pointers	12	9
Don't know	15	11
Missing	6	5
Total	133	100

(All interviews)

Table 3.8 Should the existing targets be kept?

	All		Public Health Health Promotion		Local authority Voluntary Sector	
	Number	Percent	Number	Percent	Number	Percent
Yes	36	27	2	9	16	35
No	79	59	18	82	25	54
Don't know	5	4	0	0	1	2
Missing	13	10	2	9	4	9
Total	133	100	22	100	46	100

(Selected groups)

Table 3.9 Should there be new targets?

	Number	Percent
Yes	98	74
No	12	9
Don't know	12	9
Missing	11	8
Total	133	100

(All interviews)

Table 3.10 Should the government make local targets an obligatory element?

	Number	Percent
Yes	92	69
Unsure	3	2
No	22	17
Don't know	3	2
Missing	13	10
Total	133	100

(All interviews)

respondents (53%) had found settings helpful within HOTN (Table 3.5). The team frequently found that, when interviewing those outside public health and health promotion, they needed to illustrate or explain what settings were. However, the proportion who had found settings helpful in public health or health promotion were similar to those in local government and the voluntary sector. Responses to this question may underestimate the level of support for settings-based health promotion work because the question asked specifically about support for settings in HOTN, rather than whether interviewees were in favour of settings-based work.

Over two-thirds of interviewees (68%) supported inclusion of settings in OHN (Table 3.6). They were not asked (as they were for key areas) to endorse the particular HOTN settings, but they were asked if they would like to add to them. Thirty percent of the interviewees (78% (40/51) of those responding to this question) would do so. Interviewers obtained an impression of a low level of knowledge of what the settings were, which contrasted with knowledge of key areas. Those wanting 'new settings' include some who proposed existing settings as new ones. New settings proposed included neighbourhoods, community groups, leisure and social facilities, primary health care, residential care and day centres. There were no striking differences between types of interviewees or between districts in responses to these questions.

3.4   Targets

Only 11% of interviewees found all of the HOTN targets credible, (although 12 of the 133 (9%) made the point that targets, whether credible or not, could focus and motivate action) (Table 3.7).

A much greater proportion (27%) would keep the existing HOTN targets in OHN. Health promotion and public health interviewees were less likely to want to keep the existing targets than those in local government and the voluntary sector. 74% of all interviewees would like to add new targets or indicators. 69% would make local target setting an obligatory element, and some of those who rejected this option were unhappy only with the word 'obligatory'.

They've got to, this area is especially bad, so our targets would be special cases. (Leisure manager, LA)

There were no striking differences between authorities in their responses to these questions on targets (Table 3.8-Table 3.10).

3.5   Performance management

Interviewees raised the issue of performance management at various points during the interview schedule. Their views can be summarised as follows:

♦   the introduction of performance management is perceived as a sign of commitment to delivery of the strategy, as well as the means of delivering it.

♦   performance management indicators must be achievable by those who are judged on them. *Process indicators* such as alliance formation or number of patient contacts at which appropriate lifestyle risk factors were raised are as important as health outcomes.

♦   to be achievable they should, where appropriate, take account of local baselines - there are lessons from school performance tables.

♦   where possible, there should be a known causal pathway from the performance management indicator to a health outcome.

♦   the achievement of quantifiable targets should not be at the expense of activities which address important problems but which are harder to measure.

The following examples illustrate respondents' views:

It's not a Regional Office or government priority. The chief executive gets sacked for other things but not for HOTN. People realise when there's no commitment from above, who can blame them. HOTN wasn't mentioned in our last two reviews from [region]. If [regional director] isn't hitting the chief executive over the head with it that means Alan Langlands wasn't hitting [regional director] over the head with it and Stephen Dorrell wasn't hitting Alan Langlands over the head with it. (Director of Public Health)

[The biggest inhibiting factor is] performance management of the health authority. The accountability function is discharged by the Regional Director via quarterly 'bilaterals'. Region sets the agenda for these meetings and public health issues are never on it. Ministers are not interested, it's not the 'real business'. The real business is about contracts, money, providers, activity, hospital closures and so on. Public health is seen as a completely separate issue. I had to raise public health issues to get them on the agenda. They've never asked about imm & vacc or cervical cytology screening. Public health is seen as separate...the people who count, who manage your career aren't interested. I'm concerned that the new Secretary of State is only interested in the old agenda i.e. hospitals. OK he's appointed a new Minister of Public Health but again that's making public health a separate issue. (Health Authority Chief Executive)

These views are supported by evidence of a lack of references to HOTN in corporate contracts (see Chapter 4). Other comments relating to performance management include:

Make all relevant agencies responsible for progress within their remit, like the Drugs Action Teams, which has separate but integrated targets for HA and police. Give structural employment incentives all down the health service - regions, trusts, health authorities - to achieve on OHN. Also local authority and schools. Nobody came from region to ensure we were acting on HOTN, or used HOTN action as a performance indicator with incentives and disincentives, like waiting lists. (Director of Public Health)

[Health promotion are] in a provider and it would be easier to use targets as performance indicators. That's a dangerous game, and it's not happening here. (Health Promotion Specialist)

There are two levels of target - strategic ones, say for diseases or population groups, and in theory you could also have ones for the actions possible in the cells of the matrix [in a matrix based strategy], performance indicators. (Senior Police Officer)

The government will set attainment targets for schools benchmarked against like schools, and maybe this principle could be applied for health authorities with HOTN. It enables learning from like authorities, and encourages dialogue and sharing. Perhaps there should be more sharing between districts on HOTN, a more open culture. Schools have become more open and sharing, less secretive over the last two years, and are becoming more open, to mutual benefit. (Head Teacher, nursery school)

Targets are good as long as you're not slaves of targets. People need education in their use as a management tool, and you shouldn't exclude other areas that aren't the subject of targets. I'm performance managed on burglaries and I could put all my efforts into bringing down burglaries, but that would be a short-term concern. (Senior Police Officer)

3.6 Alliances

Three quarters of respondents (99/133) thought that the encouragement to work in healthy alliances was helpful in delivering HOTN. This included 86% of those in those parts of the health sector most immediately involved (directors of public health, HOTN leads and health promotion managers), and 74% in local government and the voluntary sector. Those who did not think so included some who believed that their existing local alliances (based, for example, around Healthy Cities) had gained no support from HOTN, so this figure underestimates the level of support for alliances as a mechanism for health improvement (Table 3.11).

Responses included:

Yes, it has been at the forefront, especially in the initial stages. From the point view of leisure, you get caught up in other things because the cash hasn't been there. The willingness is there but the wallet isn't. Now we have free-standing groups [for GP referrals] and they are income generating. (Leisure manager, Local Authority)

It was the first time the government accepted the intersectoral influences on health. However it wasn't backed up by guidance to local authorities - my colleagues in environmental health didn't seem to have a copy of the document, and funding for health

Table 3.11 Is the encouragement to work in health alliances helpful in delivering the strategy?

	All		Public Health Health Promotion		Local authority Voluntary Sector	
	Number	Percent	Number	Percent	Number	Percent
Yes	99	74	19	86	34	74
No	20	15	3	14	9	20
Don't know	6	5	0	0	0	0
Missing	8	6	0	0	3	7
Total	133	100	22	100	46	100

(Selected groups)

Table 3.12 Should alliances continue to be an important way of working?
If so could more be done by health authorities or government to support them?

	Continue		More support	
	Number	Percent	Number	Percent
Yes	126	95	110	83
No	0	0	1	1
Don't know	1	1	4	3
Missing	6	5	18	14
Total	133	100	46	100

(All interviews)

education in schools was being cut at the time of the launch. (Director of Public Health)

Yes, important that it's through healthy alliances, jointly and genuinely, but you have to be careful that it's not just lip service. More often healthy alliances have to be backed by the community and spending if it is to make an impact...And, by crikey, we need some tools to evaluate healthy alliances. (HOTN lead)

Ninety-five percent would want alliances to continue to be an important way of working in OHN, with no dissent from this suggestion, and no variation between authorities or broad type of interviewee. Eighty-three percent would like to see more support for alliances of one sort or another (Table 3.12).

Typical responses to this question included:

Yes. You can't get anything done otherwise. The quality of alliances should be part of monitoring and this includes not just holding one party to account for it. (HA Chief Executive)

Yes, I think it is related to funding. There's a need to be joint funded, pots of money which not only bring people together but allow them to do things, enable them to spend the money. (Chief Officer, CHC)

Absolutely. Things could be done by both. Government should encourage alliances through Health Action Zones and Healthy Living Centres, that would be helpful. Organisations should explore

Table 3.13 Do you think there should be any change to the structure of health authorities and/or public health to facilitate *Our Healthier Nation*: for example, the idea that directors of public health should be joint appointments between health authorities and local authorities?

	DPH	HA Chief Executive	HA HOTN Lead	HP Manager	HA other	LA HOTN Lead	CHC	TOTAL
Yes	3	0	2	1	6	0	5	17
Unsure	0	0	0	0	0	2	0	2
No	1	0	1	0	1	0	3	6
Missing	4	8	7	3	3	1	0	26
Total	8	8	10	4	10	3	8	51

the potential, and key individuals will be important.
(Health Promotion Strategy Manager)

Interviewees found that existing partnerships made potential partners more skilled in and favourable towards partnership working. One respondent with considerable experience of Single Regeneration Budget funding said that in his district:

There is a culture of understanding partnership. People think of partnership as a win-win situation, and therefore they don't expect to win each time.
(TEC Officer)

Several interviews took place shortly after the deadline for Health Action Zone applications, and interviewees were optimistic and encouraged by the co-operation around the bid, which they sometimes volunteered would continue regardless of the outcome. Police and health authority interviewees cited Drug Action Teams as an effective model. Interviewees also mentioned scope for partnership building through *The new NHS* White Paper and the Crime and Disorder Bill.

I take the word alliance to mean a partnership or partnerships. It gets down to what the core business of agencies is. I'm not major in the Health Action Zone, but I am in the Drugs Action Team. An alliance is dependent on whether it is a core issue for partners. We've had a White Paper on leadership groups, [the Crime and Disorder Bill] and now there will be a leadership group of chief executives in the borough. Partners need to understand where we come from. I would regard some partnership projects as 'loss leaders'. Partnerships are about building trust. Operatives on the ground must be empowered on the ground to collaborate, there's no point in doing it just at strategic level. You have to troubleshoot the operational blocks. (Senior Police Officer)

3.7   Location of Directors of Public Health

A sub-sample of interviewees were asked about the location of Directors of Public Health, in particular, whether they should be joint appointments between health authorities and local authorities. The location of directors of public health has been debated for

some years, most recently in the Chartered Institute for Environmental Health's document *Agendas for Change*[44] which recommended that directors of public health be employed by local authorities.

These comments illustrate the range of views:

That's a seductive idea - public health departments have the opportunity to be key players, a big resource. But what's needed may just be a different emphasis from government - joint funding could be a way forward. We need a bit more time [to devote to HOTN]. (Director of Public Health)

It's difficult to say what the role of the director of public health would be in relation to the local authority now. Before 1974 the local authority did things it now doesn't do, for example it ran the ambulances and midwives and district nurses. Environmental health has changed, pollution control and health and safety have developed since 1974 and are very technical. I don't see how you'd create a role for the director of public health. We report weekly in writing to [Director of Public Health] on communicable diseases, and if there's and outbreak the 'proper officer' from the HA comes and joins our group but doesn't necessarily lead. (Environmental Health Officer)

That suggestion is in Agendas for Change. *I wouldn't want to return to pre 1974. We could use the director of public health with local resources for local health audit. Neither environmental health or public health is very strong within their organisations [i.e. being in environmental health wouldn't strengthen the director of public health's power much]. Environmental health does have the troops to get things done.*
(Environmental Health Officer)

Yes it could be a joint appointment but not back to the LA, a genuine joint appointment. I like the way public health work against medics through the HA, and we might lose that. (Joint commissioner, Social Services)

3.8   Communication - supporting documents and other resources

Several questions in the interview schedule covered the resources provided centrally to support local action - starting with the launch and roadshows in 1992, and including the documents, continuing award

Table 3.14 Was government support through the launch, roadshows, documents, Target and the health alliance awards useful locally?

All	Launch Number	Launch Percent	Roadshow Number	Roadshow Percent	Document Number	Document Percent	Target Number	Target Percent	Awards Number	Awards Percent
Yes	13	10	18	14	35	28	28	22	33	26
No	53	42	54	43	49	39	53	42	48	38
Don't know	28	22	30	24	24	19	26	21	25	20
Missing	31	25	23	18	17	14	18	14	19	15
Total	125	100	125	100	125	100	125	100	125	100
Public Health Promotion										
Yes	1	5	2	9	8	36	5	23	9	41
No	13	59	12	55	10	46	12	55	7	32
Don't know	1	5	2	9	1	5	1	5	1	5
Missing	7	32	6	27	3	14	4	18	5	23
Total	22	100	22	100	22	100	22	100	22	100
Local Authority Voluntary Sector										
Yes	6	13	8	17	12	26	13	28	11	24
No	18	39	18	39	20	44	20	44	21	46
Don't know	10	22	10	22	7	15	8	17	7	15
Missing	12	26	10	22	7	15	5	11	7	15
Total	46	100	46	100	46	100	46	100	46	100

(All interviews except HA chief executives, and selected groups)

Table 3.15 Should the government support local activity differently (documents, meetings, monitoring, response to feedback)?

	All Number	All Percent	Public Health Health Promotion Number	Public Health Health Promotion Percent	Local authority Voluntary Sector Number	Local authority Voluntary Sector Percent
Yes	93	74	19	73	35	76
No	10	8	2	9	4	9
Don't know	6	5	2	9	2	4
Missing	16	13	2	9	5	11
Total	125	100	22	100	46	100

(All interviews except HA chief executives)

scheme and *Target* newsletter. Few were popular, with around 40% of those asked this question singling out each of the resources as not useful locally. Although positive support for all these resources was low, there was variation between them, with rather more support for the documents and the awards than other items, particularly by public health and health promotion based interviewees (Table 3.14).

Three quarters of interviewees would like this type of activity handled differently in OHN (Table 3.15). Several respondents spoke negatively at what they perceived as the extravagance of the documents,

their profusion and glossy finish, and some advocated more directly worded and briefer documents for wider circulation.

[The government's] in-house magazine [doesn't] reach the public as far as I'm aware or inform the debate around health and public well-being. (Officer, Race Equality Council)

Was government support through the launch, roadshows, documents, Target and the health alliance awards useful locally?
It wasn't for us really (Local authority officer HIV/AIDS/substance use)

Table 3.16 What would be the three most useful things the government could do to ensure that the strategy is sustainable?

	Number	Percent
The strategy should be resourced properly (finance, training etc.)	63	47
The government should define a clear role for local authorities, HAs and other agencies to address the needs of the local population through intersectoral working. This may involve establishing a statutory framework.	51	38
The strategy should recognise the underlying determinants of health and/or inequalities in health.	43	32
The government should make it a high profile strategy (communicating it using appropriate language, with supplementary information, to raise public awareness inside and outside the health service).	32	24
The strategy should be devolved to the districts, so it is community focused, with local targets (and involve local people and organisations in its formulation /implementation possibly through increasing the local skills base) and more accountability (includes Health Action Zones).	30	23
The government should make the strategy truly inter-departmental, supported by coherent, consistent policies between departments and acted on down through departments to its implementation in the regions (i.e. relevant to local authorities including education).	28	21
The government should give a clear lead to the strategy on relevant policy issues (such as a ban on tobacco advertising, fiscal measures on smoking and traffic reduction/slowing measures).	26	20
The strategy should set national standards as benchmarks, with supportive documentation on setting/measuring targets and which should be more focused on output rather than inputs.	26	20
The government should set up a mechanism/organisation for monitoring quality (such as performance management), providing feedback and for advising on good practice.	13	10
The content /proposed action of the strategy should be evidence based.	13	10
The government should ensure the strategy is achievable by focusing on limited areas for action or setting realistic targets.	11	8
The content of the strategy should include other areas (such as asthma, environment (crime/traffic) and others).	9	7
The content of the strategy should be population based rather than medical/individualistic based.	8	6
The strategy shouldn't change current practice but build on what's gone before	7	5
The government should do something else with/to the strategy.	11	8

(All interviewees (N=133))

Respondents in both public health and local government expressed concern at the failure to distribute essential documents such as the HOTN White Paper to key non-NHS actors such as environmental health officers (Table 3.15). There was also concern that HOTN resources had used the language of the health service and of public health in particular - for example, in using the term 'alliance' when 'partnership' was widespread in local government.

Distribution of the special resources for particular groups of health care workers had not worked well. All of the ten GPs we interviewed had been recommended to us by their health authorities for interview for this study, but among this committed sample only two had found the GP pack[46] or *Better Living Better Life*[47] helpful. Many did not remember them, and some commented on the difficulty of sorting relevant material from the huge volume of literature that they received. None of the five interviewees in acute trusts were able to give any informed comment on the pack for hospital doctors[48].

Several respondents mentioned the need to involve the general public. A CHC member suggested:

start by getting people interested, only a small number of people know. It should be shorter and simpler, and there should be things on the telly or in soaps to say what people could do to help. Could use advertising.

3.9 The role of government

All interviewees were asked to suggest which three actions the government could take to ensure that OHN was sustainable. Respondents addressed all these types of involvement in their three priorities for government action. Their responses are summarised in Table 3.16.

Interviewees believed central government should have four key roles in a health strategy:

Providing focus and symbolic support

Central government was perceived by interviewees as having this role. Nearly a quarter of interviewees called for better communication and presentation of the new strategy, to the public and to the professionals involved.

Enabling at the local level

Over a third of interviewees (38%) mentioned the need for a statutory framework to allow key local participants, particularly local government, to work intersectorally for health with the support of their formal system. Otherwise they were vulnerable to the loss of enthusiastic key individuals who had been prepared to work for HOTN without this formal support. This response was the second most frequent. Twenty-three percent of interviewees envisaged a devolved but properly resourced structure, in which the mechanisms for achieving headline objectives were determined locally with community involvement.

Co-ordinating national action

Over one fifth of interviewees (21%) called for better cross departmental work at national level. These responses are from senior NHS employees:

Commitment at national level. Cabinet and government departments have a responsibility to feed the policy down.(Director of Public Health)

I think there does need to be a more coherent, national lead on it. In the last few years there's been confusion on different health issues which has caused a lack of confidence i.e. on substance misuse in schools, on alcohol consumption and the feeling on fiscal policy is the DoH is into it but other departments aren't supportive, they do their own thing (Director, Community Health Care Trust)

Many respondents mentioned the difficulties in working towards the sexual health targets, for example, at a time when sex education in school had been restricted by the Department for Education's circular clarifying the Education Act 1993 on sex education in schools[49]. 20% of interviewees called for a lead to be given to the strategy by national action. The field work began at the same time as the negotiation of the European Commission Directive on tobacco advertising and promotion, and the government's position on sponsorship of Formula One racing was brought up in relation to this question as well as some others. Thirteen respondents (10%) mentioned tobacco control, although the environment and other issues were also mentioned.

Healthy public policy

One third of interviewees (32%) called for the underlying determinants of health and health inequalities to be addressed through government action.

If they're serious about inequalities they must look at greater ownership by different government departments and hence down to local level. (Director of Public Health)

Table 3.17 Should the government provide additional resources?

	Number	Percent
Yes, unqualified	63	47
Yes, qualified, or No	56	42
Don't know	3	2
Missing	11	8
Total	**133**	**100**

(All interviews)

Table 3.18 How can a strategy avoid disruption to existing successful activity?

	Number	Percent
Build on what's gone before	55	41
Review what's gone before, keep successes	31	23
Give the strategy a flexible framework allowing for local consultation and priority setting	17	13
Define roles for HA, LA etc. more clearly	13	10
It won't disrupt anything: strategy has to play itself out	13	10
By having a mechanism to monitor it/give feedback	6	5
Evidence based with good justification for targets	5	4
Make it a high profile strategy	5	4
Government must make strategy truly inter-departmental	5	4
Resources (financial/human)	5	4
Focus on a few existing areas/targets	4	3
Recognise the determinants of health and inequalities	3	2
Other	22	17

(All interviewees (N=133))

All of these views of the role of government tend to imply a need for greater resources for the strategy, and the most frequent priority for government action (47% of interviewees) was the need for a better resourced strategy including administrative support for alliances, training for participants, incentives for GPs and so on. Interviewees were asked explicitly whether the government should provide more resources for OHN. Less than half said yes, and nearly as many gave a qualified or negative answer (Table 3.17).

3.10 Moving towards a new strategy

All respondents were asked how a new strategy could avoid disruption to existing successful activity. This gave respondents the opportunity to reflect and comment on how best to move on to a new health strategy. Although this question was asked of respondents prior to the publication of the Green Paper *Our Healthier Nation* many in the health service and local authorities were aware of its likely content. The results are shown in Table 3.18.

Over 40% of respondents (55/133) thought a new strategy should clearly build on or adapt the HOTN strategy and that it should not be completely new with a different focus and emphasis. According to one HOTN lead, government should:

acknowledge that there will be a gradual change and that not everything was a disaster. Build on what works, that's eminently sensible.(Assistant DPH)

Analysis by respondent type showed this view was held more strongly in HAs (43% (17/40)) than in LAs (27% (10/37)), although overall support was strongest amongst CHC and weakest amongst GPs.

Many of these respondents did not specify how the government should do this although six suggested building or broadening existing key areas. Two suggested building on the 'settings' approach while only one suggested building on existing targets. Nearly one in four respondents (31/133) thought it would be wise of the government to allow HAs to review their existing HOTN activities, being flexible enough to allow them to keep successful activities and to discard unsuccessful ones.

As one public health consultant in District C said:

I think that it's a matter for local interpretation and flexibility, working with what's good. It'll be hard for the government to be prescriptive about that. It's up to people on the ground.

Analysis by respondent type showed an almost equal proportion of HA (12/40) and LA (11/37) staff made this comment.

Flexibility in the new strategy was also considered the key to its success by 13% (17/133) of respondents. Flexibility was seen as allowing local priority setting, with the involvement of local organisations from outside the health service, within a national framework.

Ten percent (13/133) of respondents thought the government should define the role of HA and LAs more clearly, perhaps making participation in the new strategy a statutory requirement for LAs. This would ensure greater senior officer commitment to and delivery on the strategy. Both these views are re-iterated in Section 3.9 on the role of government.

Similarly, 10% (13/133) of respondents thought that the new strategy would not be disruptive, partly because the strategy had either 'played itself out' or because they were already preparing the ground for *Our Healthier Nation*. A number of ways to avoid disruption were given by the remaining respondents. Many of these issues were identical to those raised when respondents were asked 'What the government could do to ensure the strategy is sustainable?' Examples included; ensuring proper monitoring and feedback mechanisms are in place; ensuring that the new strategy is based on sound evidence, clearly justifying new areas/targets; making the strategy high profile; ensuring truly inter-departmental support for the policy within government; providing sufficient resources; and focusing on fewer key areas.

3.11   Conclusions

(i)   Interviewees considered that the key areas identified diseases which are important causes of morbidity and premature mortality, but only a quarter supported diseases as the right basis for key areas. Many supported a focus on population groups or work in settings. A strategy structured in a matrix which combines diseases, settings and population groups could provide the flexibility necessary to win the support of a wider range of partners.

(ii)   The present targets had little credibility, and the majority of the sample would like to see the indicators changed. Targets which were based on sound evidence and relevant to local baselines would carry more credibility and could form the basis for performance management.

(iii)   Many interviewees suggested that OHN be part of the performance management framework in the health service and in other sectors, and would see its incorporation in performance management as a sign of top level commitment. However, it needs to be applied with sophistication, learning lessons from other sectors (e.g. education), and should reflect the ability of local agencies to influence long term health outcomes.

(iv)   The sample was committed to working in alliances for health improvement and interviews supported a view that positive experiences of partnership for other purposes such as drugs action and economic regeneration was beneficial to partnership for health improvement.

(v)   Over a third of interviewees mentioned the need for a statutory framework to allow key local participants, particularly local government, to work in partnership for health.

(vi)   There was some support for the proposal that Directors of Public Health be appointed jointly by local authorities and health authorities, as an enabling structure for OHN.

(vii)   Communication of HOTN to most potential partners for health improvement was poor. Outside public health, some occupational groups who have a role in improving population health such as environmental health officers seem not to have received key documents. The language and concepts of most materials were familiar in public health and health promotion, but did not engage important agencies and occupational groups outside those fields.

(viii)   Interviewees would like government to take a stronger role in improving health at every level, from supporting and enabling local action to ensuring that policy decisions of government departments were taken with a view to their health impact. They were frustrated by conflicts between policies of different government departments which obstructed their work, and which seemed avoidable.

(ix)   The majority of the sample supported more resourcing for a national strategy for health, but nearly half qualified their replies to specify prescribed and purposeful spending to support structured action for health improvement at the local level.

(x)   Interviewees stressed that a new health strategy should be evolutionary rather than revolutionary. They would welcome flexibility to review current practice, allowing them to build on successful activities, and to identify local priorities through consultation with the local community.

4. THE IMPACT OF HOTN

Key points

♦ HOTN was perceived as increasing prevention activity, particularly in relation to the key areas and alliance work.

♦ HOTN was perceived as enabling health promotion efforts to be prioritised and improve co-ordination.

♦ There is some evidence for ownership of HOTN outside HA departments of public health, particularly through purchasing plans and contracts with providers.

♦ There are areas where ownership appears weaker as evidenced by lack of reference to HOTN in corporate contracts and general practice reports.

♦ The impact of HOTN on key policy documents peaked in 1993, then declined slightly thereafter.

♦ *Per capita* expenditure and health promotion expenditure as a proportion of total NHS for both the 'narrow' and 'broad' health promotion aggregate show a slight increase over the study period to a peak in 1994/5 with a gradual tailing off.

♦ There is little evidence to suggest that HOTN had anything more than a limited influence on patterns of resource allocation at local level.

4.1   Introduction

This chapter is based on the analysis of the data on the impact of HOTN at the local level in terms of changes to policies, services, behaviours/ideas, changes in organisation, and shifts in resources. Data relate to changes in prevention activity, impact on intersectoral projects, impact on policies, and shifts in resources as perceived by interviewees and as measured by an analysis of expenditure data. This

chapter also describes the impact of HOTN on health authority and local authority policies through an analysis of key documents.

4.2   Perceptions of the impact of HOTN

Health authority respondents working in health promotion and public health (N=15) were asked for their perceptions of the impact of HOTN on activity of the health authority in a number of areas including: prevention activity generally; prevention activity in the HOTN key areas; amount of spending on prevention activities; and the way prevention activities were carried out.

Most respondents (8/15) perceived that HOTN had increased the level of prevention activity generally, but particularly in relation to the key areas (10/15) and the targets (10/15). Most believed HOTN led to an increase in alliance activity (11/15) but not activity in settings (8/15). The main ways that HOTN influenced prevention activity were that it enabled efforts to be prioritised; it improved co-ordination; it gave status and legitimacy to prevention work, giving a 'hook to hang things on'.

Similar questions were put to respondents in other sectors about activity on HOTN in their spheres. Numbers are low, and conclusions must be tentative. However, these findings support a view that activity level outside health authorities is limited. Many respondents were identified through their existing involvement in alliances, and the positive responses reported in Table 4.1 below include some which were qualified by uncertainty about whether increased activity could be attributed to HOTN, so these data are likely to over-estimate HOTN activity.

Some typical responses from health promotion and public health are given below. A Head of Health Promotion said HOTN 'focused attention, but attention isn't action'. He commented:

the unit business plan [for health promotion] is not based on the HOTN key areas. But there's a lot of activity on key areas here, but it's not directly related or scientifically linked with benchmarks to HOTN targets...

A Consultant in Public Health Medicine in the same health authority said HOTN

Table 4.1 Increases in activity related to HOTN in various sectors

Sector (N)	In general	In named key area	In spending	On targets	In alliances	In settings
HAs (15)	8	13	3	10	11	6
CHCs (8)	1	4	0	0	1	0
GPs (10)	2	5	0	3	3	1
LA leads (3)	3	0	0	1	1	1
Voluntary sector strategic (3)	1	1	0	1	1	1
Police (5)	0	1	0	0	1	0
Private sector (6)	2	1	0	0	2	0

(Selected groups)

Table 4.2 Would project have happened without HOTN?

	Number	Percent
Yes	44	45
Maybe	9	9
No	31	32
Don't know	2	2
Missing	11	11

(N = 97)

Table 4.3 Impact of HOTN on Key Documents

Document Type	Mention HOTN N (%)	Mention Key Areas — Mention Only N (%)	Mention Key Areas — Structured N (%)	Mention Alliances N (%)	Mention Settings N (%)	Mention Targets — Mention only N (%)	Mention Targets — Reports Targets N (%)	Mention Inequalities — Mention Only N (%)	Mention Inequalities — Structured N (%)
Purchasing Plan (N=25)	19 (79)	9 (36)	9 (36)	14 (56)	5 (20)	11 (44)	0 (0)	4 (16)	0 (0)
APHR (N=30)	29 (96)	9 (30)	17 (56)	22 (73)	8 (26)	13 (43)	11 (36)	13 (43)	7 (23)
5 year strategy (N=5)	4 (80)	3 (60)	2 (40)	4 (80)	0 (0)	4 (80)	0 (0)	4 (80)	0 (0)
Corporate Contract (N=24)	17 (71)	11 (46)	5 (21)	16 (67)	12 (50)	15 (62)	0 (0)	4 (16)	0 (0)
Community Care Plan (N=24)	13 (54)	9 (37)	0 (0)	9 (38)	3 (13)	9 (37)	0 (0)	3 (12)	0 (0)
Provider Contract (N=12)	11 (92)	5 (42)	1 (8)	7 (58)	8 (67)	4 (33)	0 (0)	2 (16)	1 (8)
GP practice report (N=18)	3 (17)	1 (6)	0 (0)	1 (6)	0 (0)	3 (17)	0 (0)	2 (11)	0 (0)
TOTAL (N = 138)	**96 (70)**	**47 (34)**	**34 (25)**	**73 (53)**	**36 (26)**	**59 (43)**	**11 (8)**	**32 (23)**	**8 (6)**

increased it [activity in the key areas] because it gives pegs to hang things on and focused work down. It was very good to do this rather than to have a wider spread.

A former HOTN Co-ordinator in another district said HOTN

had a great effect on the work programme. We would have probably done marginal activity in the areas through health promotion, but HOTN provided us with the opportunity to increase the intent' and she continued we were able to prioritise based on local targets...there had been a concentration of work on accidents and as a result of HOTN coming along we were able to kick it and move it up, so we achieved much more...

However, a Head of Health Promotion in a third district commented:

...we had some moneys for health at work, money for health promoting hospitals, in the days when there was development money, which there isn't now. So, initially I think there was a significant impact, not just a general mushrooming of activity. But now the activity is around the determinants of health...overall it didn't influence activities at all to be frank and honest with you...it had an influence on prevention, it helped the health authority focus a little away from treatment and care but the reality is that they're still about treatment and care and the impact these have on the targets is minimal.

The following quotations illustrate that some interviewees outside the health service were positive about the role of HOTN in prioritising activities, and giving legitimacy to new activities and partnerships.

What would have happened anyway? I'd like to think I would have become more structured because people are generally more aware of their health, but there's been a much greater drive generally because of HOTN. (Chain Store Occupational Health Adviser)

Things on HIV/AIDS wouldn't have happened without HOTN, people thought it was a joke until the message came out that it's relevant to all . . .

HIV has helped partnerships with the voluntary sector. (Director, Business Partnership)

Its value will have been to raise the awareness of non-health organisations of what they can do to improve HOTN. (Local Authority Chief Officer, HOTN Alliance Chair)

We've always worked with the CHC, for example, but now we have more input (Voluntary Organisation Chief Executive)

[HOTN] led other health agencies to involve private sector. (Chamber of Commerce Chief Executive)

Some comments suggested, however, that HOTN was one among a number of initiatives and movements contributing to these effects.

There's been no process of bringing key areas into SRB bids, but we do bring health into bids. Certainly we've developed a consciousness in non-health professional for looking at health aspects of non-health issues. For example in SRB3 there's a joint board chaired by a senior HA officer. In the latest SRB bid we've built in health impact assessment. Over the last 3-4 years the awareness of the importance of links to health has grown. There was none before that , but it's growing and building rapidly now. (Local Authority Director)

Some work by the business community in health is driven by the EC - stress, safety at work and the regulations around them. (Director, Business Partnership)

4.3 Impact on health promotion projects

Another way of measuring the impact of HOTN was to ask whether the health promotion projects described in Chapter 5 would have happened without HOTN. For almost half of the projects identified by the study, interviewees thought that they would have happened without HOTN. However, for 19/44 (43%) of these, including them under the HOTN 'banner' helped obtain funding. Almost one-third of projects would not have happened without the HOTN strategy according to interviewees.

112

Table 4.4 Mention of HOTN in Key Documents by Year

Year	Mention HOTN (%)
1992 (N=12)	7 (58)
1993 (N=19)	15 (79)
1994 (N=26)	20 (77)
1995 (N=27)	20 (74)
1996 (N=38)	28 (74)
Total (N = 122)	**90 (74)**

(Purchasing Plans, APHR, Corporate Contracts only)

4.4 Impact of HOTN on key policy documents

Documents were coded according to whether they referred to HOTN and its features i.e. key areas, alliances, targets and settings. In the case of key areas and targets we distinguished between reports which just mentioned these features and those which were structured all or in part around the key areas or reported progress on targets. This is a crude measure of the impact of HOTN on policy documents, but gives some indication of the extent of ownership of the strategy.

To some degree, the analysis of documents confirms findings from the interviews that the ownership of HOTN has essentially been limited to departments of public health. Table 4.3 shows that a higher proportion of annual public health reports than other types of documents made reference to HOTN and its features. A higher proportion of annual public health reports also used the key areas to structure all or part of the report and, other than HOTN monitoring reports, were the only document to report progress towards targets. The table also indicates that HOTN has had some impact on health authority purchasing plans - over three-quarters of purchasing plans analysed mentioned the HOTN strategy and the majority of contracts with providers that were examined made reference to HOTN. The lack of performance management of HOTN described in Chapter 3 is also shown by the relatively low proportion of corporate contracts with regional offices referring to HOTN. The lack of wider ownership is indicated by fewer mentions in community care plans and GP practice reports. Table 4.4 shows the proportion of purchasing plans, annual public health reports and corporate contracts which mention HOTN by their year of publication. This shows an immediate impact of HOTN on these documents in the two years following the launch of the strategy, peaking in 1993, then tailing off slightly thereafter.

4.5 Impact on Resources - health promotion and preventive expenditure

Interviews with health authority staff show that most perceived that HOTN had not influenced overall resource allocation in their authority. This issue is explored in greater depth through the analysis of expenditure data below.

General Approach

For each of the eight HAs, a series of aggregates were constructed for expenditure in the areas of health promotion and primary prevention services. The composition of these aggregates is summarised below:

A. 'Narrow' health promotion =(1. + 2.)

1. Population based health promotion services

- ◆ designated health promotion and health education expenditure by trusts and HA health promotion units and public health departments (and earlier expenditure on health promotion via FHSA General Medical Services (GMS) cash-limited funds)

2. General Practice health promotion

- ◆ expenditure on GP health promotion schemes via GMS non-cash-limited funds.

Individually demanded preventive services = (3. + 4.)

3. Family Planning services

- ◆ Hospital and Community Health Services (HCHS) designated family planning expenditure plus GP payments for contraceptive services and expenditure on GP prescribing of contraceptives (N.B. national estimates provided by the Prescription Pricing Authority were used for 1993/94 and earlier due to non-availability of local data).

4. Cancer Screening services

♦ GP cervical cytology payments plus costs of HA (FHSA) call and recall system plus laboratory screening expenditures. Note: a national estimate for 1996/97 laboratory screening costs of £8.8650 was used in Districts B and D.

♦ expenditure on breast screening programme plus costs of operating call and recall system. Note: a national estimate for 1996/97 breast screening expenditure (£6.95 per eligible woman) was constructed

from available data 51,52, and applied in HAs B, D, E and G where local data on breast screening were not available.

B. *'Broad' health promotion & prevention =*

(Narrow health promotion + Individually demanded preventive services)

These aggregates were then expressed in terms of i) expenditure *per capita*, and ii) as a proportion of total local NHS spend on all services.

Unless otherwise stated, all expenditures in the following analysis are expressed in constant 1991/92 prices, deflated by the HCHS Pay and Prices Index.

Narrow Health Promotion

Table 4.5 and Figure 4.1 below present the mean real *per capita* expenditure on the constituents of the 'narrow' health promotion aggregate across the eight HAs.

Table 4.5 Mean real expenditure *per capita* on 'narrow' health promotion activities (£)

Year	Population Based	General Practice	'Narrow' HP
1991/92	1.64	1.42	3.06
1992/93	1.65	1.49	3.14
1993/94	1.77	1.11	2.87
1994/95	1.97	1.39	3.36
1995/96	1.88	1.26	3.14
1996/97	1.83	1.29	3.12

Constant 1991/92 prices

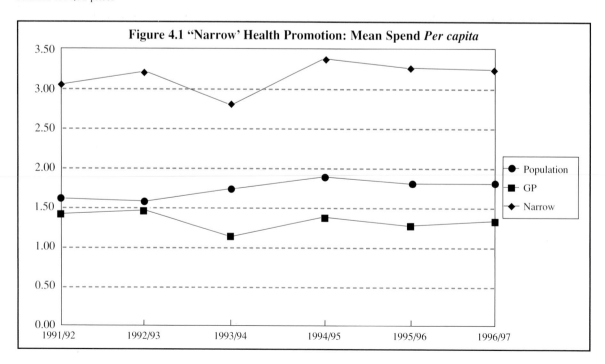

Figure 4.1 "Narrow" Health Promotion: Mean Spend *Per capita*

These data show that, averaged across all eight districts, *per capita* expenditure on population-based health promotion and prevention rose consistently over the five years to 1995/96, with a slight tailing off the following year - real *per capita* spend therefore grew by 11% over the study period. Over the whole period, in contrast, real *per capita* spend on health promotion via general practice decreased by some 9%. As a result, the 'narrow' health promotion aggregate changed less in *per capita* terms over the study period (a rise of only 2%), peaking in 1994/95 and then falling gently.

Data for each HA are displayed in Table 9.2-Table 9.4 of Appendix F and show some variation from the overall trend described above. Population based health promotion spend *per capita* rose consistently in two HAs (C,H); rose then fell in three (D,E,F); declined consistently in District A; declined and then

re-established itself in G. General practitioner health promotion spending followed the trend of a rise followed by a fall in each authority but E and G, where spending fell continuously.

Broad Health Promotion and Prevention

Table 4.6 shows real spending in two key individual demand-led preventive services (family planning and cervical cytology screening). Both indicators displayed a generally increasing trend over the study period until the 'Pill scare' of December 1995; prescribing expenditure on oral contraceptives dropped noticeably in 1995/96 and even further in 1996/97 as women switched to cheaper, older generation contraceptive pills or to other forms of contraception entirely. This impact was visible both nationally and in each study district (see Figure 4.2 below) .

Table 4.6 Individually demanded preventive services

Year	Mean Family Planning spend per woman aged 15-45	Cervical cytology spend per eligible woman aged 20-64
1991/92	13.42	3.92
1992/93	12.95	4.17
1993/94	14.22	4.25
1994/95	14.82	4.35
1995/96	14.29	4.39
1996/97	12.53	4.33

Mean real spend per capita (£),Constant 1991/92 prices

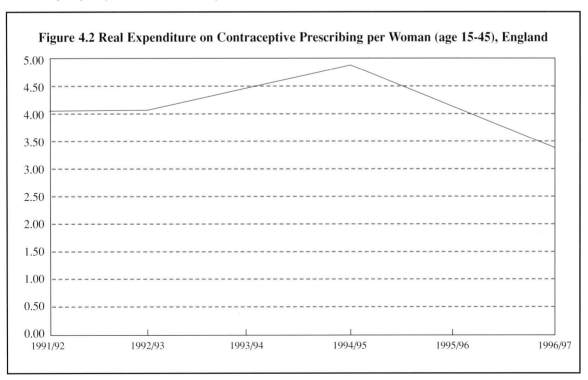

Figure 4.2 Real Expenditure on Contraceptive Prescribing per Woman (age 15-45), England

Table 4.7 Broad health promotion and prevention

Year	Narrow	Individual	Broad
1991/92	3.06	4.46	7.51
1992/93	3.14	4.41	7.57
1993/94	2.87	4.66	7.67
1994/95	3.36	4.80	8.28
1995/96	3.14	4.70	7.90
1996/97	3.12	4.30	7.48

Mean real spend per capita (£), Constant 1991/92 prices

Table 4.8 Mean health promotion and prevention spend as a proportion of total local NHS spend

Year	Narrow	Individual	Broad
1991/92	0.66	0.96	1.62
1992/93	0.66	0.93	1.59
1993/94	0.60	0.98	1.58
1994/95	0.69	0.98	1.67
1995/96	0.62	0.93	1.55
1996/97	0.61	0.84	1.45

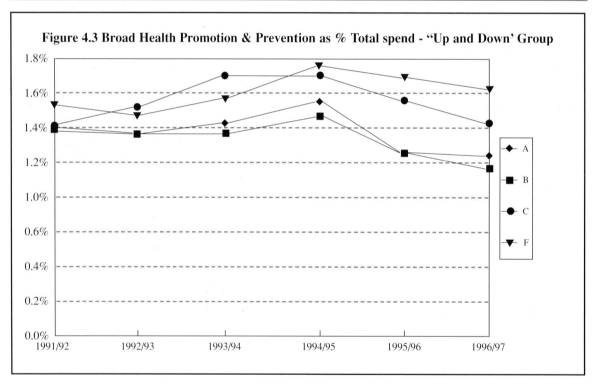

Figure 4.3 Broad Health Promotion & Prevention as % Total spend - "Up and Down' Group

When expenditure on prevention via these individually demanded programmes (family planning, cervical and breast cancer screening) is combined, and recalculated using total population, an estimate of 'broad' health promotion and prevention activity can be constructed. Table 4.7 shows that the peak in 'narrow' health promotion expenditure in 1994/95 is mirrored by the 'broad' aggregate which also reaches a peak in 1994/95, before declining in subsequent years.

District specific data are presented in Table 9.5 and 9.6 of Appendix F. With the exception of Authority H (where spend *per capita* rose continuously), broad health promotion and prevention expenditure in every HA displayed the pattern of 'rise and fall' with a peak in 1994/95.

The Resource Share of Health Promotion

When the same aggregates are examined in terms of their relationship to total local NHS spend, a slightly different pattern emerges. The share of resources devoted to 'narrow' health promotion peaked in 1994/95, and then declined slightly (Table 4.8). Clearly, the real financial growth experienced in eight authorities was not channelled proportionately into spending on these Narrow health promotion activities.

Four of the authorities clearly display this pattern of a rising resource share for health promotion and prevention which is then reversed after 1994/95. Of the four other districts, one (H) increased continuously the proportion of expenditure in this area, while spending in D, E and G declined fairly consistently over the period. Detailed data are presented in Appendix F (Table 9.7 and Table 9.9).

4.6 Conclusions

(i)   An analysis of the perceptions of the impact of HOTN on prevention activity generally indicate that HOTN increased activity, particularly in relation to the key areas and alliance work.

(ii)   The HOTN strategy is perceived as enabling efforts to be prioritised and improving co-ordination.

(iii)   Analysis of key policy documents indicates that although there is some evidence for ownership of the strategy outside HA departments of public health, particularly through purchasing plans and contracts with providers, there are areas where ownership appears weaker as shown by lack of reference to HOTN in other documents.

(iv)   The relative absence of HOTN in corporate contracts highlights the issue of the performance management of the strategy, which has been discussed in Chapter 3.

(v)   The lack of involvement of GPs in the strategy is indicated by the lack of reference to HOTN in their practice reports.

(vi)   There appears to be an increase in the impact of HOTN on key policy documents over the study period, peaking in 1993, then tailing off slightly thereafter.

(vii)   Analysis of HA expenditure data reveals a mixed picture. On average, *per capita* expenditure on population-based health promotion services by trusts and HAs in the eight districts showed a slight increase over the study period (1991/2-1996/7) - but within this mean, expenditure rose in four HAs and fell in four others.

(viii)   On average, *per capita* expenditure on health promotion activity by GPs shows a slight decrease over the same period, falling in five HAs and rising in three. The aggregate of these two measures ('narrow' health promotion) shows a slight increase over the study period, but fell back from a peak in 1994/5.

(ix)   *Per capita* expenditure for two prevention services which relate to two key areas of HOTN (family planning and cervical cytology) show an increase over the study period with a peak in 1995/6. The 'broad' health promotion aggregate shows the same increasing trend to 1994/5 with a gradual tailing off to a slightly lower level in 1996/97 than that seen at the start of the study period. In family planning services this trend was accentuated by the impact on utilisation of oral contraceptives of the 1995 'Pill scare'

(x)   Overall, expenditure on each of the components of the 'broad' health promotion aggregates grew as a proportion of total local NHS expenditure until 1994/95 - but after that year, their share of local NHS resources declined. In 1996/97, all measures of health promotion received, on average, a smaller share of NHS resources than had been the case in 1991/92.

(xi)   Overall, these data were not consistent with HOTN having achieved significant shifts in resources at local level - but this was not necessarily a primary objective of the strategy. Certainly, if HOTN had exerted an impact upon local resource priorities, this effect began to dissipate after 1994/95.

5. MECHANISMS FOR IMPLEMENTATION DEVELOPED AT LOCAL LEVEL

Key Points

- HOTN appears to have stimulated and focused intersectoral health strategies in some districts, while others have been able to progress strategies without this stimulus.

- There are three main ways the case study districts have developed local health strategies and alliances: i) under a non-HOTN label; ii) directly from HOTN; iii) HOTN 'plus', where local key areas were added to the original five.

- The different extent to which HOTN was used to focus activities for health improvement and intersectoral health strategies was reflected in varying management structures for HOTN.

- The use of contracts to involve NHS Trusts in the implementation of HOTN varied greatly - but there is support for integrating OHN explicitly into new commissioning arrangements.

- Only one HA operated a designated HOTN budget covering all HOTN development activities. Five other HAs had allocated partial (non-staff) budgets for development in certain key areas.

- Current budgeting and financial reporting mechanisms need considerable improvement if they are effectively to support decision-making across multiple settings and agencies.

- The absence of any requirement to monitor spending on HOTN development ensured that it is essentially impossible to identify or compare retrospectively the resources invested in the implementation of the strategy. If current financial monitoring and budgeting systems do not change, the same fate will inevitably befall OHN implementation.

- Six out of eight HAs had explicitly earmarked funds for alliances; amounts ranged from £2,000 to £200,000, suggesting that they were used in very different ways.

- General practitioners tend to focus on the health promotion tasks under their contracts, and did not give strong priority to strategic action for health outside this framework. This raises concern about GPs' ability to fulfil their responsibilities for population health promotion in PCGs.

- Health authorities have not found it easy to involve the police and private sector in health partnership. Police forces and some businesses are willing to engage in partnership, but prefer working on specific measures to less well-defined 'strategic' partnerships.

- CHCs and the voluntary sector have participated at various levels in implementation of HOTN and/or other strategic health policy initiatives in most districts. Poor communication of the strategy by government and HAs and funding constraints respectively have hindered this process.

5.1 Introduction

This chapter presents an analysis of the mechanisms employed at local level to implement HOTN. It begins by reviewing the general management and funding arrangements for the strategy and then describes local health strategies, partnerships and intersectoral projects. It examines how local alliances are structured and operate, the resources allocated to them and the degree of participation by alliance partners (NHS trusts, GPs, the police, the private sector, the voluntary sector and CHCs) as well as their role in health strategy.

5.2 Models of implementation

The study identified three broad models of health strategy implementation at the local level:

◆ **Non-HOTN label** - In Districts A , C and H local health strategies and alliances developed under non-HOTN labels including healthy cities and urban regeneration initiatives.

◆ **HOTN** - Districts F and G developed local health strategies directly from HOTN.

◆ **HOTN 'plus'**- Districts B, D and E have developed local health strategies using the HOTN key areas but adding local key areas and sometimes targets.

5.3 HOTN management arrangements

In almost all districts there was a HOTN lead or person identified as responsible for co-ordinating or overseeing HOTN activities. This was usually a senior member of staff within the health authority. On the whole, health authorities were split between those whose HOTN lead was either the Director of Public Health or, in one case, the assistant Director of Public Health, and those in which the responsibility was given to a senior member or head of health promotion. The exception to this was District A in which no-one in the health authority was designated with lead responsibility for HOTN. The HOTN leads situated in health promotion were directly accountable to the Director of Public Health.

In those health authorities which had someone leading on HOTN, four worked on policy and operational issues while three worked on policy issues alone. There was no apparent association between department, seniority and content of work. All the HOTN leads were employed by the health authority directly.

In Districts A, B C, G and H where HOTN was not led from health promotion, interviewees were asked how the specialist health promotion service, wherever situated, worked with the HOTN lead. Table 5.2

Table 5.1 Health Authorities A to H. Mechanisms developed at the local level to implement HOTN

Health Authority	A	B	C	D	E	F	G	H
HOTN lead	None	Asst. DPH	DPH	HP	HP	HP	DPH	DPH
Management of HOTN lead	None	DPH	DPH	DPH	DPH	DPH	DPH	DPH
Policy and/or Operational role	None	P&O	P	P	P	P&O	P&O	P&O
HOTN integration	No	No	Yes	Yes	Yes	No	Yes	Yes

Table 5.2 Health authorities A, B, C, F and G. Relationships of specialist health promotion service which do not lead HOTN to HOTN leadership

Health Authority	A	B	C	G	H
Located	PH	PH	Trust	PH	Trust
Health Promotion manager input to HA policy	Yes	Yes, Asst DPH/HOTN Lead acts as HP Manager	Yes	Yes	No

Table 5.3 Inclusion of HOTN in contracts

Health Authority	No. contracts supplied	Include HOTN in quality standards	Include HOTN in information requirements
A	0	n/a	n/a
B	2	y	y
C	0	n/a	n/a
D	1	n	y
E	5	y	y
F	1	y	n
G	2	n	n
H	1	n	n
Total	12		

summarises the structural relationships that were reported to us by HOTN leads and health promotion unit heads.

In districts A, B C and G, the Health Promotion Unit still had considerable input to HOTN strategy despite the lead being administratively separate from the Unit. In District H, input was less and the health promotion service had operational responsibilities only.

HOTN and health service contracts

The health authorities involved primary and secondary health care sectors through formal mechanisms to ensure that opportunities for implementation of HOTN in health care settings were used. Some also encouraged trusts and general practices to become involved in strategy development and implementation, project work and health alliances. Findings on trusts and general practices are reported below.

Six of the eight health authorities supplied us with one or more examples of their contracts with providers (Table 5.3) Of these, three health authorities included HOTN in their quality standards; and three included HOTN in their information requirements.

Data from interviews with health authority and trust managers also show that six health authorities had operationalised HOTN into contracts. According to interviews with trust managers, HOTN activities carried out by the trusts are monitored by health authorities in various ways (Table 5.4).

The manager of a specialist Health Promotion Unit in one district described how HOTN was operationalised into contracts in her authority:

We put health promotion and HOTN into purchasing plans. We're now changing the focus of purchasing plans to health and are putting HOTN into contracts. We [health promotion] support providers in meeting their contracts.

A consultant cardiologist in the same district described how his hospital's HOTN activities are monitored:

I'm on the medical monitoring group with health authority colleagues, we have six-monthly meetings and monitoring is as rigorous as finance or volume.

A contracts manager in an acute, community and mental health trust in another district described a more loose system of monitoring:

We don't have to do any quarterly report to them or anything. We meet regularly with the health authority and we monitor contracts there, if there's an issue they will bring it up then.

The 17 trust-based interviewees thought that OHN should be incorporated into contracts or successor mechanisms.

Local funding arrangements for HOTN

Key Areas

Only in one HA were funds explicitly earmarked for HOTN activities in the form of a HOTN designated budget. In District B, HOTN received a dedicated budget within Public Health. In 1994/95, this budget totalled over £175,000, of which half was dedicated to general support and development, and half allocated specifically to each of the HOTN key areas (plus local key areas). This budget increased further

Table 5.4 Methods of monitoring HOTN in contracts

Type of monitoring	Number of interviewees
Special HOTN meeting/report	8
Through quality mechanism	2
Integrated in routine contract monitoring	1
Through clinical effectiveness	1
No monitoring	1
Total	**13**

in following years to incorporate the Health Alliance funding described above.

Elsewhere, however, HOTN global budgets were not in evidence. The general pattern in most HAs (in public health departments and health promotion units) was for particular HOTN key areas to have non-pay expenditures allocated to them. Individual staff (or proportions of salary expenditures) were not, however, allocated to key areas, so that these 'budgets' failed to reflect the staff input going into HOTN work. This pattern of non-staff budget allocations to specific key areas was visible in five Districts (A, C, D, F, G). Because staff costs were not included, each key area typically received an allocation of a few thousand or tens of thousands of pounds only. In District G, an annual HOTN reserve was also identified (some £70,000 per year) above and beyond these key area non-pay budgets, which was allocated to small and medium projects as the year progressed.

These findings on the use of designated budgets are broadly consistent with the responses of those HA interviewees who were questioned about the impact of HOTN on resource allocation. Their responses confirmed that some specific allocation of resources to HOTN had occurred in five of the eight HAs. In the other three authorities, HOTN activity was subsumed entirely within other resource headings.

The absence of designated global budgets for HOTN (especially the failure to allocate salary budgets to HOTN) means that it is quite impossible, *post hoc*, to identify what sums any individual HA (with the possible exception of B) devoted to the implementation of HOTN. Clearly, if the dedication of resources to the implementation of a particular strategy is regarded as an important objective (sufficiently important to warrant performance management), then agencies must be required from the outset to designate the uses to which funds are being put. The failure to consider establishing a programme budgeting approach to HOTN (however simplistic) at the outset of the strategy inevitably meant that HOTN's impact on resource use can never be unambiguously described.

School Health Services

School health services are an example of a range of activities with direct relevance to HOTN (and, in turn, to *Our Healthier Nation*) whose expenditures at present cannot be monitored routinely across HAs. Data concerning expenditure on school health services could be found in only two authorities (and this only for 1996/97); the other HAs were not able to disaggregate expenditure on school nursing, medical and dental services from the much wider contracts (e.g. for general community services) in which they tend to sit.

In the two districts which were able to provide data, total NHS expenditure on school health services was well in excess of £1 million in each, and represented 0.36% and 0.38% of total NHS spend. If it is assumed that expenditure in the other districts on this item is broadly similar, it then appears that most HAs are currently unable to monitor spending on a programme which uses much the same scale of resources as their population based health promotion activities.

These problems of data availability reflect directly the absence of any form of programme budgeting within the NHS. If the new strategy seeks to monitor the use of resources by and the allocation of resources to various activities carried out in different settings, then attention needs to be given to reconsidering programme budget and financial monitoring methods. This is critically true for community health services, whose resource use remains highly opaque despite progress in costing in many other sectors in recent years.

Having reviewed the general management and funding arrangements for HOTN the next section describes the nature of local health strategies, partnerships and intersectoral projects. Consideration is also given to funding arrangements and the leadership of alliances.

5.4   Local health strategies and alliances

Interviewees were asked whether there were locally developed strategies, whether distinct local areas and targets had been formulated, and whether there was a local strategic-level alliance. They were also asked what links they had made with local agencies to implement HOTN strategies. These questions were asked of the Director of Public Health, the Head of Health Promotion and the HOTN lead if this was a

Table 5.5 Local HOTN mechanisms as reported by key informants

Authority	Local strategy	Local alliance	Local key areas	Local targets
A	Yes	Yes	Yes	Yes
B	Yes	Yes	Yes	Yes
C	Yes	Yes	No	No
D	Yes	No	Yes	Yes
E	Yes	Yes	Yes	Yes
F	Yes	Yes	Yes	No
G	Yes	Yes	Yes	Yes
H	Yes	No	No	No
Total	8	6	6	5

(Directors of Public Health, HOTN leads and health promotion managers)

Table 5.6 Involvement in strategic alliances - sector as reported by key informants

Authority	Local Authority	Voluntary Sector	Private Sector	Police
A	Yes	Yes	Yes	No
B	Yes	Yes	Yes	Yes
C	Yes	Yes	No*	Yes
D	Yes	Yes	Yes	Yes
E	Yes	Yes	No*	Yes
F	Yes	Yes	No*	Yes
G	Yes	Yes	Yes	Yes
H	Yes	Yes	Yes	Yes
Total	8	8	5	7

* Private sector actors have not been involved in strategic planning although a few companies, usually mainstream retailers, have been involved in co-operative projects.
(Directors of Public Health, HOTN leads and health promotion managers)

Table 5.7 Involvement in strategic alliances: LA departments as reported by key informants

Authority	Environmental Health	Social Services	Education	Leisure	Housing
A	Yes	Yes	Yes	Yes	No*
B	Yes	Yes	Yes	Yes	Yes
C	Yes	Yes	Yes	Yes	Yes
D	Yes	Yes	Yes	Yes	Yes
E	Yes	Yes	Yes	Yes	Yes
F	Yes	Yes	Yes	Yes	Yes
G	Yes	Yes	Yes	Yes	No
H	Yes	Yes	Yes	Yes	Yes
Total	8	8	8	8	6

*Most of the LA's housing stock was sold off. However, some of the local housing trusts have been involved in alliances.
(Directors of Public Health, HOTN leads and health promotion managers)

different person. All authorities reported having strategies, six reported local alliances, six reported having added local key areas, and five reported developing locally specific targets. All reported involving the local authority in strategy implementation, including in most cases every relevant department. All reported involving the voluntary sector, five reported involving the private sector and seven the police (Table 5.5-Table 5.6).

However, these reports reflect varying degrees of involvement, some of it quite slight, and they do not distinguish between past and current involvement.

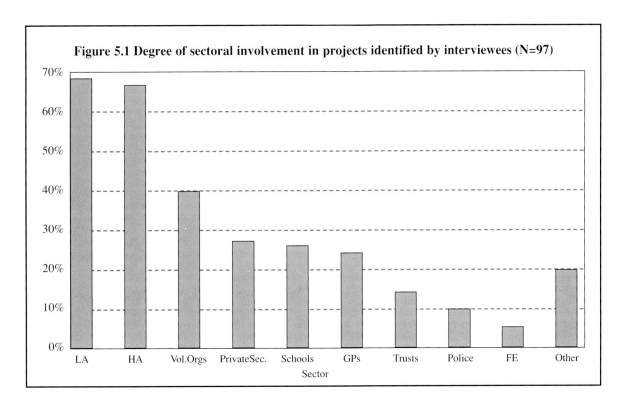

Figure 5.1 Degree of sectoral involvement in projects identified by interviewees (N=97)

Table 5.8 Description of project topic and type, lead agency and funding source

Project Topic	Number	Percent	Lead Agency	Number	Percent
HOTN key areas	51	53	LA	30	31
General Health Improvement	22	21	HA	21	22
HOTN risk factors	11	11	Multi-agency	12	12
Non HOTN areas	7	7	Voluntary Organisation	8	8
Wider determinants of health (e.g. poverty)	6	6	Healthy Alliance	5	5
			Joint HA/LA	4	4
			Police	1	1
			Other	8	8
			Missing	8	8

Funding Source	Number	Percent	Project Type	Number	Percent
Joint (other than HA/LA)	27	28	Attempts to change behaviour	35	36
Central Government (e.g. SRB, DoH, DoE)	18	19	Awareness raising	21	22
Joint Finance (LA/HA)	14	14	Improve inter-agency working and support networks	16	16
HA ONLY	13	12	Regeneration	9	9
LA only	11	11	Needs assessment	5	5
Other joint LA/HA	6	6	Strategic	5	5
None	2	2	Other	6	6
Other	4	4			
Missing	2	2			

(N = 97)

Health promotion projects

The extent and nature of involvement in projects by different sectors within a district is an indicator of the level of partnership between organisations in and outside the NHS. Interviewees were asked to identify three specific projects related to HOTN implementation - two which, in their view, had gone well, and one which had not gone so well. Ninety seven such projects were identified. Table 5.8 gives a description of project topics, type, lead agency involved and the source of funding. The majority of these focused either on HOTN key areas or on HOTN risk factors (e.g. smoking, diet) and were led either by health authorities or local authorities. Most projects were either awareness raising (for example, 'healthy eating week') or were specific attempts to change behaviours (e.g. GPs prescribing exercise). Central government and joint funding played an important role in the funding of these projects, for example, in some districts funds obtained through the Single Regeneration Budget (SRB) funded health improvement projects. Figure 5.1 shows the degree of intersectoral involvement in projects by agency. The main participants in there projects are LAs, HAs and voluntary organisations.

Resourcing Alliances

Where it could be located, financial information concerning any resources which had explicitly been allocated to support or facilitate health alliances with local authorities and other local organisations was collected from the finance departments of each of the participating health authorities. In common with most locally collected data, the very earliest records available dated from 1993/94, and several authorities had great trouble identifying any data. Table 5.9 below provides a simple summary of the scale of resources identified as having been earmarked for 'alliances' or closely analogous activities. Six of the eight authorities could point to concrete allocations to alliances or obviously analogous activities. These ranged from very small sums to a large budget in Authority B. It should be noted, however, that none of the £200,000 allocated in 1995/96 by B for its health alliance was spent - all was carried over to the following year. While overall Joint Finance expenditure *per capita* stayed relatively stable, the value of health

authority's inputs declined over the period. Table 5.10 clearly illustrates the primary pitfall of joint working and funding arrangements - that one of the partners may fail (or be unable) to maintain their commitment. While the relative share of HAs varied substantially between authorities, a clear downward trend was visible in almost all districts.

How alliances work operationally

Of the 58 interviewees involved operationally in intersectoral work for health, 10 were employed by health authorities, 34 by local authorities, three by the voluntary sector, six by the private sector and five by the police. Operational staff in HAs were employed from mainstream funds in all districts. In LAs, however, nearly one in eight operational staff interviewed were also employed using funds from specific projects. In some cases funding was mixed, both project and mainstream. In the main, funding of operational staff activity was from mainstream sources (63% (30/48)), although half the activity in the HAs (50% (5/10)), and nearly a sixth in LAs and other sectors (17% (8/48)), was co-funded with project moneys. All operational employees were line managed by their own employing agency, with the exception of a small minority of staff in LAs (9% (3/34)) who were managed jointly with an external agency. However, not all operational staff were based within their the funding institution. Two of the ten staff funded by HAs were based outside the authority, one in a trust and one in a LA, although in LAs only one of the 34 operational employees was based outside the authority itself.

For operational employees outside the health authority, their main health authority contact was most likely to be someone in health promotion (15/48) followed by the Director of Public Health (9/48) or someone else in public health (10/48).

Leadership

The extent to which leadership is shared between the health authority (and particularly the public health directorate) and other partners is a measure of partnership. Health authority, local authority and voluntary sector operational staff and interviewees in the police and private sector were asked who chaired the intersectoral alliances they worked with.

Table 5.9 Earmarked HA Resources for Health Alliances

HA	Funds identified	1993/94	1994/95	1995/96	1996/97
A	Yes	n/k	c. £50,000	nil	nil
B	Yes	c. £13,000	c. £3,000	c. £200,000	Carried over
C	Yes	n/k	nil	nil	c. £2,000
D	Yes		c. £13,000	c. £14,000	c. £10,000
E	n/k				
F	Yes	n/k	n/k	c. £6,000	c. £20,000
G	Yes	n/k	n/k	c. £66,000	c. £49,000
H	n/k				

n/k = not known

Table 5.10 Mean Joint Finance Expenditure by HA and other agencies (£ *per capita*)

Year	Health Authority	All Agencies	HA Share
1991/92	1.18	2.74	43
1992/93	1.01	2.70	37
1993/94	0.96	2.45	39
1994/95	0.64	2.38	27
1995/96	0.76	2.78	27
1996/97	0.70	2.63	27

Constant 1991/92 prices

Table 5.11 Who chairs the steering group/alliance you work with?

	Number	Percent
Health authority	13	39
Local authority	13	39
Missing	7	21
Total	**33**	**100**

(Health authority, local authority and voluntary sector operational interviewees, interviewees in the police and private sector interviewees)

Table 5.12 Who are the key people leading implementing implementation of HOTN in the health authority?

	Number mentioning
Director of Public Health	25
HOTN lead	15
Other public health	11
Any public health	31
Health Promotion Manager	22
Other health promotion	11
Any health promotion	24
Director of Finance	1
Director of Primary Health Care	2
HA Chief Executive	5
HA Chair/Member	2
HA Other	7

(Directors of Public Health, HOTN leads and health promotion managers, LA HOTN leads, Trust interviewees (N=43))

Similar proportions were chaired by HA employees and LA representatives (Table 5.11).

Directors of public health were most likely to be named by health authority and trust employees (N=43) as key individuals leading implementation of HOTN in the health authority (Table 5.12). Outside the health authority, key individuals were most likely to be employed in environmental health departments (Table 5.13).

Among the qualities that key individuals required in order to be effective, respondents were most likely to mention commitment (17/43), and an understanding of other organisations (16/43) (Table 5.14). Seven of 43 interviewees asked this question

responded that organisational rather than personal qualities made people effective, and five stressed that the qualities they identified as important for effectiveness while desirable, were not possessed by the people involved in HOTN implementation in their district.

5.5 Alliance partners

This section describes the nature of participation in each of the agencies involved in health alliances.

Alliance partners - NHS trusts

Half of the trust interviewees (9/18) reported that there was someone responsible for HOTN in the

Table 5.13 Who are the key people leading implementation of HOTN outside the health authority?

Number mentioning	Chief offficer, director or Chief executive	Other	Total
Environmental Health	10	6	16
Leisure	2	5	7
Social Services	2	8	10
Education	8	6	14
Other LA Directorate	5	4	9
Local Authority Chief Executive	-	-	5
Councillor	-	-	1
Voluntary Sector	-	-	12
Private Sector	-	-	3
Trust	2	4	6
Other Non Health Authority	-	-	10
No Non Health Authority	-	-	7

(Directors of Public Health, HOTN leads and health promotion managers, LA HOTN leads, Trust interviewees (N=43))

Table 5.14 What qualities made these people effective?

	Number mentioning
Commitment	17
Understanding of other organisations	16
Long term vision	9
Flexibility	7
Stamina	5
Competencies/skills	5
A broad view of health	5
Belief that change is possible	4
Leadership	3

(Directors of Public Health, HOTN leads and health promotion managers, LA HOTN leads, Trust interviewees (N=43))

Table 5.15 Who are the key people leading implementing implementation of HOTN within the trust?

	Number mentioning
Trust Chief Executive	4
Trust Director/Senior Manager	8
Other Management	4
Medical Staff	4
Other Healthcare Staff	8
Other	1

(Trust interviewees (N=18)

trust, although this concealed large variations in the level of engagement by these trusts. Both of the following trusts had someone responsible for HOTN.

How did HOTN affect activities in key areas?
...none, apart from the fact that people were attending the strategy groups, so that raised awareness. (Manager, community trust)
It's not in our business plan or the trust annual report...They are even struggling with the alliance thing. Our trust has never picked it up, HOTN. (Dietician at the same community trust)

There was an alliance already in place when I arrived. [This trust] is very involved. We chair two sub-groups, originally because we were a health promotion provider. Now the health promotion department has gone to the HA, and other trust staff have moved into their places. (Chief Executive, Community Trust).

The key individuals implementing HOTN that trust interviewees identified within the trust illustrated the varied extent of HOTN implementation. Those most likely to be singled out were directors and senior managers (8/18) and non-medical health care workers (8/18). Four interviewees mentioned the chief executive as a key individual within the trust (Table 5.15).

Alliance partners - GPs

Seven of the ten GPs interviewed had been involved with the health authority's HOTN work, a figure that was unsurprising given that these GPs had been identified by their HAs, and usually by the public health department. The extent of the involvement by these seven varied. Three had been involved in strategy development, one in strategy

implementation, and four in project work. Three had been involved in intersectoral alliances.

GPs took a narrow, medical approach to health promotion, rather than one which included addressing wider determinants of health, at least in their own work. Predictably the work they did in the health promotion element of their contract with the health authority fell within this medical model. They undertook secondary prevention and disease management activities for people with existing ischaemic heart disease, diabetes and asthma, they targeted disease prevention interventions at their older patients, they implemented national screening programmes, and they provided well man and well woman clinics. One GP had a teenagers' clinic, and one saw a need for a clinic for this age group. The use of the term 'health promotion' for these disease prevention and disease management tasks is different from the more usual meaning.

This medical view was also reflected in GPs' views of HOTN. They were asked how HOTN had influenced the amount and type of activity they did, and the extent to which they worked towards targets, or in alliances and settings. GPs were split in their views with 8/10 who thought it had negligible or no impact on their work in key areas, and 2/10 who thought it had increased their activity. Typical comments included:

How did HOTN affect how much activity the practice did in the key areas?
I don't think it did at all.

How did HOTN affect which activities your practice did?
It may have influenced service change in mental health. But again, I'm not over-convinced, it may have happened anyway.

How did HOTN affect which activities your practice did?

We wouldn't have done anything which wasn't in it. From now, health promotion activities would have to be the ones in HOTN.

The last group included one who believed patients' health overall had suffered because of HOTN.

. . we might not have treated asthma and diabetes. We wouldn't have done health checks on healthy individuals or put aside staff to chase cervical smears. It takes a lot of resources, and may have saved one or two lives, but we could have offered a lot of treatment with those resources.

It was clear that some GPs made no distinction between HOTN and disease prevention schemes that were required under their contract or covered by incentive payment schemes.

The medical view of health promotion which equates it only with disease prevention was understandable under a division of labour which gave GPs responsibility for patient care, and gave health authorities the lead on population health. However, the new arrangements under the NHS White Paper will give Primary Care Groups a wider responsibility to 'promote the health of the local population' of natural communities of around 100,000 people. The level of awareness shown by the GPs interviewed did not suggest that they were prepared for this task. The leverage of accountability that the health authority holds over Primary Care Groups is unlikely to be sufficient alone to strengthen the population perspective of GPs, without a greater basic understanding than was shown by the sample. The research team did not have the opportunity to talk to other practice team members, but there may be scope to broaden the perspective on population health through a requirement for multi-disciplinary leadership of Primary Care Groups.

Compatibility of HOTN with current GP management structures

GPs were asked how well they thought the current GP contract fitted with HOTN. Three saw a reasonably good fit, four thought there was a potentially positive effect that was not exploited, and three thought there was no effect. None saw any conflict.

Of the seven GPs who were fundholders, four saw fundholding as producing a benefit to HOTN and three saw no effect. A GP said

Fundholding has helped to pay to bolster services. It's allowed us to fund for example the community psychiatric nurse, we had the flexibility. It's an incentive in prescribing, for example to examine our lipid lowering prescribing more carefully.

Health promotion specialists were likely to be more cynical. One said:

Some GP fundholders used their underspends on health promotion - for example one has bought a lot of cycle helmets, but I'm not sure how he'll use them. Those who purchase health visitors don't recognise their public health function.

GPs and OHN - the future

HOTN leads and GPs were asked what could be done to involve GPs and primary health care teams more fully in OHN.

Although 7/10 GPs were interviewed after the publication of the NHS White Paper, few were looking ahead to the implications for Primary Care Groups. Suggestions from GPs were:

It shouldn't be primary care based. It needs to be a general policy of promoting health. Medical people shouldn't be involved.

Ought to be involved more, but I don't know how it would be feasible - possibly through the commissioning group.

Continue to involve us, get our input. LMC reps are involved in the key area strategies now, continue that.

Continued incentives and the publication of any evidence that it all works. If there's no payback then it won't be continued.

You would have to make the planning process bottom up rather than top down. The problem is one

of commitment, and the way to get the commitment is to make it relevant to the people carrying it out and, or course, it's relevant if they have had a hand in the planning.

Give us some breathing space, sit back and look at what we're doing, we do need more staff time at all levels, doctors and nurses, administration, everybody.

HOTN leads made the following proposals for involving GPs:

They need a mindset change almost in what health promotion means. It's not just seeing individuals in PHC locally, but identifying the population's health needs at the population level and then working with others in the community to change it. So it's not them being isolated in their practice, it needs to be effected where health is created.

The brief should be extended and not just cover prevention but wider health promotion activities.

Acknowledge the health promotion work they're already doing. More work needs to be done to encourage a public health focus, and take health promotion out of the GP contract because all it's done is made health promotion like something discrete and difficult. Health promotion should be integral to primary health care, and a lot of primary care work is good health promotion but it's not recognised as such. Let's get back to Alma Ata.

Weak congruence between the responses from GPs and the responses from HOTN leads shows a poor understanding of GPs by the HOTN leads, which may be a widespread problem in health promotion and public health. One health promotion specialist gave her perspective on a lack of mutual understanding:

People in health promotion think GPs and other clinical workers understand health promotion and public health but they don't.

These findings give rise to concern that if health promotion and public health do not appreciate the constraints under which GPs were contributing to HOTN, they would not understand how to motivate and involve them, particularly in their new broader role.

Alliance partners - the Police

Interviews were conducted with police representatives from five of the eight districts. These were senior police officers, usually with responsibility for liaising with other agencies.

In addition, a sub-group of HA and LA managers involved in HOTN were asked about the involvement of the police in alliances. Of the 19 respondents who answered, 12 said that the police were involved, five said that they were not and two did not know. According to these interviewees, the police were involved in alliances to some degree in seven out of the eight districts (see Table 5.6). However, the police officers interviewed were not familiar with HOTN, although they were able to describe their health-related activities. In most authorities, police involvement is through the Drug Action Teams (DATs) developed out of the *Tackling Drugs Together* initiative. Other areas where police are involved in joint working with the health and local authority sectors are mental health (two authorities) and accident prevention (one authority). But their involvement in alliances which could strictly be described as HOTN is limited. Police reported involvement in Single Regeneration Budget bids in two authorities and in HAZ bids in one authority. In two areas, the police have been involved in joint work in schools relating to drugs and other health issues.

The involvement of the police in *Tackling Drugs Together* was described by a senior officer in one area as follows:

Drugs is the area where we have most collaboration, although it doesn't come from HOTN, it comes from Tackling Drugs Together. *There is a County Drugs Action Team, which the Assistant Chief Constable sits on. It is felt to be a success, felt to be worthwhile, although it is hard to measure and there has been a rise in drug use. At sector level there are 11 drug and alcohol reference groups. Alcohol is felt to be a bigger problem than drugs. The groups are inter sectoral, and look at the delivery of DAT locally. Some just give information to misusers, and some also have referral schemes. They meet every two months. In 1996/97 these groups organised 76 partnership educational events aimed at demand reduction and harm reduction.* (Senior Officer)

The senior police officers interviewed were very keen to be involved in partnerships with health and local authorities. They identified links between HOTN and the Crime and Disorder Bill which encourages partnerships for crime prevention and is their equivalent of HOTN. The Bill is based on the assumption that police 'can't do it alone' and requires the setting up of local intersectoral leadership groups. These police officers want to be more involved in OHN but want help in how this can best be achieved:

Outside our core business we want to be told what you expect from us, rather than just your strategic aims. (Senior Officer)

In developing a partnership I need to know what they can offer me, and what I can offer them. (Liaison Officer)

Some argued for a statutory framework for partnerships while another argued

Partnerships tend to be notional, they're possibly not formalised usefully. DAT is over formalised, there's too much paper, we're overwhelmed. (Senior Officer)

Alliance partners - private sector

Interviews were conducted with representatives of the private sector in six of the eight districts, although only five of these knew anything about HOTN. It was difficult to find representatives from the private sector to interview mainly due to their lack of involvement in HOTN work. Those interviewed were all from private sector umbrella organisations such as chambers of commerce or training and enterprise councils (TECs), apart from one interviewee from a large retail chain store. A sub-group of HA and LA managers involved in HOTN were asked whether the private sector were involved in alliances. Of the 22 respondents who answered, 13 said that the private sector was involved, eight said that it was not and one did not know. According to these interviewees, the private sector were involved in alliances to some degree in all eight districts, although the research team could

only find people to interview in five. In one area there was private sector involvement in the healthy city project and in three areas there has been some private sector involvement more recently through SRB and HAZ bids. The area which had the most (but still limited) involvement of the private sector in healthy alliances was where the chief executive of the chamber of commerce was also a non-executive director of the local acute trust. An occupational health adviser from the retailers was not involved in alliances but had used HOTN in her work:

We have a thing called a 'Health Plan' at a company level ....and as far as I'm aware they're based around HOTN

. And then we fill in the gaps from the stuff we get from head office; in summer it's sun and skin care; and in winter it's alcohol...which is fairly typical. The main structure we do - healthy eating, cancer, heart disease, smoking - comes from the HOTN...all of those.

Two other private sector interviewees were involved in health at work projects but several others knew nothing about it.

The message about HOTN and therefore for OHN is that there are elements of the private sector which want to get involved but their involvement needs to be made clear. The private sector are less tolerant of bureaucracy and want to see action. One chief executive of a chamber of commerce remarked:

I get concerned because there is endless talk about strategy and not enough action.

Another chief executive of a chamber of commerce whose organisation had originally been involved in some alliance meetings gave up due to frustrations with the bureaucracy. His message to prospective partners in healthy alliances was:

Don't involve business unless you have something specific to offer us or something specific you want us to do, or we will think you are wasting our time.

Table 5.16 Is your organisation involved with any health alliances?

	Vol. Sec. (N=5)	CHCs (N=4)
HOTN or other strategic health alliance	2	3
Operational alliance reporting to strategic health alliance	1	2
Other health alliance	3	2
Alliance on non health issue with health component (e.g. SRB partnership)	1	1

(Strategic level voluntary sector interviewees and CHC interviewees)

Alliance partners - voluntary sector and CHCs

Strategic level voluntary sector interviewees (5) and CHC interviewees (4) who were involved in alliances were asked for details of those alliances. Responses are given in Table 5.16.

Some of these respondents were involved in up to four alliances, suggesting opportunities for learning and cross fertilisation of intersectoral alliances.

Role of CHCs in a national strategy

Senior staff from Community Health Councils in all but one district were asked what the role of consumers/patients in a national health strategy should be.

As might be expected from an organisation established to represent the views of patients and carers in the NHS, most thought that there was an important role for them to play.

The majority of CHC interviewees saw local consumers/patients and carer's views, or indeed the public's view, informing local implementation of the national strategy not the contents of the strategy itself. Most emphasised the need for local HAs to seek the views of their residents.

I think HAs should seek more pro-actively the view of the public. It's not easy to do, it's not just taking a series of snap shots but you have to build them up over-time through education and so on. (Deputy Chief Officer)

All HAs should take on board discussions and communication with the local population on targets. (Chief Officer)

A number of approaches were mentioned. Some CHC officers stressed that 'consultation must be seen to go on and that patients/users and carers perspectives are taken on.' This could happen by 'discussions and communication' or by the use of interview schedules carried out independent intermediaries. One officer advocated a community development approach, 'finding out what people's own health priorities are.' Several officers pointed out some of the inherent difficulties with these methods such as bias, with unrepresentative views being represented as those of the public.

A few interviewees from CHCs mentioned the need to involve or at least listen to the public's concerns at the national level while one respondent pointed out the need to incorporate the expertise and practical experience of the voluntary sector. These officers saw the public's views as complementary to a health strategy, not supplanting the views of health experts. This was to avoid the so-called 'Cinderella services' (e.g. mental health), losing out to the public's preference for the more visible 'acute services and GP healthcare.'

...government needs to know what's important to patients/consumers about health which isn't necessarily the same as what health staff might think. (Deputy Chief Officer)

There needs to be a close act between health experts, where they think you can make progress in the Cinderella services and the public, what they want. (Chief Officer)

By and large, respondents felt the government should have done more to communicate HOTN to the public using language which was appropriate so the strategy would 'connect with the people, be real to them'. Any attempt to seek the views of the public would, therefore, need to be accompanied by an information/education campaign and a mechanism (perhaps apart from CHCs) to incorporate their views. One CHC member saw the role of patients and carers in a national health strategy as encouraging personal responsibility: cancelling appointments in good time, returning borrowed equipment promptly and not clogging A&E departments with minor problems. Clearly, the notion of a national health strategy, or indeed HOTN, had not touched them.

Role of the voluntary sector

Six senior Voluntary Sector Council (VSC) staff from four districts were asked what they thought the role of voluntary organisations in a national health strategy should be. All saw a role for voluntary organisations either at a national or local level, while several saw a role in both. Most interpreted this role to be a dialogue between the voluntary organisations and government or the NHS at the appropriate level. For example, in developing national strategy, national representatives of the voluntary organisations could work with government/NHS, while in the strategy's implementation local voluntary organisations could engage in planning and decision making with local government/health authorities.

Most VSC officers saw their members making a valuable contribution to a national strategy by 'articulating the consensus and interests of vulnerable members of the community' and/or by sharing expertise in specific areas e.g. with disabled or elderly people. The majority thought that voluntary organisations should be involved with policy implementation at a local level or 'at least listened to'. One VSC Officer advocated the evolution of services that the voluntary sector deliver to complement the strategy, 'as long as they remain independent and that the work is in their own constitution', while another officer claimed that direct input into planning and decision making would 'make sure statutory bodies are accountable', giving voluntary organisations more than 'moral authority...when sitting with those who control resources.'

In one way or another, all VSC respondents thought that in order to fulfil these roles government would need to be more supportive, giving:

encouragement and support to those implementing strategy so they can work with voluntary organisations, especially small ones.(VSC Manager)

and that it would be helpful to have 'more official push' to bring the voluntary sector into intersectoral activity.

For most respondents, if there was to be real participation at both a national and local level, then support would also have to include financial support as lack of resources meant there was 'no capacity to get involved'. For some, what was needed was core funding not competitive bidding for short-term grants:

...money should be available, appropriate to the need. So if it's valid for the Afro-Caribbean community to do it, then the Asian community should do it. I think this would also lead to more joint work and would give the LA a better idea of what work to do. It also reduces the party-political approach.(VSC Director)

Development funds, 'although a good vehicle', were thought to be too restrictive, constraining innovation. One officer advocated funds should be available to pay travel and childminding for voluntary sector representatives as:

People assume voluntary reps have nothing better to do, when they do. They are often volunteers on very low incomes. There should be [...]encouragement to treat voluntary sector reps with respect, value their knowledge...encouragement from government to local statutory agencies. (VSC Chief Executive)

Many voluntary organisations and charities 'go for cure rather than prevention' but they are still well positioned to and do influence individual behaviour. They are also good at collecting information and highlighting issues concerning the more vulnerable members of the society as well as having expertise and practical experience in dealing with the problems facing specific client groups. Thus, most voluntary organisations believe they have a role to play in informing policy development at a national level, while at a local level they believe they should be involved in its implementation, whether helping to plan local services/ activities or enabling voluntary sector services to evolve to complement it. Such an active role would require government to recognise some of the resource constraints placed on the voluntary sector while addressing the shortcomings of current funding mechanisms. Most of the VSC representatives interviewed saw voluntary sector activity as complementing government programmes and not substituting for state responsibilities.

5.6 Conclusions

(i) The different extent to which HOTN was used to focus activities for health improvement and intersectoral health strategies was reflected in varying management structures for HOTN.

(ii) Involvement of trusts in HOTN through the contracting mechanism varied from specific requirements and detailed reporting to some vaguer and less closely monitored work or no inclusion in contracts. Trust interviewees supported implementation of OHN being integrated into commissioning arrangements under *The new NHS* White Paper.

(iii) All authorities reported having health strategies, and six out of eight reported having health alliances, with all reporting wide intersectoral involvement in strategy implementation.

(iv) HOTN appears to have stimulated and focused intersectoral health strategies in some districts, while others have been able to progress strategies without this stimulus.

(v) There are three main ways the case study districts have developed local health strategies and alliances: i) under a non-HOTN label; ii) directly from HOTN; iii) HOTN 'plus', where local key areas were added to the original five

(vi) Only one HA operated a designated HOTN budget covering all HOTN development activities. Five other HAs had allocated partial (non-staff) budgets for development in certain key areas.

(vii) The fact that only two HAs could identify their spending on school health services (and then only for 1996/97) suggests that current budgeting

and financial reporting mechanisms may need considerable improvement if they are to support decision-making effectively across multiple settings and agencies.

(viii) The absence of any requirement to monitor spending on HOTN development, and the continuing absence of any programme budgeting framework for the NHS conspired to ensure that it is essentially impossible to identify or compare retrospectively the resources invested in the implementation of the strategy. If current financial monitoring and budgeting systems do not change, the same fate will inevitably befall OHN implementation.

(ix) Six out of eight HAs had explicitly earmarked funds for alliances; amounts ranged from £2,000 to £200,000, suggesting that they were used in very different ways.

(x) General practitioners tend to focus on the health promotion tasks within their contracts, although some have doubts about the health benefits of this work. Provision of direct patient care and management dominated their work and they did not give a strong priority to strategic action for health outside this framework. Lack of understanding of population issues suggest that some GPs are not prepared for their new role in Primary Care Groups (PCGs) as outlined in *The new NHS* White Paper[11]. Involving GPs in health strategy development will not only require strengthening their population perspective but also an improved understanding of the constraints GPs are under by HAs.

(xi) CHCs have participated at various levels in HOTN and/or other strategic health policy initiatives. Despite this, most CHC interviewees saw a greater need for the views of patients, carers and the public to inform the implementation of national policy (although not its contents) and local policy. More effective communication of the strategy by government and proactive consultation by HAs would help this to be accomplished.

(xii) The voluntary sector has also participated at various levels in HOTN and/or other strategic health policy initiatives in all districts. Involvement has drawn on the sector's skill and expertise in working with specific clients groups although activity has been constrained by lack of resources. This supports their belief that they have an active role to play in development of a national strategy and its implementation at a local level.

(xiii) Health authorities have not found it easy to involve the police and private sector in health partnership. Both police and some businesses are willing to engage in partnership. They would like to be told of specific actions that they can take, and of any benefits there might be to their own work - it is probably best to keep them informed at strategy development stage, and involve them more actively at implementation when they can contribute specific actions. Communication with them is important - material should be relevant and show awareness of what their core business is.

6. FACTORS INFLUENCING IMPLEMENTATION OF HOTN

Key Points

◆ Seven key factors emerged as influencing the implementation of HOTN: lack of resources; support from central government; organisational structures within or between organisations; the quality of partnerships; commitment of organisations and individuals; demographic characteristics of the local district; and LA cultural and political factors.

◆ Lack of resources as a barrier to HOTN implementation was indicated by: (a) it was cited by one-third of interviewees as a barrier to implementation; (b) an analysis of individual health authorities' patterns of expenditure suggesting that population-based health promotion may be a 'soft target' and may be reduced to achieve savings; (c) an increase in the share of total population-based health promotion funding spent on HIV/AIDS prevention activities, suggesting that some HAs are using this ring-fenced budget to cross-subsidise other health promotion activities.

◆ This raises the issue of the importance of ring-fenced resources in the implementation of a national health strategy.

◆ Structural features of local agencies can support or impede HOTN. Those which facilitate partnership working, which strengthen the importance of health improvement within agencies and which protect it from the resource demands of other functions of health authorities and local authorities are particularly important.

◆ Interviewees perceive the national strategy as supporting implementation to some degree by giving legitimacy to action. However, many called for a statutory framework to enable key local participants to work intersectorally for health, and to protect the strategy from the demands of other functions and the loss of key staff.

◆ The quality of partnership is viewed as important for implementation of a health strategy, and can be reinforced by a supportive culture and incentives to partnership such as those provided in the Single Regeneration Budget.

◆ Committed individuals can be catalysts to action, especially if they are in a senior position. Competing pressures from other responsibilities of organisations can account for lack of commitment by some organisations, or for commitment not being translated into action. A statutory framework for the health strategy would encourage development of commitment of individuals and organisations at every level.

◆ Socio-economic features were reported as influential in strategy implementation. A health strategy needs to acknowledge the importance of the socio-economic determinants of the health of the local population if it is to be credible with those responsible for implementation locally.

◆ Local authority cultural and political features may affect implementation of HOTN, although this was a stronger factor in some districts than in others. Local authorities which had a tradition of commitment to health promotion had better relations with their health authorities.

6.1 Introduction

This chapter describes the factors which were perceived to have influenced the implementation of HOTN, the work of alliances and the success of intersectoral projects. Seven key factors emerged as influencing the implementation of HOTN: lack of resources; support from central government; organisational structures within or between organisations; the quality of partnerships; commitment of organisations and individuals; demographic characteristics of the local district; and LA cultural and political factors. Interviewees were asked a number of questions on these initiatives from which the themes in this chapter are drawn (results are given in Table 9.11 to Table 9.20 in Appendix G). Data from the expenditure analysis which support interview data in identifying lack of resources as an influential factor are also presented.

6.2 Resources

When resources were mentioned, it was almost invariably negatively - lack of resources was perceived as a barrier to implementation. Over a third (36%) of interviewees mentioned lack of resources as a factor inhibiting HOTN locally. One in ten mentioned it as obstructing alliances, and lack of resources was identified as a barrier to success for 29 of 97 intersectoral projects.

What was the biggest inhibiting factor? *The other priorities of this health authority: acute care and large teaching hospitals. The health authority focusing on secondary care issues and not taking a broader perspective...*(Consultant in Public Health)

Resources and poor communication...(CHC Chief Officer)

Resources were mentioned by 31% of interviewees asked what more the government or HAs could do to support alliances. Some respondents specifically mentioned that financial or human resources were needed. For some, financial resources should be long-term or ring-fenced to protect them from reallocation to other budgets while others indicated that staff needed skills, advice and training on working in alliances. More LA staff (43%, 16/37) than HA staff (28%, 11/40) mentioned that resources from the government would help support alliances.

Table 6.1 Mention of lack of resources as a barrier to HOTN implementation by district

	A (N=17)	B (N=17)	C (N=15)	D (N=15)	E (N=18)	F (N=16)	G (N=18)	H (N=17)
Mentioned by Number (%)	9 (53)	17 (100)	10 (67)	9 (60)	13 (72)	13 (81)	13 (72)	11 (65)

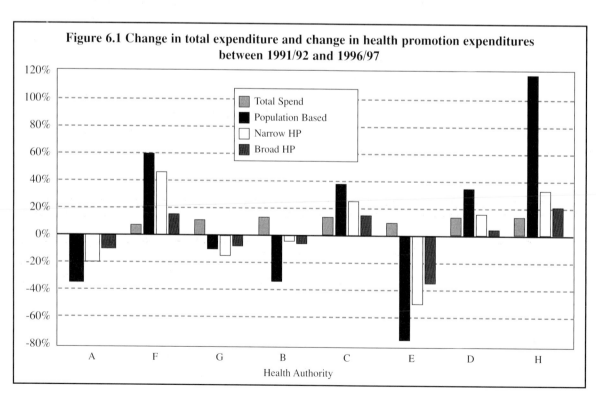

Figure 6.1 Change in total expenditure and change in health promotion expenditures between 1991/92 and 1996/97

The need for more resources was mentioned at some point in the interview by all respondents in District B, with the fewest mentions being in District A (53% of respondents) (Table 6.1). This distribution bears a closer relation to the distribution of Under-Privileged Area Score (a measure of population need for GP care, given in Table 2.1) than to the resources received by health authorities (Table 2.2 and Table 2.3).

Positive references to the impact of resources on HOTN implementation included the availability of special funding such as HOTN funds or Single Regeneration Budget grants. Availability of funding was mentioned as a factor for success for 27 of 97 intersectoral projects.

6.3   Total Expenditure and Funding

Examination of health authority expenditure and funding confirmed that resources were an important factor influencing implementation of HOTN. It would seem reasonable to assume that, all else being equal, if total NHS expenditure increases, health promotion expenditure will follow. Figure 6.1 therefore presents rates of change in total NHS spend and health promotion expenditure during the study period. They illustrate that no such relationship existed. Indeed, health promotion expenditure in all categories rose in four HAs, and fell in four, apparently without much relationship to total expenditure trends. All that can really be said is that the largest increase in discretionary population-based health promotion spending took place in District H, the biggest resource gainer - but that the largest decrease in population-based health promotion spending was not in District A (which scarcely increased total expenditure over the period).

There was no significant relationship between total *per capita* expenditure and population-based health promotion expenditure *per capita*. Furthermore, when the rate of change of the variables was examined the correlation was weak, with the rate of change of total expenditure explaining only nine per cent of the variation in health promotion expenditure. The regression coefficient was borderline significant (p=0.054), which would be consistent with a limited relationship between increasing overall expenditure and increasing health promotion expenditure.

Data were also collected on annual surpluses and deficits for each HA. These data are not presented in tabular form to prevent the identification of participants. No statistically significant relationship between deficit/surplus status and population-based health promotion was apparent, although Authority H had the fewest and smallest deficits over the six year period. District B had cut health promotion expenditure, and by 1996/97, ran proportionately the largest deficit of all the HAs. Interestingly, District E returned a financial surplus in 1996/97, having run a large deficit the previous year. It is possible that reductions in population-based health promotion activities that year were part of the price paid to achieve financial balance. Clearly, though, such a link cannot be proved or disproved from the available data.

Nonetheless, there are some grounds to suggest that population-based health promotion activity may be a 'soft' target - certainly the fact that four out of eight authorities had actively disinvested from this area

Table 6.2 Frequency of financial deficits by HA

HA	Years in deficit (N)
A	4
B	4
C	5
D	5
E	3
F	5
G	3
H	2

over the study period is significant. Structurally, it is hard (or indeed impossible) for HAs to achieve savings in the other components of broad health promotion and prevention activities. As a result, disease-focused, demand-led preventive programmes will continue to operate largely on 'automatic pilot' regardless of the local financial context, while resources for population-based health promotion may well be sensitive to financial pressures.

Relationship with AIDS Prevention Funding

Health Authority AIDS Control Act Reports contain returns on expenditure and allocations for AIDS and HIV services, including HIV prevention. Crucially, authorities receive 'ring-fenced' funding specifically to conduct HIV prevention activities. These figures cannot be directly integrated into the analysis presented above, as the HIV prevention spend reported is already captured within the population-based health promotion aggregate above; furthermore, it is widely accepted that the HIV prevention expenditure estimates are painted with a very broad brush. Table 6.3 presents mean HIV prevention expenditure *per capita* based upon AIDS Control Act Reports, and then presents this expenditure as a proportion of the population-based health promotion expenditure aggregate.

Two trends are apparent from this table. First, HIV prevention expenditure also peaks in 1994/95, like the larger aggregate of which it is a part. Secondly, HIV ring-fenced funding appears to have grown in importance as a source of total population-based health promotion funding (although its importance reduced in 1996/97).

Considerable caution must be exercised in interpreting the data on HIV Prevention expenditure in AIDS Control Act Reports, given the considerable scepticism (indeed, cynicism) shown by many NHS staff when discussing them. Taken at face value, however, Table 6.3 appears to contain one crucial message - in 1996/97, over half of all population-based health promotion activity in the eight HAs was financed through ring-fenced HIV prevention funds. Presentation of these data by district for 1996/97 is even more interesting (Table 6.4).

A literal interpretation sees District A and District E funding their entire population-based health promotion activities through HIV prevention funds. One might ask whether it is a coincidence that District A was the HA which has effectively received no real

Table 6.3 HIV Prevention Expenditure *per capita*

Year	Mean Reported HIV Prevention Expenditure (£ per capita)	HIV Prevention Spend as % of Population-based Health Promotion
1991/92	0.43	30
1992/93	0.59	45
1993/94	0.44	37
1994/95	0.59	45
1995/96	0.68	54
1996/97	0.62	52

Constant 1991/92 prices (Source: AIDS Control Act Reports)

Table 6.4 HIV prevention spend as % of population-based health promotion, 1996-97

HA	HIV Prevention Spend as % of Population-based Health Promotion, 1996/97
A	98
B	No data
C	36
D	45
E	100
F	19
G	52
H	12

funding increase since 1991/92 - or that District E had made large reductions in its health promotion activities that year following its earlier deficit. In contrast, HIV prevention funds provided only a small proportion of financing for population health promotion in the high growth District H. It is possible to argue that HIV prevention funds can therefore be used opportunistically by HAs to 'cover up' deprioritisation of health promotion activities. Alternatively, though, a positive message can be found - that ring-fenced funds do achieve their aim in ensuring that an irreducible minimum of resources are applied to priority areas - hence providing an important backstop even when HAs face severe financial problems.

6.4   Support from central government

Respondents identified two aspects of government policy which were influential in implementing HOTN and forming alliances, and which should be developed in a future strategy (see Section 3.9). First, within the HOTN strategy itself the legitimacy that HOTN gave to activities which might not otherwise have taken place was found useful. Secondly, government's own actions at national level in enabling local action were seen as influential for local implementation.

One in seven interviewees (13%) named the legitimising effect of HOTN (for activities such as involving the LA, or working on HIV) as the 'single biggest enhancing factor' in their district, and over 40% (54/133) said the government should define clearly the roles for HAs, LAs and other organisations in the strategy.

The variation in respondents' views on these features by district (given in Table 6.5) did not seem to relate to the presence of resource and structural barriers,

nor to the district characteristics in Table 2.1 or the organisational arrangements in Section 5.3. For example, in District C where respondents were likely to report structural barriers to HOTN implementation there was a positive view of the legitimising role of the health strategy, and respondents were less likely than those in other districts to report the lack of a structural framework as a barrier or call for this kind of framework in a new strategy.

6.5   Structural factors

Structural factors were frequently mentioned as supportive factors or barriers to HOTN implementation. These factors could relate to the interface between the HA and other organisations (such as coterminosity or the number of LAs to which a HA relates), or could be internal to the HA (such as reorganisation, or the location of the health promotion service), or internal to another organisation.

Table 6.6 reports variations by district in how frequently six aspects of organisational structure were mentioned during the interview as supports or barriers - the interface between the HA and other agencies, structural features of the HA itself, and structural features of other agencies within the HA's district, particularly the LA

Structures at the interface between organisations

Structural factors at the interface between organisations were mentioned as facilitating alliances by 30% of the interviewees and as obstructing alliances by 40%. Coterminosity was considered a factor which influenced HOTN implementation (4/39 and 5/30 of those answering these questions respectively) and was likely to be cited as facilitating alliances.

Table 6.5 Mention of roles of government as supports or barriers to HOTN implementation by district

Mentioned by Number (%)	A (N=17)	B (N=17)	C (N=15)	D (N=15)	E (N=18)	F (N=16)	G (N=18)	H (N=17)
Legitimising action as a support	4 (24)	1 (6)	7 (47)	2 (13)	6 (33)	3 (19)	4 (22)	1 (6)
Absence of a supportive framework as a barrier	13 (77)	13 (77)	8 (53)	5 (33)	11 (61)	10 (63)	11 (61)	11 (65)

Table 6.6 Mention of structural features as supports or barriers to HOTN implementation by district

Mentioned by Number (%)	A (N=17)	B (N=17)	C (N=15)	D (N=15)	E (N=18)	F (N=16)	G (N=18)	H (N=17)
Positive features at the interface between organisation	5 (29)	3 (18)	4 (27)	5 (33)	2 (11)	7 (44)	5 (28)	5 (29)
Negative features at the interface between organisation	5 (29)	9 (53)	8 (53)	5 (33)	8 (44)	5 (31)	7 (39)	6 (35)
Positive features of HA	2 (12)	1 (6)	6 (40)	6 (40)	1 (6)	5 (31)	3 (17)	6 (35)
Negative features of HA	3 (18)	8 (47)	4 (27)	3 (20)	7 (39)	4 (25)	4 (22)	6 (35)
Positive features of other agencies	5 (29)	6 (35)	1 (7)	2 (13)	3 (17)	4 (25)	8 (44)	2 (12)
Negative features of other agencies	2 (12)	6 (35)	6 (40)	3 (20)	5 (28)	4 (25)	2 (11)	8 (47)

Coterminosity is very important, and the structure of local authority departments is supportive . . .[The Local Authority] is always in chaos. Coterminosity is an advantage, we have excellent relations with them. (Head of Health Promotion).

Four study HAs (A, C, G and H) related to a single unitary LA. Features of the interface between LAs were relatively more likely to be positive and less likely to be negative only in A among these four. In fact, the views on this aspect of organisational structure were among the most negative and least positive in one of these four, District C. This may be explained by the strongly differing political views of the HOTN strategy, and the appropriateness to their political perspective, which over-rode the benefits gained from relating to only one HA. The most positive and fewest negative views of structural features between agencies came from District F, a rural county where the HA related to seven district councils and a county council. Respondents' positive comments referred to coterminosity with the county council achieved relatively recently in the April 1996 NHS boundary changes (Table 6.6).

Health authority organisational structures

Barriers within the HA were mentioned by 21 of 107 interviewees as obstructing alliances. Organisational restructuring and staff turnover (possibly as a consequence of restructuring) were considered to be features of the HA which influenced HOTN

implementation, with 18% (7/39) and 13% (5/39) of respondents reporting these factors respectively.

In 1995 the HA had been so busy reorganising it had done very little strategic, including HOTN. The Chief Executive has come from Social Services - learning the NHS is a huge thing. The change in regional personnel was another thing. These things take eyes off the ball [i.e. the strategy]. (Director of Public Health)

Reorganisation was not always seen as having a negative influence. One Director of Public Health reported:

Over the past five years the merger with the FHSA...relations were sticky prior to the merger and the FHSA kept primary care away from the secondary care agenda.

The structure of health promotion in HAs was thought to have a positive bearing on implementation of HOTN. Horizontal or cross departmental structures were highlighted, particularly in districts which reported employing a community development approach to their health strategy.

We've got very good locality teams here...in health promotion...there are certain departments we have good networks with. The move from centralisation to locality teams has been quite a constructive move. (Manager, Voluntary Service Council)

In an ideal world I would like health promotion and public health to be across the whole organisation, we would be part of public health and part of the health authority and would have an input into each directorate and the Chief Executive, and not be an add on. (Manager, Health Promotion Unit, managed by public health within the HA at 'arm's length')

The most positive view of the HA's organisational structure came from District D, where 40% reported at some point in the interview that these features facilitated HOTN, while only 20% responded that the HA's structure was a barrier. This may be explained by the increase in LA interest in HOTN since the HA's development of a locality health promotion structure based on the boundaries of its five local authorities. In District A, respondents were relatively unlikely to report features of the HA organisational structure as barriers or facilitating factors, while Districts B and E interviewees were likely to report both negative and positive aspects (Table 6.6).

Local authority organisational structures

LA organisational structure was mentioned as a feature which influenced HOTN implementation by 5 of 30 interviewees and as an organisational factor obstructing alliances by 34%. Unitary status meant that health policies could be applied consistently across all areas of council work so they *'run through everything'*. In contrast it was thought *'more difficult to form partnerships'* the greater the number of LAs a HA was coterminous with. A DPH explained:

All LAs are different, all have different mechanisms for looking at health issues.

Some city councils in study districts had sought unitary status under the Local Government Review. This process was considered disruptive to co-operation within local government as it created uncertainty and tensions between county and city councils.

Difficulties with the relationship between HAs and LAs were compounded by the LAs' organisational arrangements. In some LAs directorates worked largely independently of each other without a strong

corporate approach across the authority. This kind of vertical organisational structure led to lack of co-ordination and communication between departments and made it difficult for HAs to develop relations across them.

The most positive and least negative view of the role of other agencies' organisational structures in HOTN implementation came from District G. Both HA and LA interviewees there spoke approvingly of the LA's recent reorganisation which attempted to overcome vertical divisions between services. Most negative and fewest positive views of LA organisational structure and its role in HOTN implementation came from Districts C and H. In District C, this was probably a result of the Council's large size, strong departmental identity and fragmentation across the city. In District H, HA and voluntary sector respondents reported failure of some directorates in the unitary authority to work collaboratively with each other or with other agencies, a problem which had recently been addressed by the simultaneous replacement of several directors (Table 6.6).

6.6   Quality of partnership

The quality of partnership was mentioned by 19% (24/128) as the 'single biggest factor' enhancing HOTN implementation in their district. Poor partnership was mentioned negatively as an inhibiting factor in their district by 8% of interviewees. More specifically, good partnership was seen as an organisational factor facilitating alliances by 23% of respondents and poor partnership was seen as obstructing alliances by 6%.

Was there anything about the way that the organisations were set up and run that facilitated your work? *Co-operation between officers in other agencies through our regular work.* (Environmental Health Officer)

The management style [of the health authority] did not encourage genuine multi-agency working. The new Chief Executive changed all that. However, it took some time before people had the confidence in this style of working. (Director of Public Health)

Quality of partnership was an important influence on the success of the 97 intersectoral projects studied, with

Table 6.7 Were there any issues around ownership and accountability of alliances, or responsibility for alliances?

	Number	Percent
Yes, serious	20	19
Yes, minor	14	37
No	19	18
Missing/Don't know	28	26
Total	**107**	**100**

(All interviewees except HA Chief Executives, GPs and CHC interviewees)

Table 6.8 Mention of quality of partnership as a support to HOTN implementation by district

	A (N=17)	B (N=17)	C (N=15)	D (N=15)	E (N=18)	F (N=16)	G (N=18)	H (N=17)
Mentioned by Number (%)	8 (47)	5 (29)	6 (40)	4 (27)	3 (17)	9 (56)	6 (33)	8 (47)

shared ownership being a factor for success for 22, and problems with the partnership being a barrier to success for 20.

The issues of ownership, accountability and responsibility for action in alliances were explored with a specific question (Table 6.7). Nearly one in five reported serious problems, with the majority of respondents involved having encountered only minor problems or none.

Were there any issues around ownership of alliances, accountability of alliances or responsibility for action? *There are, it's down to the variable priority given by organisations. If membership is too junior it raises questions of accountability.* (Welfare Rights Manager)

No, because the healthy schools award is funded by the health authority, therefore they are responsible, but it works well with me working with them on this, very well. I lead on drug issues because it is funded by the local authority, but it works well because we've been so long together. (LEA Personal and Social Education Adviser)

No, it's all led by [Director of Public Health]. (Local Authority Health and Safety Officer)

Positive views of the quality of partnership were reported most frequently in Districts F, A and H, and least frequently in District E, interestingly, with a

highly structured framework for partnership (Table 6.8). In District F, partnership was around a HOTN alliance, in District A around a local health strategy based on a Healthy City model, and in District H around long standing locality-level partnerships for economic regeneration which were increasingly involving the HA. This finding reinforces the conclusion in Chapter 4 that a variety of models of health strategy implementation should be supported.

6.7 Commitment - key individuals and senior officers

Overlapping aspects of commitment emerged as factors influencing HOTN implementation - the importance of key individuals (who might be senior or junior in an organisation), commitment of individuals at senior level in organisations and overall commitment across organisations. These aspects could not always be distinguished, and the distinction may sometimes be unclear in practice.

Organisational commitment

All interviewees were asked how strong they felt the commitment to HOTN was in their organisation. Respondents were asked about commitment to HOTN of their HA, main service providers and local organisations. Answers were scored either very strong, quite strong, or weak/none. Organisations coded 'very strong' tended to be actively involved in strategy development and strategic planning,

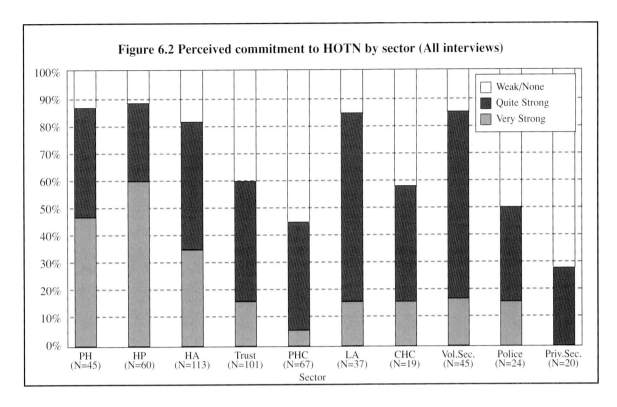

Figure 6.2 Perceived commitment to HOTN by sector (All interviews)

those coded 'quite strong' were involved to various degrees in operational issues or a number of projects, and the participation of organisations coded 'weak/none' had been patchy, dwindled or was non existent. The results are summarised in Figure 6.2.

Health promotion departments were perceived to be highly committed to HOTN with nearly 60% of those asked indicating commitment was very strong. The commitment of public health departments was perceived to be less with around 47% coded very strong while in the health authority as a whole such a response dropped to around 35%. The commitment of trusts was perceived to be less with only 16% of those who answered coded very strong, while commitment of primary health care was thought to be weak or non existent by over half of those asked (57%).

Outside the health service, local authorities and the voluntary sector were felt to be similarly committed, both being marginally more committed than NHS trusts. Commitment in the private sector was perceived to be the weakest.

Lack of organisational commitment was likely to be a barrier to the success of intersectoral projects (mentioned in relation to 18 of 97 projects).

Some respondents suggested that commitment to HOTN was used as a label to serve the concerns of organisations.

They recognise that we're not going to drop it, and throw it at us when they want more money and can present it as HOTN. (Consultant in Public Health Medicine)

Local voluntary groups used the HOTN to ask what the HA was doing. (Health Promotion Manager) The commitment of an organisation may owe more to the efforts of an individual within the organisation than to genuine corporate commitment.

In the community trust there is commitment...but in the acute trusts clinicians still need a lot of persuading that health promotion is their responsibility. The exception has been the cardiology department which has been working in the CHD area. The HA tends to work with a few individual clinicians who are enthusiastic. (Director of Public Health)

Senior staff commitment

Senior staff commitment in HAs was mentioned as a feature influencing HOTN by 36% (14/39) of those asked. Thirteen of these 14 respondents said senior commitment had had a positive influence. Respondents tended to emphasise that commitment had to be to 'health' rather than just health services:

Key decision makers in organisations drive how the organisation sees its role and how it works. Over 15 years we've had five Chief Executives, all with different ways of working. The previous one was very service oriented, but the present one is into health improvement. (Health Promotion Strategy Manager)

The Chief Executive before the current one was only interested in hospital issues, his personal values and beliefs didn't fit with the HOTN agenda, it was a major obstacle. (Health Promotion Manager)

Some respondents were explicit about the benefits that senior support can bring. As the Director of Public Health in District G put it:

The current Chief Executive is also committed which brings managerial support.

In District F:

Both Directors of Public Health have had a key role. There was enough support to get the alliance and development fund running and a worker for the alliance...(Head of Health Promotion)

Key Individuals

Key individuals were mentioned by 10% (13/128) as the biggest single enhancing factor for HOTN implementation. Nearly one in five (18%) mentioned key individuals as an organisational factor facilitating alliances, and 14% mentioned unhelpful individuals as obstructive to alliances.

Individual commitment by HA staff or access to skills and experience found in HAs were considered important for the implementation of HOTN with 15% (6/39) of respondents (the majority HA staff) mentioning this factor. In some cases this was put down to their knowledge and expertise in a particular area while in others it was their skill in building alliances.

Certainly, a major influence has been persons who have been given a lead role i.e. [the Consultant in Public Health]. He appeared to be committed and he was very good at setting up alliances. I have them now and they're still quite strong. (Head of Health Promotion)

However, one respondent did not perceive the skill/knowledge base in HA staff to be broad enough to implement HOTN effectively.

...drivers for HOTN have been in public health consultants. They needed more multi-disciplinary teams to make it work. (Health Promotion Manager) Individual staff commitment to the HOTN strategy in the LA was seen as an important factor in bringing LAs on board (6/30). This contrasts with HAs where senior commitment was thought to be more important than the role of key individuals, perhaps due to the lack of a clear role for LAs (see Section 3.9).

Personalities in the LA have been very important, without commitment and personalities it won't work. (Health Promotion Manger)

In some cases, the enthusiasm of key individuals was thought to be responsible for getting the senior management more involved.

It was more individuals who took a key interest and brought their directors along rather than the other way around. There was never a strong steer from the DoE [for other agencies] to get involved...so if it hadn't have been for key individuals there might have been an impasse. (Public Health Consultant)

Variations by District

The role of commitment of senior officers of local agencies, and of key individuals at any level, were least likely to be mentioned as facilitating in District G (Table 6.9) despite a strong lead from the Director of Public Health who had personally contacted LA officers and members and other agencies, and who chaired most alliance groups.

In District H there was a contrast between frequent reports of the facilitating role of key individuals and a lack of reports of senior commitment. The LA had

Table 6.9 Mention of senior commitment and key individuals as supports to HOTN implementation by district

Mentioned by Number (%)	A (N=17)	B (N=17)	C (N=15)	D (N=15)	E (N=18)	F (N=16)	G (N=18)	H (N=17)
Senior Commitment	4 (24)	3 (18)	2 (13)	2 (13)	4 (22)	4 (25)	2 (11)	2 (12)
Key Individuals	5 (29)	2 (12)	3 (20)	5 (33)	6 (33)	7 (44)	1 (6)	8 (47)

experienced internal conflict (referred to under structural features above) while the HA had experienced high staff turnover at senior level, and continuity depended on commitment of operational and voluntary sector employees, often at locality/neighbourhood level.

Influences on commitment

Competing political pressures, national and local, were frequently given as an explanation for low levels of commitment. In HAs, changing government priorities to accommodate politically sensitive issues such as winter pressures, waiting lists and 'balancing the books' meant that health strategy tended to get put on the back burner.

The Chief Executive was supportive enough to see something had to be done, but not to put resources into it. Prevention is secondary to sickness care when the chips are down, especially now we have a deficit. (Head of Health Promotion)

A number of HA agendas were, in part, dominated by local issues.

[HOTN] feels very peripheral just at the moment because the main focus is the acute service review happening in [District]. (HOTN Lead)

Work pressures, especially in the voluntary sector, lead to organisations being more reactive than proactive in their commitment to health.

People want to see improvements in health of people they work with but are bogged down in the immediate activities...[it's] harder to engage people in longer term strategic issues. (Worker in Voluntary Service Council)

6.8   Factors relating to the local population

Divisions within districts between affluent and deprived areas were identified as influencing implementation of HOTN by over half the respondents asked (23/39), while nearly one in five respondents (18% (7/39)) mentioned socio-economic factors such as poor housing and drugs and crime. Social and economic deprivation or the poor state of the local economy were mentioned by 13% (5/39) of respondents.

The east-west divide, we need to target the west. It's a multi-cultural community and there are neighbouring communities with very different cultures, closed communities, and we have to tailor our services. (Manager, Health Promotion Unit)

We have extremes, clearly there's a lot to do. There's an East/ West split, there are more acute needs in the east of [the district]. HIV, sexual health - because of the population and location. (Assistant DPH)

Some HAs were involved in intersectoral groups set up to tackle local poverty and health inequalities. In District F an anti-poverty group was established under the HOTN alliance, and in District D, the local health alliance group set up a Food and Low Income Network. However, for one respondent:

HOTN has been the least meaningful where deprivation is the highest, where people are worrying about where the next penny is coming from. (Head of Health Promotion)

The frequency of references to population health and health determinants by study districts does not follow the distribution of proxies for population health used in this study - Underprivileged Area score, SMR, and NHS spending (Table 2.1, Table 2.2 and Table 2.3). Districts A and F are the 'healthiest' by all these measures but interviewees in these districts were relatively likely to mention local population factors as barriers to HOTN implementation (Table 6.10). Both these HAs were addressing the health needs of population sub-groups within their relatively healthy districts.

6.9   Local authority cultural and political features

Of those asked about features of the LA influencing HOTN implementation, one in five respondents (6/30) indicated that the political views of the LA were important. An interviewee from an area with two-tier local government said:

Politics came into it - Labour run councils thought it was a Tory policy because it was disease focused. Tory authorities liked it. Some key members made a difference. (Head of Health Promotion)

While undoubtedly this was true in some districts it does not reflect the picture of council involvement in health strategy in every district, as this interview illustrates.

Because it was Conservative government initiative largely, in the City Council there was a definite cultural antipathy towards it...a local councillor who's now in parliament was very much trying to espouse the values of HFA rather than the HOTN approach...and the two are not compatible. He used it as a stick with which to beat the HOTN policy, he thought HFA was a more holistic and a better strategy. (HFA Co-ordinator)

Some Labour councils, especially those with a long standing commitment to health issues, still got involved. One county council, became involved precisely because the HA and the local district councils were *'very conservative with a small "c"'* and it feared the opportunity for intersectoral work on health might be lost.

In District B, the rift between a pro-HOTN Labour council and a long-standing Conservative council had a detrimental affect on the HA's attempt to build district-wide alliances, with one authority refusing to 'put their name to the same projects' for political reasons. However, the change in political control at one of the councils has created a new opportunity to work on health.

There was a big change politically in [District B], it was a Tory council which was way behind the times, it didn't have very good support for the voluntary sector, so the present council had 23 years of neglect to deal with. Previously, they refused to accept that there was any drug problem here so they've had to turn around. (Voluntary Service Council Manager)

A Councillor on this authority said:

The Conservatives, I have no record of them being interested. In 1994, Labour took over so it's rising now mainly due to me. I'm a member now. I'm starting from a different point.

Party politics was most likely to be mentioned as a barrier in District G (Labour throughout the period of HOTN implementation) and District A (Conservative throughout this period) (Table 6.11). In District G HA interviewees reported hostility to

Table 6.10 Mention of aspects of population health as barriers to HOTN implementation by district

	A (N=17)	B (N=17)	C (N=15)	D (N=15)	E (N=18)	F (N=16)	G (N=18)	H (N=17)
Mentioned by Number (%)	5 (29)	5 (29)	2 (13)	4 (27)	0 (0)	3 (19)	6 (33)	3 (18)

Table 6.11 Mention of Local Authority party politics as a barrier to HOTN implementation by district

	A (N=17)	B (N=17)	C (N=15)	D (N=15)	E (N=18)	F (N=16)	G (N=18)	H (N=17)
Mentioned by Number (%)	4 (24)	3 (18)	3 (20)	0 (0)	2 (11)	2 (13)	5 (28)	2 (12)

HOTN among councillors, although not among officers. In District A, LA members had been unenthusiastic about the health strategy which was sustained by partnership at senior officer level. A strong tradition of health promotion in the LA or the LA's view of health was also influential in HOTN implementation, each being mentioned by 5/30 interviewees. Some LAs were committed to health promotion or had a broad vision of the EHO's public health role, leading to good relations with the local HA. Indeed, some LAs had pressed for or successfully negotiated a lead role in a small number of alliances. However, some authorities viewed HOTN as relating to individual lifestyle and could not see its relevance to them, while other LAs viewed health in economic terms only. Thus, an authority's view of health and its public health function were important to its attitude towards HOTN and the kind of relationship formed with the local HA .

6.10   Conclusions

(i)   Seven key factors emerged as influencing the implementation of HOTN: lack of resources; support from central government; organisational structures within or between organisations; the quality of partnerships; commitment of organisations and individuals; demographic characteristics of the local district; and LA cultural and political factors.

(ii)   Lack of resources as a barrier to HOTN implementation was indicated by: (a) it was cited by one-third of interviewees as a barrier to implementation; (b) an analysis of individual health authorities' patterns of expenditure suggesting that population-based health promotion may be a 'soft target' and may be reduced to achieve savings; (c) an increase in the share of total population-based health promotion funding spent on HIV/AIDS prevention activities, suggesting that some HAs are using this ring-fenced budget to cross-subsidise other health promotion activities.

(iii)   This raises the issue of the importance of ring-fenced resources in the implementation of a national health strategy.

(iv)   Structural features of local agencies can support or impede HOTN. Those which facilitate partnership working, which strengthen the importance of health improvement within agencies and which protect it from resource demands other functions of health authorities and local authorities are particularly important.

(v)   Interviewees saw the national strategy as giving some support to implementation by giving legitimacy to action. However, many called for a statutory framework to enable key local participants to work intersectorally for health, and to protect the strategy from the demands of other functions and the loss of key staff.

(vi)   The quality of partnership is viewed as important for implementation of a health strategy, and can be reinforced by a supportive culture and incentives to partnership such as those provided in the Single Regeneration Budget.

(vii)   Committed individuals can be important catalysts, and can be influential if they are in a senior position. Competing pressures from other responsibilities of organisations can account for lack of commitment by some organisations, or for commitment not being translated into action. A statutory framework for the health strategy would encourage development of commitment of individuals and organisations at every level.

(viii)   Socio-economic features were reported as influential in strategy implementation. A health strategy needs to acknowledge the importance of the socio-economic determinants of the health of the local population if it is to be credible with those responsible for implementation locally.

(ix)   Local authority cultural and political features may affect implementation of HOTN, although this was a stronger factor in some districts than in others. Local authorities which had a tradition of commitment to health promotion had better relations with their health authorities.

7. IMPACT ON NON-HOTN AREAS

Key points

♦ Strategic activity and activity involving alliances and targets, or based in innovative settings is low in the non-key areas (childhood immunisation, asthma, diabetes) compared to the level and type of activity in the HOTN key areas.

♦ There may have been a slight increase in 'HOTN-type' activity where these areas are designated as local key areas.

♦ Work is based largely on well established mechanisms in primary health care. These mechanisms need strategic management probably best ensured at the national level.

♦ These areas do not seem to have suffered as a result of attention to HOTN key areas.

♦ The inherent characteristics of these three areas probably led to the development of a different pattern of activity.

7.1   Introduction

The three 'non-key' areas were childhood immunisation, asthma and diabetes. Each could have met the HOTN key area selection criteria, in that:

they are major causes of premature death or avoidable ill health

effective interventions are available offering hope for improvement in health

it is possible to set objectives and targets and monitor progress towards them

The study examined the amount of strategic and intersectoral work done in these areas, in relation to that done in the key areas. Four possible explanations might account for differences between activity in these areas and the key areas, with some overlap:

(i)   work in the non-key areas was unaffected by HOTN, but might have developed differently had they been key areas

(ii)   activity in the key areas increased, and alliance work in those areas developed, at the expense of this type of work in non-key areas

(iii)   experience gained on HOTN key areas was diffused more widely, so that the non-key areas benefited from the growing experience within agencies of strategy development, use of targets, alliance working and work in settings, with these methods increasingly employed in the non-key areas

(iv)   the non-key areas were different types of health issue from the key areas, and that difference led to both a different pattern of activity and the decision not to select them as key areas

The analysis below is based on interviews with directors of public health, HOTN leads, health promotion managers and general practitioners.

Childhood immunisation

No district reported any strategic work on childhood immunisation, although two had made special efforts to improve uptake in low-uptake areas. There were some multi-disciplinary service groups, but no alliances as they are understood within HOTN. Work was to the national targets, driven by the GP contract, and this mechanism seemed to work well. There was some move to explore settings in Authority A where there was a large 'traveller' population.

The childhood immunisation programme is delivered primarily via general practice, with remuneration via the system of target coverage payments. However, some immunisation continues to be carried out via community health services, although the relative importance of their role varies from district to district. The table below summarises local NHS expenditure on the child immunisation programme via payments to GPs and community health services. This exercise highlighted one anomaly relating to the vertical nature of the immunisation programme. Vaccine supplies for the child immunisation programme are financed centrally; a single central contract exists between the Department of Health and Farillon for the manufacture and distribution (including cold chain management) of all vaccines for this programme.

The Department of Health provided data on immunisation uptake rates and eligible populations for all districts for the study period. These were combined with local data on GP payments and trust expenditures, and with estimates of national expenditure on vaccines. It is clear from Table 7.1 below that expenditure on the immunisation programme has remained essentially stable throughout the study period - the dip in 1992 to 1994 reflects lower uptake rates for MMR vaccine during those years. By the end of the study period, the proportion of local NHS resources devoted to the childhood immunisation programme had declined from 0.39% to 0.32% (excluding vaccines).

Table 7.1 Mean expenditure on childhood immunisations

Year	Mean cost per immunised child	Vaccine Costs	Total per immunised child	Immunisation % of total NHS Spend
1991/92	145.90	53.17	199.07	0.39
1992/93	123.50	50.41	173.91	0.35
1993/94	131.09	51.67	182.76	0.36
1994/95	153.37	45.63	199.00	0.38
1995/96	146.10	52.40	198.50	0.35
1996/97	145.34	53.76	199.11	0.32

Table 7.2 Strategic development activity in non-HOTN areas

Health Authority	Childhood Immunisation	Asthma	Diabetes
A	Settings-based work	Developing strategy Settings-based work	
B		Local key area	Local key area
C		Settings-based work	
D		Service user involvement in service group Settings-based work	Linked to healthy schools
E			Service user involvement in service group Targets based on St Vincent Declaration
F			Service user involvement in service group
G		Collaboration with LA on pollution Settings-based work	Service user and community involvement in service group
H			Led from public health in same way as key areas. Service user involvement in service group. Targets based on St Vincent Declaration

Asthma

Authority A was just developing a strategy, and Authority B had identified asthma as a local key area and was basing its work on a HOTN model. Apart from these, no authority had attempted to work strategically in this area. Some multi-disciplinary service-based groups had drawn up disease management guidelines. Authority D's group involved service users. In Authority G there had been work with the environmental health department on pollution, but this had not been linked to the work of the service-based group. Asthma prescribing was a common topic for primary health care audit. GP work was structured through the contract and chronic disease management payments, and training had been provided for practice staff. Four authorities mentioned guidelines for schools.

Diabetes

Authority B had designated diabetes a local HOTN key area and attempted to work on a HOTN model. Work in Authority H was led by a public health specialist, giving diabetes the same status and structure as a key area. Like asthma, this was an area where guidelines were commonly developed by multi-disciplinary service based groups to co-ordinate the work of primary and secondary care, and training was provided for primary care staff. More authorities had involved users in their multi-disciplinary group - two mentioned the British Diabetic Association, and one 'the voluntary sector and the local community'. Two authorities reported using the St Vincent Declaration as a basis for targets, again driven by the GP contract and chronic disease management payments. In one authority there was a link to healthy schools work.

7.2   Conclusions

Strategic activity and activity involving alliances and targets, or based in innovative settings is low in the non-key areas compared to the level and type of activity in the HOTN key areas conducted by even the most inactive authorities. However, the impression gained was of areas which were highly service based, and in this context, diligently managed through efficient mechanisms. One

Director of Public Health said of childhood immunisation:
There's no written strategy. This health authority does well on immunisation, it's one of the best due to the hard work of GPs and health visitors.

The study found, in relation to the four explanations proposed above:

(i)   key area status, given to diabetes by two authorities, and to asthma by one, had slightly raised the amount of HOTN-type activity

(ii)   there was a little diffusion of HOTN methods into these areas

(iii)   these areas did not seem to have suffered as a result of attention to HOTN key areas

(iv)   the scope for intersectoral work is low - childhood immunisation coverage is well-served by efficient procedures geared to achieving national targets, and present knowledge of the natural history of asthma and diabetes does not give the evidence base for intersectoral primary prevention, except where that work already overlaps with prevention of other health problems (road traffic accidents in the case of asthma, and CHD with diabetes). The characteristics of these three areas probably led to their not being selected as key areas, and also to a different pattern of activity developing.

(v)   the absence of strategic development activity in childhood immunisation is consistent with the widespread perception that this is a 'self-managing' vertical programme, primarily conducted via the GP contract, and which does not need to be worried about greatly at local level. It is, however, important to note that an absence of strategic overview may compromise the programme's ability to foresee and respond to demand-side problems, such as changing public perceptions of vaccine safety. Clearly, though, strategic overview of this particular programme might be best conducted at national level.

8. LESSONS LEARNED FOR IMPLEMENTATION OF A NATIONAL HEALTH STRATEGY

Key points

1. A range of models of implementation of OHN should be supported to allow for variation in local circumstances and previous developments in health strategy.

2. OHN should address the underlying determinants of health and inequalities. A matrix model has many advantages, enabling explicit consideration of both disease and population-based models of health. (see figure 8.1)

3. There is an unresolved issue about where responsibility for the strategy should rest and the public health function should be kept under review in the light of changes in the NHS.

4. Regardless of the detailed arrangements within the NHS, communication needs to be improved to widen ownership of OHN outside the NHS.

5. If the momentum of the strategy is to be sustained, it needs to be firmly embedded in a performance management framework. This should include monitoring the process of implementation as well as the outcome, and should enable resources connected with the strategy to be identified, isolated and monitored.

6. There is a need for a statutory framework to allow key local agencies, particularly local government, to work in partnerships for health. Other incentives for partnerships should also be considered.

7. Targets are a necessary tool for prioritisation, but must be credible and local development of local targets should be encouraged.

8. Central government has a key role to play but it is essential that there is a consistent message across government that is in support of OHN. Central government should also foster the development and dissemination of an evidence base.

9. It will be important to increase the role of key stakeholders, in particular the public, the private sector and those working in primary care.

10. Consideration should be given to ring-fenced funding for the implementation of OHN.

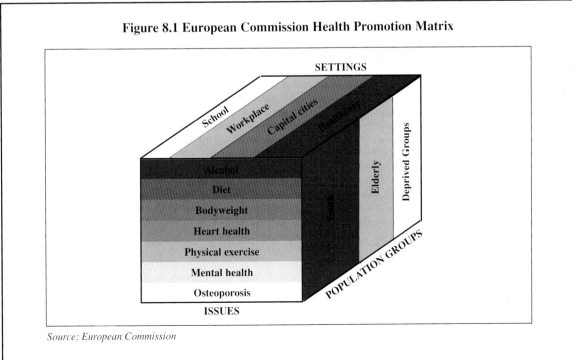

Figure 8.1 European Commission Health Promotion Matrix

Source: European Commission

8.1   Introduction

This chapter draws out the main lessons for the implementation of OHN from this study of the implementation of the HOTN strategy. These have been grouped under nine headings, although there is considerable overlap between them.

8.2   Range of models of implementation

This study has found a great deal of work being undertaken in the development and implementation of local health strategies in all eight case study districts. Different models of implementation of HOTN have been developed in different districts according to local circumstances. These models range from districts which developed local health strategies and alliances directly from HOTN; those which developed them using HOTN and adding to it ('HOTN plus'), and those which developed local health strategies and alliances under a non-HOTN label such as healthy cities or urban regeneration. It is important that this range of models is supported at the national level and that flexibility is encouraged in the development of health strategies and partnerships under whatever banner is most appropriate locally.

8.3   Philosophy underlying HOTN

A major criticism of HOTN confirmed by this study was that it did not address the underlying determinants of health and illness, and inequalities in health status. This acted as a barrier to implementation at the local level because the strategy had less credibility, particularly with local authority and voluntary sector partners, for example in Districts B and F. Despite this, many of the case study districts included these issues in the development of their own local health strategies, for example Districts B, F and H. Not surprisingly, therefore, respondents called for the new national health strategy to address the determinants of health, and inequalities.

The second issue concerning the underlying philosophy of a national health strategy is not as unanimous. There is a divergence of opinion about whether the strategy should be centred on a population- or disease-based model. This division does not directly mirror organisational loyalties as might be expected - the call for population-based model comes from NHS, local authorities and the voluntary sector. Given this division and given that a health strategy has at least five broad audiences who use different languages: i.e. the NHS; local authority; voluntary sector; the public; and the private sector, it does not make sense to suggest that the strategy should be based around one model rather than another. Instead, the strategy should incorporate more explicitly a matrix working whereby both models are included. An example of this is the matrix used by the European Union health promotion programme[45] (Figure 8.1).

In addition to using this matrix model, the strategy needs to be marketed differently to different audiences so that they can relate to it in their own language. This would mean, for example, producing documents relating to the strategy for different audiences (see under 'Communicating the strategy' below).

8.4   Responsibility for the strategy

This study raises the question about where responsibility for the national and local health strategies should lie. Should responsibility necessarily rest with the NHS given that most of the determinants of health lie outside its responsibility? Wherever the responsibility finally rests, it is important that the government should clearly define what the roles of NHS organisations and local authorities are. Some interviewees called for a statutory framework and this clearly relates to the proposal for a 'duty of partnership'.

The question of responsibility for the strategy also raises the issue of where the public health function should sit, particularly in the context of *The new NHS* and the development of Primary Care Groups (PCGs). There was some support in the study for the proposal that directors of public health be appointed jointly by local authorities and health authorities, as an enabling structure for OHN. The report of emerging findings of the CMO's project to strengthen the public health function in England rejects the need for organisational and structural change at this time. However, given the huge changes that may take place in the organisation of the NHS over the next ten years, it is important to keep this under review so that the public health function does not get left behind.

The new NHS White Paper proposes fewer and larger health authorities. The implications for health partnerships need to be thought through as this study confirms the importance of coterminosity and the difficulties of trying to relate to too many local authorities in these partnerships.

8.5 Communicating the strategy

Communication is important for wider ownership of OHN. Too often we found ownership of HOTN limited to public health departments within health authorities. This study found that communication of HOTN to most potential partners for health improvement was poor. Outside public health, some occupational groups who have a role in improving population health (such as environmental health officers) seem not to have received key documents. The language and concepts of most materials were familiar in public health and health promotion, but did not engage important agencies and occupational groups outside those fields.

It is also evident that an obvious gap in the HOTN strategy was involvement of the public both at the national and local levels. The strategy needs to be communicated to the public in an exciting and imaginative way. Similarly, there are opportunities to get the private sector involved in the strategy at the local and national levels and this needs to be communicated to them.

Supporting documents produced by central government need to be aimed at different audiences (not just the NHS) where appropriate, and a balance must be struck between user-friendly documents and 'glossiness'.

8.6 Sustaining the momentum

Clearly it is a challenge to sustain momentum for a national public health strategy which has to continue for 10-20 years to produce results in the 'short-termist' climate which besets the political

environment and the NHS in particular. The NHS has been subject to large-scale organisational changes in the past ten years and will continue to experience such changes in the coming years. Other agencies vital to the strategy's implementation are also likely to undergo great changes. In this context, a national health strategy needs to be flexible enough to adapt to these changes and regularly renew itself to maintain its relevance.

OHN therefore needs to be firmly embedded in the work of Government departments and local agencies which must implement it. As a minimum, it needs to be shown to be high on the agenda of the Department of Health and the NHS through the performance management framework (see under 'Monitoring the Strategy' below). Health authority chief executives and other senior managers should be judged on their performance on implementing OHN as well as on their ability to manage waiting lists.

Process monitoring and performance management

This study indicates strong support for monitoring the strategy not just in terms of its health outcome targets but also in terms of implementation. Local agencies want to be monitored on the basis of process targets such as partnerships/alliances and the quality of those relationships, as well as on how far they have met their CHD target. It is clear from the data that HOTN has not been monitored by regional health authorities/regional offices in the same way as finance and activity is. OHN needs to be part of the performance management framework for all NHS organisations. Currently the consultation document on a national framework for assessing performance[12] only includes the monitoring of health improvement by SMRs. The *processes* of health strategy implementation need to be monitored andmonitoring could, for example, focus on Health Improvement Programmes which have to be developed by health authorities.

Statutory framework

Consideration should be given to the development of a statutory framework to encourage partnerships for health at the local level. This would facilitate the participation of LAs in intersectoral action.

Currently, the absence of a statutory framework means that intersectoral action and LA health promotion activity may face cuts when resources are under pressure. Other incentives for partnerships should also be considered to support the commitment of individuals and organisations necessary for implementation.

Monitoring resources

The use of resources in the implementation of HOTN was not monitored at either national or local level in any systematic way, not least because the financial systems in use both at the time and today could not support any intelligent monitoring process. The absence of monitoring in itself made HOTN activity vulnerable relative to areas perceived as more pressing. Financial systems have not changed, and essential implementation activity for OHN will be just as vulnerable to deprioritisation if HAs are under financial pressure. A key lesson of HOTN is therefore that, if OHN implementation is to remain a priority, the resources connected with the strategy must be identified, isolated and monitored (regardless of their source) *from the outset*. This may not necessarily require a general programme budgeting framework to be developed for the whole NHS - but it does require a local, comprehensive budget to be established for OHN which incorporates all the resources (especially human) closely involved in strategy implementation and delivery.

8.7   Targets

The majority of respondents in the study found targets a helpful way to prioritise and focus efforts. However, there are a number of ways in which this review of HOTN provides lessons for the development of targets in OHN:

- national targets must be credible i.e. based on sound and convincing evidence

- encouraging the development of local targets is important

- the use of process targets both locally and nationally would be useful e.g. monitoring the development of

partnerships/alliances (see under 'monitoring' above)

- data from interviews with professionals outside the health sector indicates that there are both negative and positive lessons to be drawn from the experience of measuring performance in education and in the police force

8.8   Role of central government

The clear message from this study is that those implementing the strategy on the ground need to feel supported by central government in terms of national policies which are consistent with the strategy. It is difficult to maintain momentum and enthusiasm for the strategy at local level if national policies are in conflict with it e.g. not taking a firm line on tobacco advertising and sponsorship.

Respondents in this study are keen to have an evidence base for their work. While we are aware some work has been conducted in this area, there is scope for an R&D initiative in public health and health promotion to bring this work together and fill in the gaps.

8.9   Increasing the involvement of key stakeholders

This study has identified the need to increase the involvement of three key stakeholders at both the national and local levels: the public; the private sector; and primary care.

The public

We have already referred to the lack of communication of HOTN to the public and how this must be improved for OHN. Ways also need to be found of involving the public at the local level in implementation of OHN.

The private sector

Health authorities have not found it easy to involve the private sector in health partnerships. Some businesses are willing to engage in partnership. They would like to be told of specific actions that they can take, and of any benefits there might be to their own work - it is probably best simply to keep them informed at strategy development stage, and then to involve them at the implementation stage when they can contribute specific actions. Communication with them is important - material should be relevant and show awareness of what their core business is. It would be helpful if a lead on involving the private sector could be taken at a national level by the Department of Health.

Primary care

Involvement of GPs and the primary health care team in the implementation of OHN is vital if it is to succeed. In terms of GPs' commissioning role in, for example, PCGs, they need to be involved at a strategic level with health authorities and other agencies. How this can be achieved given the constraints on their time is difficult to imagine. However, the development of PCGs should be conditional on their ownership and involvement in local health strategies (via Health Improvement Programmes).

8.10   Resourcing the strategy

The government must express clearly the priority it attaches to differing levels of activity in strategy implementation. The absence of earmarked or ring-fenced funding for HOTN probably sent an implicit message about the priority attached to the strategy; certainly, the absence of active monitoring of local expenditure on HOTN implementation appears to have lowered its priority in the eyes of local NHS decision-makers. Government should actively communicate its decision on each of the following resource issues:

♦   whether OHN is to receive new funds from central government.

♦   if so, are they to be ring-fenced? Ring-fencing tends not to be popular at local level, and does not sit comfortably with locally-led decision-making - but it does appear to have ensured the survival of some population-based health promotion activity in Health Authorities who had greatly reduced local resourcing for these activities.

♦   whether these funds are for strategy implementation or for 'service delivery' (e.g. Healthy Living Centres etc.). Successful strategy implementation may well require greater resourcing for essentially 'managerial' activities, and this fact should not be shied away from.

♦   does the strategy seek to increase activity and resourcing for 'health promotion' activities by shifting local resources? Or is this not a relevant objective?

Current resourcing mechanisms within the NHS (let alone across different agencies) leave much to be desired in their ability to illustrate the true application of resources and to facilitate informed decisions on resource allocation. Key areas of expenditure are embedded in general contracts and funding agreements (especially those for community health services), which cannot be disaggregated to satisfactory levels at present. The real importance of these shortcomings lies not in the fact that they render monitoring impossible, but in the fact that they obscure and obstruct accurate situation analysis and hence reduce the quality of decision making.

The structural changes which will accompany *The new NHS* White Paper may be undermined by a failure to address these issues of programme budgeting and resource allocation. Resources will need to be apportioned between Primary Care Groups and central public health functions - and the clear implication of the expenditure analysis reported above is that, in practice, current financial systems will not support such a disaggregation. Serious consideration must therefore be given (with some urgency) to developing more appropriate programme budgeting arrangements for public health, health promotion and preventive activities.

The importance of intersectoral working across multiple settings raises the question of whether such a new programme budgeting system should be developed for the NHS alone. In the absence of more fundamental functional reorganisation, perhaps a form of 'matrix' programme budgeting, cutting across agencies, functions and settings is in fact required.

9.   APPENDICES

Appendix A
Table 9.1. Detailed breakdown of type of interviewee by health authority district

Appendix B
Interview schedule used for the Directors of Public Health

Appendix C
List of documents requested from health authorities

Appendix D
Financial data obtained from Department of Health

Appendix E
List of local expenditure data requested

Appendix F
Financial data tables

Table 9.2 Real *per capita* expenditure on population based health promotion by district (£ *per capita*)

Table 9.3 Real *per capita* expenditure on general practice delivered health promotion (£ *per capita*)

Table 9.4 Real *per capita* expenditure on 'narrow' health promotion (£ *per capita*)

Table 9.5 Real *per capita* expenditure on individually demanded preventive services (family planning, cancer screening)

Table 9.6 Real *per capita* spending on 'broad' health promotion and preventive services

Table 9.7 Resource share of 'narrow' health promotion (% total NHS spend)

Table 9.8 Resource share of individual demand-led preventive services (% total spend)

Table 9.9 Resource share of 'broad' health promotion and prevention activities

Table 9.10   Expenditure per immunised child excluding vaccines (£ per immunised child aged 2)

Appendix G Tables showing the factors influencing HOTN implementation locally

Table 9.11   What is the single biggest factor enhancing HOTN in your district?

Table 9.12   What is the single biggest factor inhibiting HOTN in your district?

Table 9.13   Were there any factors about the way organisations were set up and run that facilitated alliances?

Table 9.14   Were there any factors about the way organisations were set up and run that obstructed alliances?

Table 9.15   What features of the HA have influenced HOTN implementation?

Table 9.16   Features of the HA's area that influenced HOTN implementation

Table 9.17   Features of the HA's local authority/ies (structure, history, culture, individuals that influence HOTN implementation)

Table 9.18   Could more be done by health authorities or government to support alliances?

Table 9.19   Projects - Factors for success

Table 9.20   Projects - Barriers to success

9.1   Appendix A

Table 9.1 Detailed breakdown of type of interviewee by district

Type of Interviewee	A	B	C	D	E	F	G	H	Total
Health Authority									
HA Chief Executive	1	1	1	1	1	1	1	1	8
Director of Public Health	1	1	1	1	1	1	1	1	8
Director of Health Promotion	1	0	1	0	1	1	1	1	6
HOTN Lead	1	2	0	2	1	0	1	1	8
PH/HP operational employee	1	1	3	1	1	1	0	2	10
Trustsα									
Chief Executive	0	0	0	0	1	1	0	0	2
Senior management figure	3	3	1	1	2	1	1	1	13
Operational staff member	0	1	0	1	0	0	1	0	3
General Practitioners									
Non-fundholders	1	0	0	0	1	1	0	0	3
Fundholders	0	1	2	1	1	0	1	1	7
CHC									
Chief/Deputy Chief Officer/Member	0	1	1	1	1	1	1	2	8
Local Authority									
Environmental Health	1	0	0	1	2	2	3	0	9
Social Services	0	1	1	0	0	1	1	0	4
Education	0	1	0	1	1	1	2	1	7
Leisure	0	0	0	0	0	0	1	1	2
Housing	0	0	0	0	2	1	0	0	3
Other	3	1	2	0	1	0	0	2	9
HFA/Healthy Alliance	1	0	1	1	0	0	0	0	3
Voluntary sector									
Voluntary councils	0	2	0	1	1	1	0	1	6
Voluntary organisations	1	1	0	0	0	0	1	0	3
Private Sector	1	0	1	1	0	1	1	1	6
Police	1	0	0	1	0	1	1	1	5
Total	17	17	15	15	18	16	18	17	133

α This includes interviews with members of staff from Acute, Community and Mental Health Trusts

9.2   Appendix B

Interview schedule - Director of Public Health

Name of organisation:

Name of respondent:

Title of respondent :

Length of time the respondent has been in that post :

Interviewer Name:

Type of interview			Department
Health Authority			Public Health
Local Authority			Health Promotion
Trust			Other (write in)
Primary care			
Voluntary Sector			
Community Health Council			
Other (write in)			

Date:

Duration of interview :

Thank you letter sent: [date]

Face to face interview:

Telephone interview:

Key:

Local Authority: C - County   Trust: A- Acute
                      D - District   C - Community
                      U - Unitary   M- Mental health
                                          A & C- Acute & community
                                          C & M- Community & mental health

1.	**What is the single biggest factor enhancing or inhibiting HOTN in your authority.**
	1 What is the single biggest enhancing factor?
	2 What is the single biggest inhibiting factor

2.	**What do you think of Health of the Nation**
	key areas: CHD & stroke, Cancers, Mental illness, HIV/AIDS & sexual health, Accidents
	1 Did the strategy meet an existing policy need?
	2 Has the strategy been adaptable to local circumstances?
	3 Do the key areas identify important problems?
	4 Could the key areas have been based around population groups, or something else, rather than around diseases?
	5 Are the targets credible?
	6 Is the encouragement to work through healthy alliances helpful in delivering the strategy?
	7 Is the encouragement to work in 'settings' helpful in delivering the strategy?
	8 Was government support through the launch, roadshows, documents, *Target* and the health alliance awards useful locally?
	9 Was the fact that the strategy followed an extensive consultation important to how it is perceived?
	10 Has national policy activity such as interdepartmental groups and raising tobacco tax on health grounds been important to local implementation of the strategy?
	11 Can you sum up how your view has changed since the launch?

3.	**What was done to adapt HOTN to local needs**
1	Have you developed a local health strategy? If so, how was this done - mainly by the HA or alliances or collaboration?
2	Did you consult the community? How (CHC, surveys, media)?
3	What features of the <u>health authority</u> (structure, history, culture, individuals) have influenced HOTN implementation?
4	What features of the HA's <u>local authority/ies</u> (structure, history, culture, individuals) influenced HotN implementation?
5	What features of the HA's area (population, economy, geography) influenced HOTN implementation?
6	Did you have a local launch of the strategy?
7	What local HOTN documentation did you produce?
8	What local targets did you develop?
9	Did you add any new local <u>key areas</u>? What?

4.	**How is health of the nation organised within your authority**
1	
a.	Is there a HOTN lead?
b.	If so, is this person operational, or policy-setting only?
c.	Is this person employed by the health authority or by a trust?
d.	How does the DPH work with this person?
2	How is HOTN activity integrated with other activities such as contracting, service strategies, purchasing plans?
3	
a.	Did you set up key area implementation groups?
b.	If so, who was on them?
c	Are they cross-directorate and/or intersectoral?
4	Is the present structure different from what was originally set up? Why?
5	[If applicable] How have past mergers influenced the present structure?
6	Have you made any joint appointments with <u>other</u> organisations?

5.	Who are the key people leading implementation of HOTN locally

striking egs, not necessarily for each key area and setting

1 Within the HA? (what directorate, what function, how senior)

2 Outside the HA? (what organisation and function)

3 What qualities made these people effective?

4 Were professional/managerial boundaries ever a problem - how?

6.	What made local healthy alliances successful, or less successful?

striking e.g.s not comprehensive list

1 Who has been involved in alliances?
a Local authority departments
  i social services
  ii education
  iii environmental health
  iv housing
  v leisure
b Voluntary sector
c Private sector
d Police
e Primary care

1 Were all alliances HA led?

2. Were there any issues around ownership of alliances, accountability of alliances or responsibility for alliances?

3. Was there anything about the way that the organisations were set up and run that <u>facilitated</u> alliances?

4. Was there anything about the way that the organisations were set up and run that <u>obstructed</u> alliances?

5. Did any organisational-cultural issues between different organisations arise?

7.	What difference did HOTN make to prevention in the health authority - what happened because of HOTN and what would have happened anyway?
	1 How did HOTN affect how much activity the authority did in the key areas?
	2 How did HOTN affect what activities the health authority did?
	3 How much did it affect the way the health authority worked (targets, alliances, settings)?
	4. Is it your impression that HOTN influenced overall resource allocation?
	5 Were specific resources allocated to HOTN activities? [Impression only]

8.	We are also looking at three non-key areas where the criteria for key area status might have been met: childhood immunisation, diabetes, asthma
	For each of them could you briefly summarise: **a. how local strategies have developed** **b. whether you have worked using HOTN features (targets, alliances, settings) in these areas?** [criteria were: major cause of premature death or avoidable ill-health; availability of effective interventions; feasibility of target setting and monitoring] 1 childhood immunisation 2 asthma 3 diabetes

9.	How strong do you feel the commitment to HOTN currently is?
	1 Within your public health department?
	2 Within health promotion?
	3 Across the health authority?
	4 Across your main service providers?
	5 Across primary care?
	6 Across other local organisations?

10.	**What would you advise the government to do differently from HOTN, and what to preserve, in *Our Healthier Nation***

1. What would be the <u>three</u> most useful things the government could do ensure that the strategy is sustainable? [over the timescale of the interventions which in some cases could be 20 years or more.]

2. How can a new strategy avoid disruption to existing successful activity?

3. Should the government keep all existing <u>key areas</u>?

4. Should there be new <u>key areas</u>?

5. Should the existing <u>targets</u> be kept?

6. Should there be new <u>targets</u>?

7. Should the government make local targets an obligatory element?

8. Should alliances continue to be an important way of working? If so, could more be done by health authorities or government to support alliances?

9. Do you think there should be any change to the structure of health authorities and/or public health to facilitate *Our Healthier Nation*: for example the idea that directors of public health should be joint appointments between health authorities and local authorities.

10. Should the new strategy include work through settings? If so, should settings be added to or strengthened?

11. What could be done to involve GPs and primary health care teams more fully in *Our Healthier Nation?*

12. Should the government provide additional resources?

13. Should the government support local activity differently (documents, meetings, monitoring, response to feedback)?

14. Should the government act differently on national policy?

11.	**Is there anything else we haven't covered that you would like to add?**

9.3   Appendix C

Documents requested from Health Authorities

Documents	1992/93	1993/4	1994/5	1995/6	1996/7
HA Purchasing plans					
Annual public health reports					
5-year HA strategies					
HA corporate contract with region					
Community care plan					
Other Health of the Nation documentation e.g. HOTN annual report, HOTN launch document					
At least 1 and up to 5 e.g.s of provider contract if the contract has been used to implement HOTN					
FHSA corporate contract					
FHSA Annual plan					
Practice annual report for up to 3 selected GPs (any year)					

9.4   Appendix D

Authority and Trust Accounts Dataset

Data supplied by Department of Health SPB ATA

Expenditure Data Required for each Health Authority

Period: Annually, 1 April 1991 to 31 March 1997

Variable	Source/Comments
Total expenditure	HAA1
Surplus/Deficit	
Joint Finance Total expenditure by HA	HFR20
Joint Finance Total expenditure all agencies	Joint Finance
Genito-Urinary Medicine Out-patient expenditure	Speciality programme Cost return
Health Programme Support:	District Summary FR12
	(if not available, please provide by DMUs)
Immunisation	
Surveillance	
Screening	
Contact Tracing	
Health promotion / education	
Family Planning	
Histopathology in DMUs	FR11
Mental Illness:	Day case patients expenditure
Drug abuse	
Alcoholism	
Other specialities:	
Drug abuse	
Alcoholism	

Expenditure Data Required for each Health Authority

Primary Care data, 1996/97 only

Variable	Source/Comments
Practice staff	HAA04A
Hospital purchases	Purchase of healthcare by GP Fundholders
Drugs	
Other from Savings	
GMS cash limited	HAA04A
GMS non cash limited	Purchase of Primary Healthcare by HA
Pharmaceutical	
General Dental	
General Ophthalmic	
Department of Health Initiative Funding	
Immunisation:	HFR12
Childhood higher target	GMS Fees & Allowances Expenditure
Childhood lower target	
Pre-school Booster higher target	
Pre-school Booster lower target	
Vac/Imms (non target)	
MMRII	
HiB (if any)	
Cervical Cytology higher target	
Cervical Cytology lower target	
Contraceptive services ordinary	
Contraceptive sources IUD	
Health promotion sessional fees:	
Unbanded scheme	
Banded scheme - Band 1	
Banded scheme - Band 2	
Banded scheme - Band 3	
CDM Diabetes	
CDM Asthma	
transitional	
Supply of syringes/needles	

Expenditure Data Required for each FHSA

Period: Annually, 1 April 1991 to 31 March 1996

Variable	Source/Comments
Total expenditure	FAA01
Surplus / deficit	Income & expenditure account
FHSA Administration Revenue	FAA05 then FAA08 notes to the
FHSA Administration Capital	income and expenditure account
GP Fundholding	Note 2.2
Practice Staff	
Hospital Purchase	
Drugs & Appliances	
Other from savings	
GMS Practice Expenditure	
Revenue	
Capital	
Practice Fund Management Revenue	
Practice Fund Management Capital	
FHS Non-cash limited	
General Medical Services	
Pharmaceutical Remuneration	(then total from 1993/94)
Pharmaceutical Drugs & Appliances	
General Dental	
General Ophthalmic	
Immunisation:	FFR03 GMS Non Cash Limited Expend
Childhood higher target	FFR02 " "
Childhood lower target	
Pre-school Booster higher target	
Pre-school Booster lower target	
Vac/Imms (non target)	
MMRII	
HiB (if any)	
Cervical Cytology higher target	
Cervical Cytology lower target	
Contraceptive services ordinary	
Contraceptive sources IUD	
Health promotion sessional fees:	
Sessional fees for health promotion clinics (total)	(1991/92, 1992/93)
Old Scheme	(93/94 to 95/96)
New scheme	(93/94 to 95/96)
Transitional	(93/94 to 95/96)
Supply of syringes/needles	

Expenditure Data Required for each trust

Period: Annually, 1 April 1991 to 31 March 1997

Variable	Source/Comments
Genito-Urinary Medicine Out-patient expenditure	TFR2A Code 113 (expend 063)
Paediatric Community services	TFR2F expend 073
Immunisation	102
Surveillance	
General:	
Screening	111
Contact Tracing	
Health promotion / education	117
Family Planning	113
Laboratory / pathology	
Histopathology	
Mental Illness:	TFR2F expend 070
Drug abuse	907
Alcoholism	908
Other specialities:	
Drug abuse	914
Alcoholism	915

9.5   Appendix E

Expenditure survey - list of data requirements and sources

Aggregate HA Data

1.1   Total HA annual expenditure from 1990/91. Please provide HA spend for each predecessor HA, and FHSA spend (cash limited/non cash limited, GMS and other)

1.2   Total population data by age band/sex by year from 1990/91 for all relevant areas (i.e. predecessor authorities) [ONS/OPCS]

1.3   Cervical cytology target populations (i.e. women aged 20-64 less exclusions) from 1990/91

1.4   Breast screening target population if available

1.5   Target population for child immunisations (children reaching second birthday in previous 12 months) since 1990/91 [e.g. KC51]

1.6   Explanation of changes in and impacts of capitation funding formulae on district since 1990/91

Health Promotion Expenditures

2.1   Expenditure on/through Health Promotion Units annually since 1990/91 [e.g. DHQ or HPU expenditure statements, possibly health promotion contracts if statements not available, Speciality and Programme Cost Return HFR22 for earlier years]

2.2   General Public Health departmental expenditures annually since 1990/91, with as much breakdown as possible by function/activity. Particular focus on resources explicitly devoted to *Health of the Nation (HOTN)* activities [DHQ expenditure statements, discussion with key budget holders etc.]

2.3   Trust based health promotion activities annually since 1990/91 [provide contact point in each relevant trust and make appropriate introductions]

2.4   GMS health promotion activity annually since 1990/91 [expenditure on GP health promotion clinics by type, number of clinics by type p.a.; then expenditure via banding scheme, number of GPs in each band etc.]

2.5   Other primary care health promotion [e.g. FHSA funded health promotion facilitator posts, health promotion training for practice staff]

Key Areas and Programmes

Sexual Health

3.1   AIDS Control Act reports (financial, activity and incidence statistics) annually since 1990/91

3.2   Expenditure on NHS Family Planning services annually since 1990/91, plus any detail on special services for teenagers [HFR22 for early years, trust expenditure statements and/or contracts]

3.3   Expenditure on GP contraceptive services annually since 1990/91 [total GP GMS contraceptive payments p.a., number of GPs providing contraceptive services p.a., data on prescribing of key contraceptives]

3.4   Expenditure on GUM services annually since 1990/91 [Trust expenditure statements, and/or contracts]

3.5   Expenditure on other sexual health projects [e.g. Joint Finance, etc.]

Cancers

3.6   GP cervical cytology payments annually since 1990/91, with details of level of attainment/coverage [GMS data]

3.7   Expenditure on cervical cytology provided via Family Planning Service annually since 1990/91 [FPS expenditure statements if available]

3.8   Laboratory screening costs of cervical cytology [? part of pathology contract?]

3.9   Costs of operating call and recall system centrally [any FHSA/HA staff specifically tasked to cervical cytology]

3.10   Skin cancer initiatives via Health Promotion Units, GPs, Dermatology clinics etc. [various sources including expenditure statements, discussing any previous campaigns with relevant staff etc.]

3.11   Expenditure on breast cancer screening programme since HA assumed responsibility; suitable contact point at Regional Office to obtain data prior to this time

3.12   Stop smoking activities - will be derived from multiple sources listed above

Childhood Immunisations

3.13   Annual expenditure on GP immunisation payments, details of target attainment and coverage

3.14   Expenditure on immunisation via Community clinics [Trust data]

3.15   Expenditure on total vaccine supplies [source to be identified]

Revised list of data requirements
21 January 1998

Following the agreement from the Department of Health to extract data on our behalf from the HA/FHSA/trust annual accounts database, and the identification of AIDS Control Act data at central level, I am delighted to report that the remaining requirement for local level data collection is substantially reduced. Below please find a table which presents those data items which we are still asking you to prepare locally if available (all items which do not figure in the annual accounts). The table indicates whether the data is likely to be held at HA level, or where it should be obtained direct from Trusts. Please note that there is one item which was not on my original request, but which has subsequently become important - expenditure on school nursing and school medical services. While this data may need to come from Trusts, I would be grateful if you could check at HA level (e.g. to see if amounts were specified in contracts etc.).

HA Based Data	Trust Based Data
1.2 Population by age/sex band by year from 1991/92	2.3 trust based health promotion activities since 1991/92
1.3 Cervical cytology target populations from 1991/92	3.8 Laboratory screening costs of cervical cytology
1.4 Breast screening target population	3.14 Expenditure on immunisation via
1.5 Child immunisation target populations	community clinics
1.6 Explanation of changes in and impacts of capitation funding formula since 1991/92	School nursing and school medical services expenditures
2.2 Public health departmental expenditures, with as much breakdown as possible, for all available years	
2.5 Other primary care health promotion (e.g. facilitators etc.)	
3.3 Prescribing of oral contraceptives by GPs since 1991/92	
3.8 Laboratory screening costs of cervical cytology	
3.9 Costs of operating call and recall system for cervical cytology	
3.10 Skin cancer prevention initiatives	
3.11 Breast cancer screening programme expenditures	

9.6   Appendix F Financial data tables

Table 9.2 Real *per capita* expenditure on population based health promotion by district (£ *per capita*)

Year	A	B	C	D	E	F	G	H
1991/92	1.59	1.06	1.73	1.40	2.56	1.02	1.53	2.28
1992/93	1.35	0.67	1.77	1.68	1.96	1.08	1.17	3.51
1993/94	1.35	0.65	2.35	1.70	2.13	1.09	1.15	3.70
1994/95	1.35	0.76	2.35	2.48	2.24	1.85	1.11	3.62
1995/96	0.64	0.59	2.53	1.91	2.21	1.74	1.42	4.03
1996/97	0.99	0.71	2.44	1.90	0.68	1.63	1.37	4.90

Constant 1991/92 prices District A, D, G: 1992/93 and 1993/94 estimated

Table 9.3 Real *per capita* expenditure on general practice delivered health promotion (£ *per capita*)

Year	A	B	C	D	E	F	G	H
1991/92	1.28	1.06	1.23	1.33	1.42	1.03	1.48	2.53
1992/93	1.36	1.51	1.57	0.95	1.48	1.09	1.69	2.28
1993/94	0.88	1.13	1.38	0.89	1.28	1.36	0.76	1.17
1994/95	1.34	1.54	1.37	1.37	1.40	1.32	1.43	1.38
1995/96	1.26	0.77	1.25	1.65	1.33	1.31	1.21	1.28
1996/97	1.25	1.32	1.28	1.31	1.32	1.31	1.22	1.32

Constant 1991/92 prices

Table 9.4 Real *per capita* expenditure on 'narrow' health promotion (£ *per capita*)

Year	A	B	C	D	E	F	G	H
1991/92	2.87	2.12	2.95	2.73	3.97	2.05	3.01	4.82
1992/93	2.71	2.18	3.34	2.63	3.44	2.17	2.86	5.79
1993/94	2.24	1.79	3.73	2.59	3.41	2.45	1.92	4.86
1994/95	2.69	2.30	3.72	3.85	3.64	3.17	2.55	5.00
1995/96	1.90	1.35	3.78	3.56	3.54	3.05	2.64	5.31
1996/97	2.25	2.03	3.72	3.21	2.00	2.94	2.59	6.22

Constant 1991/92 prices

Table 9.5 Real *per capita* expenditure on individually demanded preventive services (family planning, cancer screening)

Year	A	B	C	D	E	F	G	H
1991/92	4.01	4.87	4.17	4.30	5.52	4.46	4.60	3.73
1992/93	4.03	5.05	4.08	4.17	5.04	4.50	4.53	3.84
1993/94	4.45	5.07	4.68	4.26	5.02	4.73	4.70	4.38
1994/95	4.50	5.26	4.93	4.35	5.13	5.04	4.86	4.35
1995/96	4.33	5.76	4.51	4.21	4.79	4.82	4.74	4.42
1996/97	3.89	4.44	4.35	4.18	4.28	4.65	4.40	4.23

Constant 1991/92 prices Includes GP contraceptive prescribing

Table 9.6 Real *per capita* spending on 'broad' health promotion and preventive services (£ *per capita*)

Year	A	B	C	D	E	F	G	H
1991/92	6.88	6.99	7.13	7.03	9.50	6.52	7.61	8.55
1992/93	6.74	7.23	7.42	6.80	8.48	6.67	7.39	9.63
1993/94	6.69	6.86	8.41	6.85	8.43	7.18	6.61	9.25
1994/95	7.19	7.56	8.64	8.20	8.77	8.21	7.41	9.35
1995/96	6.22	7.11	8.29	7.77	8.32	7.87	7.37	9.73
1996/97	6.13	6.47	8.07	7.39	6.28	7.60	6.99	10.45

Constant 1991/92 prices

Table 9.7 Resource share of 'narrow' health promotion (% total NHS spend)

Year	A	B	C	D	E	F	G	H
1991/92	0.59	0.41	0.59	0.59	0.92	0.47	0.66	1.06
1992/93	0.55	0.41	0.69	0.56	0.77	0.48	0.65	1.21
1993/94	0.48	0.35	0.75	0.53	0.73	0.53	0.41	1.01
1994/95	0.57	0.44	0.73	0.75	0.75	0.68	0.53	1.04
1995/96	0.39	0.24	0.71	0.70	0.71	0.65	0.54	1.04
1996/97	0.46	0.36	0.67	0.61	0.42	0.63	0.52	1.20

Table 9.8 Resource share of individual demand-led preventive services (% total spend)

Year	A	B	C	D	E	F	G	H
1991/92	0.82	0.95	0.83	0.92	1.28	1.03	1.01	0.82
1992/93	0.82	0.95	0.84	0.88	1.13	0.99	1.02	0.80
1993/94	0.96	1.01	0.94	0.86	1.07	1.03	1.01	0.91
1994/95	0.96	1.01	0.97	0.85	1.06	1.09	1.02	0.91
1995/96	0.89	1.04	0.84	0.83	0.97	1.04	0.96	0.87
1996/97	0.79	0.78	0.78	0.80	0.89	0.99	0.88	0.81

Table 9.9 Resource share of 'broad' health promotion and prevention activities (% total spend)

Year	A	B	C	D	E	F	G	H
1991/92	1.40	1.37	1.42	1.51	2.21	1.50	1.67	1.89
1992/93	1.37	1.37	1.52	1.44	1.90	1.47	1.67	2.01
1993/94	1.44	1.36	1.70	1.39	1.80	1.56	1.43	1.93
1994/95	1.53	1.45	1.70	1.60	1.81	1.77	1.55	1.95
1995/96	1.28	1.28	1.55	1.53	1.68	1.69	1.50	1.91
1996/97	1.25	1.14	1.45	1.41	1.31	1.62	1.39	2.01

Table 9.10 Expenditure per immunised child excluding vaccines (£ per immunised child aged 2)

Year	A	B	C	D	E	F	G	H
1991/92	60.51	110.50	164.54	128.48	184.25	169.09	252.57	97.24
1992/93	99.19	73.72	167.14	132.38	170.82	143.81	115.91	84.99
1993/94	103.75	117.39	161.74	128.83	170.19	143.12	117.65	106.07
1994/95	115.90	108.97	174.03	143.89	179.43	160.56	230.98	113.18
1995/96	111.57	124.51	180.97	110.96	176.01	125.20	229.42	110.13
1996/97	120.46	110.83	189.89	116.52	111.77	161.72	248.77	102.78

9.7 Appendix G

Factors perceived as influencing implementation of HOTN

Table 9.11 What is the single biggest factor enhancing HOTN in your district?

Respondents mentioning	Total	Percent
Partnership in local organisations	24	19
HOTN legitimises activities (e.g. partnership, LA's role, HIV)	17	13
Key individuals (high quality, commitment, good relations between)	13	10
HA structure including location of health promotion	12	9
Health status of local population	10	8
Other positive attributes of HA	8	6
Positive attributes of local agencies or organisations other than HA	7	5
Other attributes of locality (geography, economy etc.)	7	5
Quality and commitment of health professionals	6	5
National factor	1	1
Other	4	3
No factor/DK	12	9
Missing	7	6
Total	**128**	**100**

(All interviewees except police)

Table 9.12 What is the single biggest factor inhibiting HOTN in your district?

Respondents mentioning	Total	Percent
Lack of resources/ resource pressure of health service	33	26
Apathy/lack of awareness of general public	14	11
Poor partnership in local organisations	10	8
Organisational/structural barriers within/between local organisations	10	8
HOTN is based on a medical/disease model	7	6
Lack of commitment/ownership in local ownership	7	6
Lack of recognition of inequalities in healthy area	7	6
HOTN has a lifestyle approach/doesn't consider environmental/socio-economic factors	6	5
Low priority/lack of commitment by health authority	4	3
Local or national party political factor	4	3
Poor health status of local population	4	3
Other attributes of locality (geography, economy)	4	3
Lack of effective measures in HOTN for implementation	4	3
Lack of cross departmental working by government	1	1
Other	1	1
No factor/DK	6	5
Missing	7	6
Total	**128**	**100**

(All interviewees except police)

Table 9.13 Were there any factors about the way organisations were set up and run that facilitated alliances?

Respondents mentioning	Total	Percent
Structural factors between local agencies	33	31
Partnership of local organisations (inc. history of , commitment to)	25	23
Key individuals (high quality, commitment, good relations between)	19	18
Structural factors within other local agencies	17	16
HA structure inc. location of HP	9	8
HA other positive attributes (commitment etc.)	5	5
Other positive factors within local agencies	4	4
Other national factor	4	4
HOTN legitimising (inc. partnership, LA's role in health etc.)	2	2
Other	1	1
No factors/DK	20	19
Missing	27	25

(All interviewees except HA Chief Executives, GPs and CHC interviewees(N=107))

Table 9.14 Were there any factors about the way organisations were set up and run that obstructed alliances?

Respondents mentioning	Total	Percent
Organisational structural barriers between other local organisations	43	40
Organisational/structural barriers within other local organisations	34	32
Organisational/structural barriers within the HA	21	20
Obstructive/unhelpful key individuals	15	14
Local or national party-political factors	10	9
National limits on resources	10	9
Poor partnership in local organisations	6	6
HOTN being based on the medical model	6	6
Other national factors	2	2
Other	7	7
No factors/DK	9	8
Missing	24	25

(All interviewees except HA Chief Executives, GPs and CHC interviewees (N=107))

Table 9.15 What features of the HA have influenced HOTN implementation?

	Total	Percent
Demographic factor	21	54
Senior staff commitment	14	36
Organisational restructuring	7	18
Individual staff member's skill, knowledge, commitment	6	15
Staff turnover	5	13
Cross department integration of HP	5	13
Strong HP ethos in HA	5	13
Coterminosity	4	10
Community/public involvement	3	8
Monitoring	2	5
HA organisational relations	2	5
Political views	1	3
Other	4	10

(DPHs, HOTN Lead/Managers in HA and LA, CHC, voluntary sector (N=39))

Table 9.16 Features of the HA's area that influenced HOTN implementation

	Total	Percent
Inequalities/divides	23	59
Environmental conditions	7	18
Deprivation/ economic factor	5	13
Lack of resources (human/financial)	4	10
Presence of funding	3	8
Size of HA	2	5
Voluntary sector/community activity	2	5
Other	3	8

(DPHs, HOTN Lead/Manager in HA/LA (N=39))

Table 9.17 Features of the HA's local authority/ies (structure, history, culture, individuals that influence HOTN implementation)

	Total	Percent
Political views	6	20
Individual staff member's skill, knowledge, commitment	6	20
Coterminosity	5	17
Strong HP ethos in HA	5	17
Unitary status	5	17
LA's view of health or HOTN and health	5	17
LA's organisational structure	5	17
LA's public health role	4	13
Senior staff commitment	3	10
Demographic factor	3	10
Staff turnover	2	7
Cross-department integration of HP in HA	1	3
Other	2	7

(DPHs, HOTN Lead/Manager in HA/LA (N=39))

Table 9.18 Could more be done by health authorities or government to support alliances?

	Total	Percent
Define roles for HA,LA etc. more clearly	54	41
Resources (human/financial)	41	31
Government must make strategy truly inter-departmental	17	13
By having a mechanism to monitor/give feedback	5	4
Give credit/reward good work	4	3
Make it a high profile strategy	4	3
Single stream funding arrangements	4	3
Raise the profile of strategy but not do not impose it	3	2
Give the strategy a flexible framework for local consultation and priority setting	3	2
Recognise the health impact of policies in all government departments	3	2
Senior staff commitment	3	2
Incentives to participate in alliances	3	2
HAZ/HLC should encourage alliances	2	2
Review the strategy annually	2	2
Alliances are down to individuals	2	2
Recognise the determinants of health and inequalities	2	2
Realistic/review targets	2	2
Using of contractual arrangement between purchasers/providers	2	2
Other	13	10

(All interviews)

Table 9.19 Projects - Factors for success

	Total	Percent
Met an existing need	27	28
Resources available	26	27
Shared Ownership by partners	21	22
Built on well-established relationships	19	20
Committed individuals	17	18
Accessible to target group	12	12

(N = 97)

Table 9.20 Projects - Barriers to success

	Total	Percent
Lack of resources	29	30
Problem within the partnership	20	21
Lack of commitment by partner organisations	18	19
Lack of consultation with/problem with involving target group	15	15
Partners have too many commitments	12	12
Poor consultation/relations with target audience /poor preparation	12	12

(N = 97)

10. REFERENCES

1.   *The Health of the Nation: A Strategy for England.* London: HMSO, 1992.

2.   World Health Organization. Regional Office for Europe. *Targets for Health for All.* Copenhagen: WHO, 1995.

3.   Public Health Service. *Healthy People 2000: National Health Promotion and Disease Prevention.* Washington DC: Department of Health and Human Services, 1990.

4.   *The Health Survey for England 1992.* London: HMSO, 1994.

5.   *The Health of the Nation: One Year On.* London: HMSO, 1993.

6.   *Fit for the Future.* Second Progress Report on the Health of the Nation. London: HMSO. 1995.

7.   Target Newsletter of the Health of the Nation, Issue 13. London: HMSO, October 1995.

8.   Report by the Comptroller and Auditor General. *Health of the Nation: A Progress Report.* London: National Audit Office. August, 1996.

9.   Tessa Jowell. Public health strategy launched to tackle root causes of ill health. London, 7 July 1997. http://www.coi.gov.uk/coi/depts/GDH/coi0362d.ok.

10.   Secretary of State for Health. *Our Healthier Nation: A contract for Health.* A consultation paper. London: Stationery Office, 1998.

11.   Secretary of State for Health. *The new NHS. Modern, Dependable.* London: Stationery Office, 1997.

12.   NHS Executive. *The new NHS: a national framework for assessing performance.* Leeds: NHSE, 1998.

13.   Department of Health. *Chief Medical Officer's Project to strengthen the public health function in England.* London: Department of Health, 1998.

14.   Hunter D. Breaking down barriers. *Health Service Journal* 1991 101:5272;19.

15.   Cornish Y, Russell-Hodgson C et al. *Review of Health of the Nation in North Thames.* London: South East Institute of Public Health, 1997.

16.   McCarthy M. The Health of the Nation: the way forward Health care UK 1994/95. *Annual review of health care policy.* Ed. Harrison A. King's Fund Policy Institute.

17.   Harvey J, Fralick E. Targeting neglect. *Health Service Journal* 1997 107:5564;26-7.

18.   Appleby J. Feelgood factors. *Health Service Journal* 1997 107:5560;2426.

19.   Green J. *Evidence and policy in accident alliances.* Final study report for the NHSE North Thames Organisation and Management Group. HRSU, London School of Hygiene & Tropical Medicine. June 1998.

20.   Delaney F. Making connections: research into inter-sectoral collaboration. *Health Education Journal* 1994 53;474-85

21.   London Research Centre. *Health alliances: A study of inter-agency collaboration in health promotion.* South West Thames Regional Health Authority, 1993.

22.   Rathwell T. Pursuing health for all in Britain - an assessment. *Social Science and Medicine* 1992 34; 169-82.

23.   Bloxham S. A case study of inter-agency collaboration in the education and promotion of young people's sexual health. *Health Education Journal* 1996 55:389-403.

24.   Nocon A, Small N, Ferguson B. Made in heaven. *Health Service Journal* 1993 163:5381;24-26.

25.   Costongs C, Springett J. Joint working and the production of the City Health Plan: the Liverpool experience. *Health Promotion International* 1997 12:9.18.

26.   Royston GHD. A monitoring and evaluation framework for the implementation of 'The Health of the Nation'. *In Managerial Issues in the Reformed NHS*. Ed, Malek M, Vacani P, Rasquinha, P Davey. 1993 John Wiley & Sons, Chichester.

27.   Speller V, Funnell R, Friedli L. Multisectoral collaboration for health: evaluative project. In *Research and change in urban community health*. Ed: Bruce N, Springett J, Hotchkiss J, Scott-Samual A. Avebury 1996.

28.   Funnell R, Oldfield K and Speller V. *Towards healthier alliances: a tool for planning, evaluating and developing health alliances.* HEA & Wessex Institute of Public Healt, (1995.

29.   Minutes of Evidence Taken Before the Committee of Public Health. Appendix 2. Health of the Nation: a progress report (PAC96-97/37). Hansard 6 November 1996 31.

30.   NHS Executive Anglia & Oxford/North Thames/South Thames. *Defining the essential: the functions, roles and costs of health authorities and GP purchasers.* NHS Executive North Thames, November 1996.

31.   Public Health Foundation. Measuring state expenditures for core public health functions. *American Journal of Preventive Medicine* 1995 11(suppl.2):58-73.

32.   Studnicki J. Evaluating the performance of public health agencies: information needs. *American Journal of Preventive Medicine* 1995 11(Suppl.2):75-80.

33.   Donaldson C. Economics, public health and health care purchasing: reinventing the wheel? *Health Policy* 1995 33:79-90.

34.   Madden L, Hussey R, Mooney G, Church E. Public health and economics in tandem: programme budgeting, marginal analysis and priority setting in practice. *Health Policy* 1995 33:161-168.

35.   Miller P, Parkin D, Craig N, Lewis D, Gerard K. Less fog on the Tyne? Programme budgeting in Newcastle and North Tyneside. *Health Policy* 1997 40:217-229.

36.   Jones C and Wright K. Programme budgeting revisited: special reference to people with learning disabilties. *Health Services Management Research* 1997 10(4):255-265.

37.   Brambleby P. A survivor's guide to programme budgeting. *Health Policy* 1995 33:127-145.

38.   Pettigrew AM. *The Awakening Giant*. Oxford: Basil Blackwell, 1995.

39.   Pettigrew AM. Ferlie E, McKee L. *Shaping Strategic Change*. London: Sage, 1992.

40.   Burgess R. *In the Field: An Introduction to Field Research*. London: George, Allen and Unwin 1984

41.   Office for National Statistics (formerly Office of Population Consuses and Surveys). *Key population and vital statistics:* local and health authority areas. Series VS PP1, 1991 to 1994.

42.   Glaser BG, Strauss AL. *The Discovery of Grounded Theory*. Chicago: Aldine, 1967.

43.   Webb EJ, Champbell DT, Schwartz RD, Sechrest L. *Unobtrusive Measures: Non-reactive Research in the Social Sciences*. Chicago: Rand McNally, 1966.

44.   Commission for the Environment. *Agendas for change*. London: Chartered Institute for Environmental Health, 1997.

45.   European Commission. *1998 Work Programme of the Community Action Programme on Health Promotion, Information, Education and Training*. GEST 9V/F/3 Luxembourg: European Commission DGV.

46.   Department of Health/Royal College of General Practitioners/British Medical Association. *The Health of the Nation - what you can do about it*. An information pack from general practitioners for general practitioners. London: Department of Health 1996.

47.   Department of Health/General Medical Services Committee/Royal College of General Practitioners. *Better Living. Better Life*. Resource pack for general practitioners. Henley on Thames: Knowledge House, 1992.

48.   Department of Health. *The Health of the Nation - what you can do about it*. An information pack by hospital doctors for hospital doctors. London: Department of Health 1995.

49.   Department for Education. Education Act 1993: *Sex Education in Schools*. London: DFE, 1994 (Circular 5/94; 6 May).

50.   National Audit Office. *The Performance of the NHS Cervical Screening Programme in England*. London, The Stationery Office 1998.

51.   Committee of Public Accounts. *Health of the Nation: A Progress Report* (PAC96-97/37). 6 November 1996.

52.   Department of Health. *Breast Screening Programme, England:* 1995-96. Statistical Bulletin 1997/3.

Printed in the UK for The Stationery Office
J61202, C10, 10/98, 5673.